# COSMOPOLITAN *Twain*

*Mark Twain and His Circle Series*
TOM QUIRK, EDITOR

# COSMOPOLITAN *Twain*

EDITED BY **Ann M. Ryan**

AND **Joseph B. McCullough**

University of Missouri Press
Columbia and London

Copyright © 2008 by
The Curators of the University of Missouri
University of Missouri Press, Columbia, Missouri 65201
Printed and bound in the United States of America
5  4  3  2  1      12  11  10  09  08

Library of Congress Cataloging-in-Publication Data

Cosmopolitan Twain / edited by Ann M. Ryan and Joseph B. McCullough.
       p. cm.
    Includes bibliographical references and index.
    Summary: "From New York City to Vienna to the suburban utopia of Harford, Twain spent most of his life in an urban environment, generating writings that marked America's movement into the twentieth century. Rather than the nostalgic voice of America's rural past, Twain was a visionary of a cosmopolitan future"—Provided by publisher.
    ISBN 978-0-8262-1827-8 (alk. paper)
    1. Twain, Mark, 1835–1910—Homes and haunts. 2. Twain, Mark, 1835–1910—Travel.   3. Cosmopolitanism in literature.   4. Cities and towns in literature.   5. City and town life in literature.   6. Twain, Mark, 1835–1910—Settings.   7. Twain, Mark, 1835–1910—Psychology. 8. Modernism (Literature)—United States.   I. Ryan, Ann M.   II. McCullough, Joseph B.
    PS1334.C67  2008
    818'.409—dc22

                                    2008040157


⊗™ This paper meets the requirements of the American National Standard for Permanence of Paper for Printed Library Materials, Z39.48, 1984.

Designer: Kristie Lee
Typesetter: The Composing Room of Michigan, Inc.
Printer and binder: Thomson-Shore, Inc.
Typefaces: Berkeley, Astaire, Aristocrat

Title page illustration courtesy Mark Twain Papers and Project, Bancroft Library, University of California, Berkeley.

**Ann:**

*In loving memory of Liz Salvagno*

**Joe:**

*In memory of my mother and father and for Jessica, who often makes me laugh and who makes me very proud*

# Contents

# Acknowledgments

We owe our thanks to a great many people for their support, guidance, and expertise. We would like to thank Robert Hirst and the staff of the Mark Twain Project of the University of California, Berkeley, for both their assistance and their permission to use materials from the archive, and we would also like to thank Bob for his generous insights into this project. At the Mark Twain House and Museum, we owe thanks to Patti Philippon, who was instrumental in providing resources for Kerry Driscoll's essay. Additionally, we appreciate the kindness extended to this project by the entire staff of the Mark Twain House, particularly Jeffrey Nichols, who helped us to experience firsthand Twain's cosmopolitan lifestyle. We are grateful to the Center for Mark Twain Studies at Elmira College, and especially to Barb Snedecor for making available the many resources of Quarry Farm. We would like to thank as well Mark Woodhouse of the Gannett-Tripp Library at Elmira College for lending us his expertise. Kenneth Johnson from the reproduction department of the Library of Congress's digital collection made a complicated process much less daunting. And we also owe our thanks to the Barrett Collection at the University of Virginia for giving us permission to reproduce an image of Twain, resplendent in his top hat, and to Stephen Railton, whose Mark Twain in His Times Web site makes these images so accessible. And we are most particularly grateful to Ms. Alexandra Lidov for her permission to use the work of her husband, Arthur Lidov, whose drawing of Mark Twain has contributed greatly to this volume. Finally, we would like to acknowledge Tom Quirk, editor of the Mark Twain and Circle Series, whose support and sage advice throughout this project cannot be overstated.

Joe would also like to acknowledge Gina Sully, a Ph.D. student at UNLV—who also hails from Buffalo—for calling to his attention critical information about Buffalo, New York, during Twain's stay there. Finally, he would like to thank Judy, yet again, for her loving companionship, friendship, and good cheer, along with her uncanny ability to keep him focused and on task, without which this project would have remained a good idea only.

Ann would like to thank the Le Moyne College Research and Development Committee for its support of this project; the President of Le Moyne College, John Smarelli; as well as the Provost, Linda Le Mura, both of whom have encouraged and supported scholarship at Le Moyne. She would also like to thank the Chair of the English Department, Chris Warner, for helping her to make this project a priority, and Julie Grossman and Patrick Keane, also of the Le Moyne College English Department, for their generous readings of her work. She would like to thank Michael Kiskis, for being the Dean to her Jerry, and she owes a great deal of thanks to Kerry Driscoll, whose investment in this project has been stalwart and inspiring.

Ann would also like to thank her parents, Jeanne and John Ryan, who managed—somehow—to make 4908 Westview Drive feel like a fairly cosmopolitan place. Finally, she owes special thanks to Tom Kennedy, independent scholar and loving curmudgeon, for his sharp-eyed reading of her essays and for his affectionate support of the author.

# Abbreviations

| | |
|---|---|
| *CofC* | *Clemens of the "Call": Mark Twain in San Francisco.* Ed. Edgar M. Branch. Berkeley: University of California Press, 1969. |
| *CTSS1* | *Mark Twain: Collected Tales, Sketches, Speeches, & Essays, 1852–1890.* Vol. 1. Ed. Louis J. Budd. New York: Library of America, 1992. |
| *CTSS2* | *Mark Twain: Collected Tales, Sketches, Speeches, & Essays, 1891–1910.* Vol. 2. Ed. Louis J. Budd. New York: Library of America, 1992. |
| *ETS2* | *Early Tales and Sketches, 1864–1865.* Volume 2. Ed. Edgar M. Branch and Robert H. Hirst. Berkeley: University of California Press, 1979. |
| *FE* | *Following the Equator: A Journey around the World.* New York: Dover Publications, 1989. |
| *HF* | *Adventures of Huckleberry Finn.* Ed. Victor Fischer and Lin Salamo et al. Berkeley: University of California Press, 2001. |
| *IA* | *The Innocents Abroad or, The New Pilgrim's Progress.* New York: Modern Library, 2003. |
| *Interviews* | *Mark Twain: The Complete Interviews.* Ed. Gary Scharnhorst. Tuscaloosa: University of Alabama Press, 2006. |
| *L1* | *Mark Twain's Letters, Volume 1: 1853–1866.* Ed. Edgar M. Branch, Michael B. Frank, and Kenneth M. Sanderson. Berkeley: University of California Press, 1992. |

L2            *Mark Twain's Letters, Volume 2: 1867–1868.* Ed. Harriet Eli-
              nor Smith and Richard Bucci. Berkeley: University of Cal-
              ifornia Press, 1990.

L3            *Mark Twain's Letters, Volume 3: 1869.* Ed. Victor Fischer
              and Michael B. Frank. Berkeley: University of California
              Press, 1992.

L4            *Mark Twain's Letters, Volume 4: 1870–1871.* Ed. Victor Fis-
              cher and Michael B. Frank. Berkeley: University of Cali-
              fornia Press, 1995.

L5            *Mark Twain's Letters, Volume 5: 1872–1873.* Ed. Lin Salamo
              and Harriet Elinor Smith. Berkeley: University of Califor-
              nia Press, 1997.

L6            *Mark Twain's Letters, Volume 6: 1874–1875.* Ed. Victor Fis-
              cher, Michael B. Frank, and Harriet Elinor Smith. Berke-
              ley: University of California Press, 2002.

*Letters*     *Mark Twain's Letters, Volume 2.* Ed. Albert Bigelow Paine.
              New York: Harper and Brothers, 1917.

LLMT          *The Love Letters of Mark Twain.* Ed. Dixon Wecter. New
              York: Harper and Brothers, 1949.

LOM           *Life on the Mississippi.* Boston: James R. Osgood, 1883.

MFMT          Clemens, Clara. *My Father, Mark Twain.* New York. New
              York: Harper Brothers, 1931.

MTA           *Mark Twain's Autobiography.* 2 Vols. Ed. Albert Bigelow
              Paine. New York: Harper and Brothers, 1924.

MTHHR         *Mark Twain's Correspondence with Henry Huddleston Rogers,
              1893–1909.* Ed. Lewis Leary. Berkeley: University of Cali-
              fornia Press, 1969.

MTH&M         Mark Twain House and Museum, Hartford, Connecticut.

MTHL1         *Mark Twain-Howells Letters, Volume 1.* Ed. Henry Nash
              Smith and William M. Gibson. Cambridge: Harvard Uni-
              versity Press, 1960.

MTOA          *Mark Twain's Own Autobiography: Chapters from the North
              American Review.* Ed. Michael J. Kiskis. Madison: Univer-
              sity of Wisconsin Press, 1990.

| | |
|---|---|
| MTP | Mark Twain Papers and Project, Bancroft Library, University of California, Berkeley. Unpublished Material. |
| MTPO | Mark Twain's Letters, 1876–1880. Ed. Victor Fischer, Michael B. Frank, Harriet Elinor Smith et al. Mark Twain Project Online. Berkeley: University of California Press, 2007. |
| MTTMB | *Mark Twain's Travels with Mr. Brown: Being Heretofore the Uncollected Sketches of Mark Twain Written for the Alta California.* Ed. Franklin Walker and G. Ezra Dane. New York: Alfred A. Knopf, 1940. |
| N&J2 | *Mark Twain's Notebooks and Journals, Volume 2 (1877–1883).* Ed. Frederick Anderson, Lin Salamo, and Bernard L. Stein. Berkeley: University of California Press, 1975. |
| P&P | *The Prince and the Pauper.* Berkeley: University of California Press, 1983. |
| RI | *Roughing It.* The Oxford Mark Twain. New York: Oxford University Press, 1966. |
| SMTHL | *Selected Mark Twain–Howells Letters, 1872–1910.* Ed. Frederick Anderson, William M. Gibson, and Henry Nash Smith. Cambridge: Belknap Press, 1967. |
| SNO | *Sketches New and Old.* New York: Oxford University Press, 1996. |
| Speaking | *Mark Twain Speaking.* Ed. Paul Fatout. Iowa City: University of Iowa Press, 1976. |
| TA | *A Tramp Abroad.* New York: Oxford University Press, 1996. |

# COSMOPOLITAN *Twain*

# Introduction
## Mark Twain and the Cosmopolitan Ideal

ANN M. RYAN

THE problem of geography—that is, of establishing regional and national boundaries, of marking natural phenomena, or even of defining performative spaces—often dominates our perceptions of Mark Twain. The critic of Twain's fiction, almost of necessity, becomes a kind of literary cartographer, mapping the divisions and fault lines that define Twain's persona and that construct his narrative agendas. Whether or not these geographic signposts, as well as the psychological claims they carry, are unique to the life of Mark Twain or more widely emblematic of the chaotic shifts in nineteenth-century American identity, they have significantly organized responses to the author and his work.

Mark Twain has been represented as the embodiment of an idyllic South (and its most sustained critic), as a northerner and an easterner (and, therefore, complicit in propagating the values of both), as a post-transcendentalist, at once worshipping and eulogizing Eliot's "River God," and alternately as an icon or a caricature of the West.[1] In his world travels, Twain can be read

---

1. T. S. Eliot, "Introduction," *Adventures of Huckleberry Finn* (New York: Chanticleer Press, 1950). See also Jonathan Arac, *Huckleberry Finn as Idol and Target: The Functions of Criticism in Our Time* (Madison: University of Wisconsin Press, 1997), and Joseph Coulombe, *Mark Twain and the American West* (Columbia: University of Missouri Press, 2003).

as both the imposing agent of Edward Said's imperial Occident and the original voice of America, exposing the sham of Europe's cultural hegemony and the detritus of its history. Finally, critics have suggested that place is less important for Twain than space, most prominently the stage. Here they mean both the stages upon which he performed and the wider public stage that Twain seemed—through the marketing of his image and his persona—almost to invent. While these varied readings highlight how Twain, chameleon-like, adapted his personae to the various landscapes he inhabited, they also point toward what I would characterize as the modernity of Mark Twain. As Twain traveled and lived in a variety of nations and places, he acquired languages, costumes, poses, and politics until he became one of the first truly cosmopolitan, world citizens. In response to each of the cities this volume will explore, Twain generated fiction and nonfiction prose that marked America's movement into the twentieth century and toward the darker realities that make possible this cosmopolitan state. For if the celebrity persona of "Mark Twain" represents one of the important byproducts of urbanity—he is in many ways an artificial person, an amalgam of imagination, industry, and technology—Samuel Clemens, the author of that mask, narrates the impoverished truths that frequently make this artifice such a powerful commodity. Twain anticipates American modernism: the intractability of race and nation, the tyrannies of industrialism and religion, and the promise, as well as the illusion, of a transnational, transhistorical, transcendent individuality. His narrative insights also resonate uncannily with the literary and political theories of a postmodern and postcolonial world.

This urban legacy has, nevertheless, often been elided by Twain critics, who favor instead Twain's rural origins and his mythologizing of them. At the beginning of the twentieth century, Van Wyck Brooks and Bernard DeVoto began the first serious characterization of Twain based upon his rural associations. Their contentious readings carved out a fault line that continues to inform critical responses to Twain's work. Van Wyck Brooks famously argued that Twain was a victim of the East, and of the Langdon influence specifically: "From the moment of his marriage his artistic integrity, already compromised, had as a matter of fact, been virtually destroyed." In response DeVoto claimed that Twain was not a failed artist, but an original representative of frontier America, "umbilically tied" to the Mississippi: "Whatever else this frontier humorist did, whatever he failed to do, this much he did. He wrote books that have in them something eternally true to the core of his nation's life. They are at the center; all other books whatsoever are farther away." Ernest Hemingway continued this critical bifurcation when he famously claimed that "All American literature comes from a book called *Huckleberry Finn*"—except for the closing chapters of the novel, which are "just cheating." Like so many critics, before and after him, Hemingway opposed Twain's artistic integrity to what Forrest Robinson might call Twain's "bad faith."[2]

Such essentializing claims have obscured Twain's own agency in constructing these competing perceptions of himself and his fiction. Far from being the unconscious product of the West or the dupe of the East, Twain manipulated his regional investments and identifications as he produced his fiction, reworking and reimagining his identity all the while. Twain, for example, appeared as a wild Indian on the cover of *Innocents Abroad*. He played the part of an eastern dandy while traveling through the West in *Roughing It*. Twain was a confederate deserter who—in an exaggerated southern drawl—heroicized his own cowardice before northern audiences and Union veterans. He dressed in his Oxford gowns in Connecticut and wore his bathrobe on the streets of London. Twain was forever contemplating and ironizing his place—or lack of place—in the world, which makes him significantly more restless, less "umbilically tied" to any specific location, than we may want to believe. Yet, despite Twain's many relocations and self-representations, critics continue to mine the tensions mapped by DeVoto and Brooks, between Twain's western legacy and his eastern real estate, producing visions of Twain that range from social progressive and reformer to henpecked husband and sellout.

As contradictory as these readings seem to be, at least one similarity connects them. This East/West axis spins in search of the mythical "authentic" Twain who, we are told, is best embodied by his nostalgic forays into childhood and by his raucous western fictions. For Brooks, DeVoto, and their critical progeny, the great works of Mark Twain—*Huck Finn, Tom Sawyer, Life on the Mississippi,* and *Roughing it*—could never have been written if

2. Brooks, *The Ordeal of Mark Twain* (New York: E. P. Dutton, 1920), 151; DeVoto, *Mark Twain's America* (Boston: Houghton Mifflin, 1967), 321; Hemingway, *Green Hills of Africa* (New York: Simon and Schuster, 1935), 22; Robinson, *In Bad Faith: The Dynamics of Deception in Mark Twain's America* (Cambridge: Harvard University Press, 1992). See also Peter Stoneley, *Mark Twain and the Feminine Aesthetic* (Cambridge: Cambridge University Press, 1992), 1–11.

Twain's muse had not been the Mississippi, the West, small-town America, or some other untamed and untainted locus of American identity. Thus, many literary critics mirror in a more nuanced form the popular conception of Mark Twain, while marginalizing or excusing his darker and more complicated responses to American culture and history.

One of the aims of this volume is to offer a corrective to the dominant perception of Mark Twain, or at least to map out another landscape for critical inquiry, by locating Twain in the urban centers where he lived so much of his life. This collection, which directly confronts notions of Mark Twain as an embodiment of rural American values, will present a less familiar portrait of the author and his position in American culture. If Twain responds to the brutality, alienation, and hypocrisy of the modern urban state by dreaming of small southern towns and a "monstrous big river," he also resists the venality, self-importance, and bigotry of rural America by embracing the identity and ideology of "The City." Opposed to the Mississippi River, which becomes an icon of transcendent American individuality, are London, Vienna, San Francisco, St. Louis, New Orleans, Hartford, Buffalo, and New York, all of which consume Twain's small-town identity. Some casual readers, and even professional critics, are disappointed, or discomfited, or in some measure embarrassed by Twain's investment in cosmopolitan aesthetics and values; they long for a Mark Twain who represents America more organically or who honors his talents more fully. Of course, the irony here is that this urban and urbane Mark Twain may, in fact, be completely true to himself—even in the last chapters of *Huck Finn*. In other words, Twain represents that part of the American psyche formed and informed by urban experience. As for Mark Twain himself, he is no country boy longing to go fishing on the Mississippi. As the essays in this collection argue, Twain is a cosmopolitan: he is competitive, skeptical, necessarily tolerant, passionately secular, multilingual and multicultural, frankly materialistic and acquisitive. Despite the nostalgic backward glance that seems to frame much of his fiction, Twain's writing—even his most celebrated texts—evinces a progressive, modernist critique of American politics and history, a critique provoked by his life as an urban citizen.

Although most scholars and even casual readers of Twain's fiction are aware of his travels, few have calculated the effect of Twain's lifelong residency in the major cities of America and the world. Twain lived longer in

This pencil drawing by Arthur Lidov represents Twain as the embodiment of pastoral, American ideals. (Courtesy Library of Congress; used by permission of Alexandra Lidov)

New York City than in Hannibal. He resided for extended periods in London, Heidelberg, Vienna, San Francisco, Buffalo, and Hartford. During his time as a riverboat pilot, while he was purportedly falling in love with the "River God," he was also engaged in trafficking people and goods from one midwestern city to the next, arriving finally in the cosmopolis of New Orleans. While Twain did "Go West" as a young man, he was no John Muir, nor did he typify the ideals extolled by Horace Greeley. Twain recorded his impressions of the western landscape, but he was more often annoyed by the hostility of the wilderness than he was charmed by its scope or majesty, nor did he apply the diligent labor or entrepreneurial imagination to the West's natural resources that might have made his fortune. Twain's first motivation in heading West was to avoid the horrors of the Civil War; only later, and almost by accident, did he mine for either mineral or literary gold. Even here, Twain was drawn to a city, San Francisco, where he would begin his first sustained analysis of the mechanisms and rhythms of urban life: criminal acts and the sensational treatment of them; the pretentious and playful lives of the rich and famous; the friction and attraction between the races. After less than four years out West, a period that included a trip to Hawaii, Twain returned East—to New York, Buffalo, and Hartford—never again to reside in the wilds or at the margins of American life.

Twain's urban experience has been predominantly represented as a series of pauses in an overall transient life. The fact that Twain set up domestic spaces in London or Vienna or New York is presented as a necessary hiatus in his frenetic travels, dictated by logistics more than by design. However, to characterize Twain as a tourist suggests that he did little more than take his show on the road. Such a reading privileges the commodity of "Mark Twain," while it obscures the lasting effect of his travels. Twain, of course, diligently contributed to the perception that he is an American export, marketing his image and selling his fiction as if both were simply commercial products, until eventually "Mark Twain" becomes a kind of literary Coca-Cola. Even beyond reinforcing the image of Mark Twain as the prototypical American, these performances effectively propagated what would become a hegemonic American culture. As he moved from nation to nation and place to place, Twain processed his experiences through what he termed his creative "machine," resulting in the prose and the performances that would earn him world acclaim. Twain's metaphor is telling in that it frames his

This 1896 photograph taken by Alfred Ellis in London shows Twain in the habiliment of the urban sophisticate. (Papers of Mark Twain, MSS 6314, Clifton Waller Barrett Library of American Literature, Special Collections, University of Virginia Library)

travels as both a capitalist and an imperial enterprise. Samuel Clemens used
Europe, the Middle East, Africa, and the South Pacific as raw materials that,
once acted upon by his imaginative machinery, enabled him to create a distinctly American product: the narrative voice and persona of Mark Twain.
This was both the process and the conceit that made possible a work such
as *Innocents Abroad* and that ensured the popularity of Twain's comic performances. Twain's distinctive American voice—western, irreverent, ironic—
remained remarkably consistent, whether he was undermining Old World
pretensions, for example, or exposing the icons of the Holy Land. Twain understood the power of his persona and would, like Edgar Bergen with Charlie McCarthy, trot this sometimes wooden self out upon the stage and produce the commodity for which he was being paid. That his audiences and
readers were—and to some extent still are—convinced of the authenticity
of this character is a tribute to the genius of Twain as both performer and
artist.

To confuse this performing persona with the person of Mark Twain, a
transference made so absolutely by his reading public that Twain felt sometimes trapped by the image he had crafted, is to miss the complicated literary and political evolution precipitated by his cosmopolitan life. In the introduction to their volume on cosmopolitan theory and practice, Carol A.
Breckenridge, Sheldon Pollock, Homi Bhabha, and Dipesh Chakrabarty describe one of the distinguishing aspects of a cosmopolitan identity: a feeling of being at once displaced and interconnected, of being both unified and
eclectic. They suggest that the cosmopolitan has acquired, by necessity and
sometimes by design, "ways of living at home abroad or abroad at home—
ways of inhabiting multiple places at once, of being different beings simultaneously, of seeing the larger picture stereoscopically within the small."[3] By
the time he reached his professional and artistic maturity, "Mark Twain"—
the artist and the artifice—embodied this cosmopolitan ideal. Twain described the tourist in *Innocents Abroad* as one who travels for the pleasure of
returning home, a "consummate ass" who may adopt a veneer of sophistication, but who remains relatively unchanged by the journey (*IA*, 121). Although Twain represented himself as just such an ass, over time his alle-

3. Breckenridge, Pollock, Bhabha, and Chakrabarty, "Cosmopolitanisms," in *Cosmopolitanism*, ed. Breckenridge et al. (Durham: Duke University Press, 2002), 11.

giances and his values shifted; no longer content to be a hometown hero, he became, instead, a citizen of the world.

In this move from the parochial to the global, Twain is less unique than we might suppose. As was the case with many other Americans during the late nineteenth century, Twain's horizons were broadening rapidly. Cities across the globe were assuming their modern dimensions, adapting to the technologies of modernity and acquiring the massive populations needed to sustain their economies. Concurrent with the westward expansion of nineteenth-century America was the growth of its urban centers. New York, Chicago, Boston, and San Francisco all more than doubled over the course of the century as immigrants, displaced workers, bohemians, and entre-preneurs converged upon American cities. Meanwhile, London ended the nineteenth century with a population of 6.7 million people, making it the largest city in the world, with New York and Paris close behind. Mark Twain was one of those millions, and he did not merely travel to or through American and European cities, recording his witticisms along the way; he sought them out. Twain was an urban citizen for most of his adult life, and even on those occasions when he set up his home in a suburban space—whether renting a villa outside Florence or transplanting his family to Riverdale, just north of New York—he was drawn into the life of the city. In his travel narratives, particularly *Innocents Abroad* and *Following the Equator,* Twain was fascinated by streets, crowds, and public spaces, by railroads and railway stations, by the language, the architecture, the smells, the food, and the sounds of cities. In his more journalistic efforts, his early letters to the *Alta California,* for example, or in his later political satires, Twain was consistently a critic of the fashions and customs of the cultural elite, of the hypocrisies of the political and religious monopolies that are headquartered in urban sites, yet his response to the urban poor was a tense oscillation between hostility and empathy, mirroring the attitudes of many urban residents. While his reactions to each of the cities in which he lived were distinct—the politics of New York, the police force of San Francisco, the behavior and look of whites in Bombay—Twain's observations of urban landscapes are also surprisingly consistent. In his descriptions of both the masses and the machinery that inhabit the urban landscape, Twain records not only the emerging infrastructure of the modern city but its ethos as well.

Having lived in so many cities around the world, Twain both narrated and embodied the cosmopolitan ideal. He moved easily through culturally, linguistically, and economically diverse environments; he spoke to royalty and to cab drivers with equal regularity and ease. As first imagined by Marshall McLuhan in the mid-1960s, the cosmopolitan transcends national boundaries and, by virtue of technological advances in travel and communication, articulates the commonality of human suffering and human potential.[4] Twain's later works, particularly such protest pieces as "King Leopold's Soliloquy" or "To the Person Sitting in Darkness," reflect an outrage made possible by having lived much of his life abroad. Yet, even in works that do not seem to be informed by either Twain's transnational identity or his global politics, Twain responded to his subject from the vantage point of the cosmopolitan: sympathetic, engaged, yet also distanced from his subject—"seeing the larger picture stereoscopically within the small." In a relatively "local" essay such as "Sociable Jimmy," for example, Twain as narrator takes pleasure in the "different" sound of Jimmy's speech, just as the humor depends upon our immediate recognition of Jimmy's humanity. Twain's outsider status—he is an adult, white, and literate—creates the interest in Jimmy's unique narrative, just as it makes possible the linguistic community that evolves between the narrator and the speaker, and between the text and the reader. The "global village" is formed by Jimmy's distinct voice, by his sociable humanity, and by Twain's careful record of both.

Yet if this narrative reflects the liberatory possibilities of Twain's cosmopolitanism, in which difference yields to community, it also represents those aspects of cosmopolitan political theory that trouble some of its critics. Twain's easy movement between cities, his global perspective, and the empathy that perspective seems to create are the products of privilege. Although Twain observed the suffering of many different people in a wide variety of contexts, he did so—like a nineteenth-century Angelina Jolie—from the window of a first-class cabin. Even Twain's pleasure in the speech of Jimmy may be read as a type of objectification, a pleasure constructed by Twain's superior position in the world. Although he did on occasion sympathize with the condition of the poor, Twain spent more of his time catering to and socializing with the elite. Twain's cosmopolitanism, like that of

4. McLuhan, *Understanding Media: The Extensions of Man* (New York: McGraw Hill, 1964).

many contemporary people, may ultimately represent the choices and comforts that modernity has created for a select few, not the extent to which
technology and globalization have liberated the impoverished many. Twain's
fiction and nonfiction prose represent both these perspectives: the haunt-
ing possibility that all of mankind is created equal, and the routine assaults
upon this ideal by organized religion, political ideology (including democracy), industrial progress (and its ensuing battery of the poor), and simple,
unadorned prejudice. Though he may never have fully portrayed his own
love affair with wealth and power, Twain routinely exposed the abuse of the
poor by the rich, and he gloried in revealing the congenital stupidity of the
privileged classes.

Yet, for all Twain's interest in the dynamics of wealth and poverty, it's fair
to say that he often avoided fictional representations of urban life. Very few
of his fictional works directly engage the life of the nineteenth-century metropolis: London appears either in its medieval or its Renaissance incarnations; Huck and Tom never explore New Orleans or San Francisco; Hannibal dominates Twain's fiction, while New York and Vienna seem only to
provide a stage for it. Certainly there are other writers more clearly invested in depicting "the city" as a setting and cultivating it as a metaphor. In fiction, Edith Wharton, Henry James, and even Melville and Poe, for example,
devote their imaginative energies to exploring the economic forces of urban
life as well as the extent to which those forces corrupt morals, commodify
culture and art, and objectify human beings. At the other extreme, poet Walt
Whitman conflates the dynamic nature of the city with the Dionysian possibilities of the Emersonian self: "Thrive, cities! bring your freight, bring
your shows, ample and sufficient rivers; / Expand, being than which none
else is perhaps more spiritual; / Keep your places, objects than which none
else is more lasting." Whitman's expanding, multitudinous city creates the
environment in which the poet, and by implication his audience, can transcend the narrow limits of a historically defined self: "What is it, then, between us? / What is the count of the scores or hundreds of years between
us? / Whatever it is, it avails not—distance avails not, and place avails not."[5]
Twain, by contrast, was more apt to despise a crowd than to embrace it; still,

5. Whitman, "Crossing Brooklyn Ferry," in *Whitman: Poetry and Prose,* ed. Justin Kaplan
(New York: Library of America, 1996), 307.

his characters—Huck, Tom Canty, Prince Edward, even Pudd'nhead Wilson and August Feldner—often yearn for the same human connection that Whitman idealizes, and they often seem to do so when they are lost in a sea of other people. If Twain is uneasy about Whitman's romance with the city, he also seems detached from the realist desire to engage and expose urban experience. Twain is no Crane or Dreiser, taking up the problem of the have-nots in the patois or the setting of the city. Yet while he does not portray, like James or Wharton, the psychological tensions of life on Washington Square or Fifth Avenue, Twain is, nonetheless, an urban writer.

Twain's avoidance of "urban narratives" is, more accurately, a strategic narrative distance. Twain made a career out of sidestepping, or as he describes it in "Private History of a Campaign that Failed," "flanking" in order to avoid direct assaults: he did so with issues of sexuality and racial identity and, in this case, with the problems of urbanity. This distance, in part a function of his humor and in part a reflection of his anxiety, allowed Twain to sweep away the surface details of city life and to engage the moral, economic, political, and ideological structures that sustain it. Twain drew upon the urban characters he encountered and the progressive ideas he absorbed in order to explore the ethical debris of modernity. Twain's mysterious strangers, for example, are quintessential cosmopolitans: their experience is diverse; their language is sophisticated; their morality is supple. They enter various small towns, from Hadleyburg to Eseldorf, and expose the self-serving theology and ethics of the inhabitants. In *Pudd'nhead Wilson*, Twain's last fictional portrait of the Mississippi, the cultural values of cosmopolitan Europe clearly trump the family values—twisted as they are—of Dawson's Landing. The Italian Twins happily escape the lunacy of America, leaving behind the random operations of its democratic institutions: "The twins were heroes of romance, now, and with rehabilitated reputations. But they were weary of Western adventure, and straightway retired to Europe."[6] Even in his *Autobiography*, a work rife with nostalgic reflections, Twain functions as a kind of mysterious stranger, returning to the people and places of his youth and promising to shock those who think they know him.

Twain's nostalgia, as represented in *Tom Sawyer* and *Life on the Mississippi*

6. *Puddn'head Wilson and Those Extraordinary Twins*, 2d ed., ed. Sidney Berger (New York: W. W. Norton and Co., 2004), 114.

may have been provoked by his early experiences in New York, San Francisco, or New Orleans; as a poor printer or struggling newspaperman he may have longed for a simpler time and place. However, under the influence of his increasingly cosmopolitan perspective, Twain's memories yielded a more sustained critique of rural America and the values it represents. In *Following the Equator*, for example, Twain describes watching "a burly German" give a servant a "brisk cuff on the jaw," which leads him back to Hannibal where his father—"a refined and kindly gentleman"—would strike "our harmless slave boy, Lewis, for trifling little blunders and awkwardnesses." Twain's imaginative journey back to Hannibal, a town where a man "had a right to kill his slave if he wanted to" is less important than its point of origin; Twain's memory forges a common bond between the American slave and the servant in Bombay, between the institutionalized and naturalized brutality of the past and its corollary in the present (*FE*, 315–52). Unlike American realists who attempt in their fiction to record the oppressive conditions of the poor, Twain bypasses these images. Instead he traces the origins of this suffering to its roots in the complacent world beyond the urban landscape.

Twain quickly moved beyond the late-nineteenth century desire to document reality and began—like the early modernist that he is—playing with representations of it. At the turn of the century, Mark Twain anticipated the themes and forms of modernism in his experimentation with linear narrative, particularly in his *Autobiography,* in his contemptuous representations of Christianity and its politics, and in his rejection of the organizing narratives of history. Twain's pseudonymous identity, however, is perhaps his greatest modernist text. In her work on photography and autobiography, Linda Haverty Rugg describes Twain as an artist who "most thoroughly grasped the power of photographic illusion. . . . In response to the uncertainties surrounding identity and ownership, he created a self-image that would also serve as a self-ironizing mask, working through photographs and an experimental, endless autobiography."[7] Twain makes the modernist assumption that names, faces, and words are no longer stable categories through which to interpret identity; instead, they are fictions capable of being revised and reinvented.

7. Rugg, *Picturing Ourselves: Photography and Autobiography* (Chicago: University of Chicago Press, 1997), 29.

Twain also makes clear in his later work that such freedom has its costs. At the turn of the century, Twain would produce gothic fantasies in which human and almost-human characters exist beyond "bigotry and narrow-mindedness," but are also beyond name, place, religion, and race (*IA*, 491). Twain's final response to urban experience as a whole comes in the form of mysterious and nameless strangers whose anonymity feels less liberating than forsaken. In *No. 44, The Mysterious Stranger,* written in part during Twain's final years in New York, Twain creates a world in which all realities . are reduced to special effects: names and identities are interchangeable; the past and the future are a random collection of sets and scenes; and the human body and face are only costumes to be worn and discarded at will. In this highly experimental and fragmentary text, Mark Twain is at his modern and even postmodern best, exchanging the claims of realism and authenticity for the attractions of pleasure and play. In *The Mysterious Stranger* Twain liberates his hero, August Feldner, from all the demands of history and identity. No. 44, his tutor, is the ultimate cosmopolitan, a universal traveler who has endless experiences but no real being or beliefs. Toward the end of the narrative he dons a minstrel-show mask, but it has no meaning for August, other than the visceral feelings of pathos and pleasure it evokes. If August is freed from the anger and guilt that accompany this costume, he is also abandoned by Twain in a world of solipsistic play and performance: "Nothing exists but You. And You are but a *thought*—a vagrant Thought, a useless Thought, a homeless Thought, wandering forlorn among the empty eternities."[8] In his letters to the *Alta California,* Twain complains about the endless distances he must travel in New York to reach his destination. August Feldner has become an exaggerated version of this urban wanderer: completely free to follow his own desires, while also utterly lost and alone.

Like another displaced and cosmopolitan American modernist, T. S. Eliot, Twain takes a long view of history and sees in it a series of disconnects and absurdities; however, instead of watching the inevitable fall of London Bridge or shoring up the fragments against his ruin, Twain represents the

8. "No. 44, The Mysterious Stranger," in *Mark Twain's Mysterious Stranger Manuscripts,* ed. William M. Gibson (Berkeley: University of California Press, 1969), 405.

losses of history as a cosmic joke, in which he is both the author of the humor and its target. In fact, the dark, satiric project of American modernism—and Eliot's *Wasteland* may be the best example of it—can claim its origins in the late writing of Mark Twain. Had Twain been born a generation later, he surely could have found an audience in the salons of Paris with Gertrude Stein and at the expatriate retreats of Eliot's London and Pound's Rome.

To represent Twain as a cosmopolitan is to reposition him within the landscape of American cultural history. By shifting the points on the map that locate Mark Twain, this volume highlights Twain's own investments in the values and the structures of modernity. More important, we hope to reveal a Mark Twain who is less static, less caste in bronze than the iconic portrait that dominates the popular culture. Despite the sepia-tinted haze that surrounds many popular and scholarly representations of him, Twain was as avant-garde as he was nostalgic. And if Twain seems somehow rooted in the world of his childhood, he became equally disillusioned by the values that world generated and defended. These essays will demonstrate the extent to which Mark Twain stepped out of the antebellum South and into the cosmopolitan world of the late nineteenth and early twentieth centuries. Ultimately, Twain defied one of his own favorite truisms, that "training is everything," that we do not rise above or beyond the limits of our education or the prejudices of our youth. Mark Twain clearly transcended his own.

Our efforts here represent an initial foray into the topic of Twain's cosmopolitanism, his modern aesthetic, and even his cultural identity—and these efforts are admittedly incomplete. We could have expanded the list of cities to include Bombay, Calcutta, Washington, D.C., Paris, Heidelberg, and many others. However, the cities contained in this volume had a sustained influence on Twain over the course of his lifetime as well as a profound affect upon his fiction and his literary identity. We begin with New York, the first major American city that Twain called home, where seventeen-year-old Sam Clemens worked as a printer while absorbing the dangerous, provocative possibilities of the metropolis. In *Adventures of Huckleberry Finn* and *The Prince and the Pauper,* Twain recorded his own evolution from Pap

Finn—the defensive, paranoid white supremacist—to Tom Canty, a cha-meleon child whose fantasies become both a fraud and a truth. I will ar-gue that, from these early angry responses, Twain eventually took pleasure in the confusion that the streets of New York invited, the play and display that blur the color of faces and mistake performers in costume for authen-tic individuals.

Next we move to the Mississippi River and the Midwest, where Bruce Michelson aligns Twain's restlessness and his seeming detachment from the urban sites he occupies with the central paradox of cosmopolitanism: that the "global" perspective requires a distance that may, in fact, amount to a lack of engagement. Michelson begins by positioning Twain in the crossfire of current debate about both the political efficacy of cosmopolitanism and the cultural valences suggested by the term. He surveys the critical land-scape and discovers a number of cosmopolitans and cosmopolitanisms: ef-fete academics who blithely dismiss both humanism and Western political engagements in Third World countries, content in what amounts to a styl-ish nihilism; advocates for cultural plurality whose work to right the wrongs of historical imperialism and the current processes of globalization provides the fodder for the aforementioned academics; and finally the privileged, transnational citizens whose political sympathies may be less refined than their sense of style and taste. Michelson's Mark Twain can, in the right light, look like any one of these incarnations of the cosmopolitan: a nihilist who nonetheless wants change; a reformer who doesn't particularly want to be bothered with the details of reform; an urbane sophisticate who longs for authentic experience. Beginning with his years as a printer in St. Louis and a riverboat pilot, Mark Twain developed, according to Michelson, a habit of detachment, becoming a "perpetual outsider," living "on land as a visitor with wages in his pocket, but never as an assimilated local." Riding the cur-rents of the Mississippi (or, as a printer, caught up in the rapid flow of words and information), Twain became swept up in the larger currents of change that would ultimately obscure the particularities of both St. Louis and New Orleans. Michelson presents us with a Mark Twain who is kinetic and un-easy, just as he is at home in almost any port or town. Twain's experience in St. Louis and New Orleans prepared him for a world in which any cos-mopolitan politics or pose is necessarily flexible and transient.

In San Francisco, Twain had his first major success as a comic writer, yet his experiences in the city, specifically his exposure to a bohemian group of talented writers, excited his ambitions to become something more than a humorist. Here, Bret Harte and Charles Webb, among others, functioned for Twain as Tom Sawyer's gang does for Huck Finn: he wanted in. In his essay, James E. Caron distinguishes between the drudgery of reporting and the thrill of literary performance. Twain's loathing for his work as a reporter does not signal his ambivalence to the issues of urban life (poverty, crime, political intrigue, and so on). Rather, it represents Twain's increasing investment in a cultural and literary identity only articulated and available in the journals (and salons) of San Francisco. Caron presents Twain as a "comic *flâneur*" who, of necessity, cultivates a certain reportorial detachment from the landscape he surveys, but who also mocks this highly artificial pose. In San Francisco, Twain discovered a comic voice that is informed by literary aesthetics and conventions, yet equally inspired by a bohemian worldview.

In Buffalo we see Twain accommodating himself not simply to domestic life but also to life as a successful member of a prominent East Coast family. Joseph B. McCullough represents Twain's experiences in Buffalo as both central to his evolving public persona and, conversely, a spur to his more untamed impulses. McCullough does not reproduce Brooks's argument that Twain's artistry suffered under the Langdon influence. If anything, Jervis Langdon emerges in this essay as the patron he was, making possible Twain's entry into the world of business, entrepreneurialism, and real estate transactions. McCullough does, however, point toward a kind of constraint at work in part due to the stability of Twain's life in the city. For the first time, Twain was a home owner, a business owner, and the head of a family. What this produced in him was a restlessness that actually inspired his wandering and his writing. In Buffalo, Twain resisted, and possibly resented, how bound he was by obligation, routine, and ownership. At the end of his tenure in Buffalo, Twain sounded, according to McCullough, a little bit like his fictional child Huck: "All I wanted was to go somewheres; all I wanted was a change" (*HF*, 15).

If Twain felt unsure of the pact he made when he married into the eastern cultural elite, if his forays onto the stage indicate that he may have been hearing "the call of the wild," Kerry Driscoll argues that by the time Twain and Livy settled in Hartford he had fixed his sights on being recognized by that community and accepted by it as well. Driscoll finds Twain at a cultural and personal crossroads, anxiously working to prove himself a member of the literati and glitterati of Hartford, yet also struggling to define his own aesthetic sensibility; all of which becomes concentrated for Driscoll in Twain's relationship to material luxuries. While traveling in Europe, Twain invested in a series of complex transactions meant to signify that he was an aesthete, involved citizen, and philanthropist, foremost among them the purchase of "an elegant music box made of 'handsome walnut root' by the Swiss firm of Samuel Troll, Fils." Driscoll reads this music box as a symbol of Twain's complex position in Hartford: Twain carefully balanced his desire to perfect his domestic surroundings against his ambition to display both taste and sophistication. In this careful analysis of the patterns of spending and shopping that involved both Twain and Livy, Driscoll finds a narrative of cultural anxiety as well as a crisis of identity. The "playlist" that the music box eventually contained became a contested space, where Twain's cultural ambitions competed with his domestic ideals. According to Driscoll, the music box—positioned in the foyer—represented the interiority (and idealized tranquillity) of Twain's domestic life in the Hartford house while simultaneously serving as a public, even cross-cultural, display of refinement and consumption.

In Twain's early visits to London, Peter Messent marks the beginning of a complex process for Twain of shifting, redefining, and at times rejecting his national identity, while at other times embracing a more nuanced form of it. Messent chooses these early visits as a starting point for more than chronological reasons; he suggests that Twain's relative detachment (a word that comes up frequently in this volume) from the conventional sights of London is a reflection of his fixation upon the human landscape. This detachment may either be a necessary first step toward becoming a world citizen or a fallacy, a privilege available only to the privileged. In other words, the entire notion of the cosmopolitan may simply be a repackaging of Western rights and assumptions, a new kind of colonialism. And while Messent's essay does not directly raise these questions, I think they're implicit in the representation of Twain as consciously pursuing the company of the social and intellectual elite of London, while also immersing himself in the national and international media available to him, thereby unconsciously shifting his worldview. Messent's essay positions Twain in the 1870s very much as a work in progress. While he was making his fortune by reifying his image as the prototypical American, he was also undermining that characterization by embracing the international politics and the multicultural perspective available in London. So, London seems to have liberated Twain from his narrowly constructed national identity, ironically enough, by granting him access to a narrowly defined cultural elite. His politics became more liberal while his taste became more refined.

Twain fully achieved this transnational voice during his time in Vienna, which Janice McIntire-Strasburg presents as a site of both political and psychological "breakthroughs." Twain discovered in Vienna a way to mediate his authentic feelings by using his artificial persona, a process that moved in two directions: outward, toward the world of politics and religion, and inward, toward his own grief and rage. As both outsider and celebrity, Twain was in the position of many cosmopolitans. His wealth and worldliness guaranteed some power within the social and political landscapes he inhabited, while the transience of his lifestyle insulated and liberated him from the dangerous consequences of political engagement. His investment in Viennese politics could be a choice, an experiment rather than a historical imperative (best represented by his seat in the Reichsrath's gallery, watching while a riot occurred). By the time he got to Vienna, Twain had a global perspective that—elitist as it was—made possible some of his more sweeping views and compelling claims about human civilization. His experiences in India and Australasia, according to McIntire-Strasburg, expose the extent to which Twain had become a member of the cultural elite (the larger, higher "balcony" in which he was now sitting). Yet this perspective, far from distancing him from local politics, allowed him to give these issues a global dimension. Twain responded to indigenous people and to the imperialists who oppressed them: he spoke out against the persecution of Jews in Vienna, the genocidal conduct of King Leopold in Africa, and the missionary hypocrisies of Christians in China. McIntire-Strasburg argues that Vienna became for Mark Twain a bully pulpit, where his politics became global and his voice became fully his own.

In what we believe to be the ultimate gesture of a cosmopolitan reading, we close the volume with a counterpoint, a view of Twain that is less urban than suburban. Michael J. Kiskis does not present Elmira as either a cultivated city or a site of sophisticated cultural and intellectual exchange—though that argument certainly could be made. That the Langdons made

Elmira their home may be enough to testify to the progressive and profitable environment of this small city. Instead, Kiskis presents Elmira, and more specifically Quarry Farm, as an alternative, possibly an antidote, to Twain's increasingly cosmopolitan lifestyle. Kiskis represents the increased need for privacy and for domestic retreat as one consequence of urban living. The mile-high hill upon which the farm rests functioned like the security fences that now surround most suburban homes. The steep hill blocked outside distractions and invasions, while also preserving for Twain an all-important view of the world beyond, below, and maybe even within. Quarry Farm became what most city dwellers dream of: a country home, a piece of utopian real estate made necessary by the madness of urban life. Although Twain never returned to the rural landscapes of his youth—nor did he want to—Elmira recovered for him, according to Kiskis, something like the imagined innocence of childhood. Like the contemporary bedroom community, Elmira became a respite for Twain and his family, a quiet retreat from which Twain could transform his perceptions of the world beyond Elmira into the fictions that would secure his fame. If this volume positions Twain as a sometime realist, a closeted modernist, and a postmodernist in disguise, Michael Kiskis reveals Twain's practices as a writer to be firmly Romantic and Victorian. Twain's fiction emerged only when he could "recall in tranquillity" his dreams of home and family. Though even in this Romantic gesture, I would argue, we can hear Mark Twain's world-weariness, his longing for a mythical home, a desire for peace that was the reflection of his cosmopolitan life.

# Mark Twain and the Mean (and Magical) Streets of New York

ANN M. RYAN

In 1853 seventeen-year-old Sam Clemens arrived in New York City after an arduous five-day trip across four states. He left his mother in Hannibal, Missouri, which, with a population of two thousand, had been chartered as a city only seven years earlier. After a short stay in St. Louis, he headed for New York City; at close to 700,000 inhabitants, it was the largest and most diverse metropolis on the continent. It would be the first time, and in many ways the last, that Mark Twain could claim to be an actual "innocent abroad," rather than the crafted impersonation of innocence that he would eventually become. At the conclusion of *Innocents Abroad: A New Pilgrim's Progress*, published in 1869, Twain declares somewhat blithely, "Travel is fatal to prejudice, bigotry and narrow-mindedness, and many of our people need it sorely on these accounts" (*IA*, 491). Yet these transforming and somewhat punitive effects of travel began for Mark Twain not in Europe or the Holy Land, where most of his assumptions and beliefs were affirmed, but in New York City, where Twain's identity was not only assaulted but dismantled and reformed.

The story of Mark Twain in New York City is in many ways emblematic of success in nineteenth-century America: a small-town boy makes his fortune and his name under the bright lights of the city. Mark Twain's experience in New York reproduces the narrative arc of the ideal cosmopolitan: in 1853 Twain arrived in lower Manhattan a lonely, frightened, angry, and awestruck teenager; thirty-nine years later he would be known as "The Belle of New York," an embodiment of New York sophistication and élan.

What I hope to establish is how Twain may have understood his own remarkable progress from regional humorist and small-town wit to urbane celebrity and literary progressive and, more important, what that progress might signal about the effects of urbanity and the broader implications for cosmopolitan identity in America. Although the notion of cosmopolitanism seems to describe global issues arising out of the twentieth and twenty-first centuries, as many philosophers and cultural critics have suggested the term casts a long shadow. Twain's biography demonstrates that how one lives in a world of "Others" was equally an issue for the nineteenth-century urbanite. Did his success, for example, represent to Twain the potential for reimagining identity (racial and national), realigning politics (global and local), and shifting resources (cultural and economic)—all transformations made possible in urban spaces? Or, did he discover—somewhere between dinner at Delmonico's and the back allies of the Five Points—the darker implications of a cosmopolitan worldview: that despite these changes in costume and context, all human experience is the same? In his later fictional experiments, Twain's understanding of the universal human community (one of the ideals that inspires some theories of the cosmopolitan) is little more than an expression of nihilism. Through his talking microbes and mysterious strangers, this aging Mark Twain reveals (and even seems to revel in) the ubiquitous and mechanistic sameness of human life, death, sin, and suffering.

Cosmopolitanism, as a political alternative to a narrowly defined (and defended) conception of identity, is more than simply the experience of diversity—more than a sampling of foods and customs and languages and clothes. It insists, according to Kwame Anthony Appiah, upon "the sort of core moral ideas increasingly articulated in our conception of basic human rights." Without imposing a globalized definition of the Right or the Good, cosmopolitans accept the fact that these Others—exotics, foreigners, distant strangers—are people, and that "People have needs—health, food, shelter, education—that must be met if they are to lead decent lives."[1] In

---

1. Appiah, *Cosmopolitanism: Ethics in a World of Strangers* (New York and London: W. W. Norton, 2006), 162–63.

his experiences in New York City and in the fiction that grew out of those experiences, Twain wrestled with these imperatives of modern urban life: that in cities we confront people whom our politics, or culture, or religion have chosen to objectify, but whom the circumstances of modernity will no longer allow us easily to ignore or exploit. Of all the cities in which he lived and worked, New York most clearly presented Mark Twain with the challenges of a cosmopolitan political ideal. In his journey toward this cosmopolitan ethos, Twain had to balance the habits of racism he had inherited against the realities of poverty and injustice that inhabited the city and that subsequently haunted his fiction.

Many of Twain's novels evince a fascination with the elements of urban life, even while set in rural communities and landscapes. In such "rural" works as *Connecticut Yankee* or *Pudd'nhead Wilson,* Twain negotiates the tension between two dynamics: a deterministic view of the world that is specifically a consequence of urban life, one dominated by beggars, threatening mobs, isolated individuals, and sudden and meaningless death; and the romantic alternative where the city offers the possibility of fantastic transformations, where paupers become princes, and race, class, and gender are shifting guises, not inexorable fates. Twain would, for example, experiment with characters who re-create their identities by simply changing their clothes; however, these powerfully suggestive transformations have their limits. Twain would likewise undermine his own models of transcendence by returning his characters and texts to their points of origin: Tom Driscoll is sold down the river and Dawson's Landing returns to its slumbers; Huck is still a homeless runaway and Jim's freedom remains negotiable; Hank Morgan returns to the nineteenth century and history is unredeemed.

I will focus on two novels that particularly echo Twain's life in New York City, *Adventures of Huckleberry Finn* and *The Prince and the Pauper.* Although other works may also claim to be "New York" stories, namely "What Is Man?" and *No. 44, The Mysterious Stranger* (both written partially in New York City), these divided fictions represent Twain's own evolution from vulnerable street child to "prince" of the city.[2] The abused, orphan boys these novels struggle to protect and redeem are, in many ways, shadows of Mark

2. In 1876 Twain halted his work on *Huck Finn* at almost the midway point of the novel, the Grangerford-Shepardson feud. Unsure that he would ever continue with Huck's autobiography, he began *The Prince and the Pauper.* Twain published *The Prince and the Pauper* in December 1881; *Adventures of Huckleberry Finn* was completed and published four years later.

Twain's turbulent early days in New York. We hear the origins of these two novels both in the 1853 letters he wrote to his family during his adolescent adventure in New York and in his 1867 journalistic letters written for the *Alta California*. In his descriptions of the streets of New York, and later its fictional double, sixteenth-century London, Twain contrasts the theatricality and glamour of the street with the human detritus that seems to be the byproduct of cosmopolitan life. The dirty beggars who populate the slums and the alleys of lower Manhattan would come to represent for Mark Twain the deterministic forces of race and poverty, later figured in Pap Finn, John Canty, and even the doomed King Edward. At the opposite extreme, the runaway Huck and the princely Tom Canty record Mark Twain's own magical experience of New York City. Sam Clemens began his life in New York clinging to the privileges of his race and railing against the shifting lines of racial and national identity. By the time he next returned to New York in 1867, Mark Twain took pleasure in the freedom of the street, in the endless possibilities it offered for performance and play. Sam Clemens, a brazen, occasionally nasty adolescent capable of casual racism and full of grand dreams, would escape what fate (and Hannibal) seemed to have in store for him and eventually become the cosmopolitan "Mark Twain."

## FROM PAUPER TO PRINCE: AN OVERVIEW OF TWAIN AND NEW YORK CITY

My focus will be upon Twain's early encounters in New York City in 1853, followed by his arrival in New York as a minor journalistic celebrity in 1867. However, because Twain's relationship to New York City spans a fifty-five-year period, my efforts here will necessarily be incomplete. A short summary of Twain's life in New York may help to indicate how much more remains to be discussed.

After his first exhilarating and traumatic experience of the city at the age of seventeen, Twain did not return to New York until 1867 and 1868, the months preceding and following the *Quaker City* excursion. The next major "phase" of his New York life is the "Belle of New York" period, 1893–1894, followed by his extended residency in New York from 1900 to 1903 and 1904 to 1908. Yet, from the time that he began the Sandwich Island lectures at Cooper's Union in 1867 to the day in 1908 when he moved to

Stormfield in Redding, Connecticut, Twain visited New York scores of times and for a myriad of reasons: New York City was most frequently Twain's last and first look at America as he traveled abroad; it was home to many of the newspapers that would market his image and to some of the journals that would transform the comic pseudonym "Mark Twain" into a literary nom de plume; New York was the site of his financial triumphs (his lucrative deals with Harper and Brothers, and his success as the publisher of Grant's memoirs), as well as the site of Twain's disastrous financial experiments and investments (the most notorious being the Paige Typesetter, Charles L. Webster & Co., and the American Plasmon Company).

In a striking contrast to the issues of poverty and marginalization that inspire my reading, Twain spent a great deal of time in the last decades of the century cultivating the friendship of the moneyed classes in New York. Not only would Henry Huttleston Rogers of Standard Oil become his friend, his patron, and his economic adviser, Twain would also surround himself with the likes of Andrew Carnegie as well as any number of New York celebrities and socialites. In addition, New York City was Mark Twain's most sustained performance space. He either belonged to or was a guest of some of the most prestigious clubs and societies in New York: the Lotos Club, the St. Nicholas Society, the Nineteenth Century Club, and others. He spoke at fund-raisers for everything from hurricane victims in Galveston to the Hebrew Technical School for girls. He spoke at memorials, at annual banquets, at literary club meetings, at dinners for the press, for political organizations, and at his own birthday parties. In the later part of the nineteenth century, it seemed that for any sort of gathering or celebration, Twain had both the formal wear and the speech to fit the occasion. Twain drew crowds not only in the various clubs and halls where he lectured but also on the city's streets, docks, museums, and restaurants. When he returned to New York in 1900 after a four-year absence, he was thronged by reporters and fans, and his arrival in the city was reported by every major newspaper. Twain appeared regularly in New York's papers (in letters to editors, in photographs, and etched into cartoon form), and his picture eventually adorned cigar boxes and tobacco products. For the latter portion of the nineteenth century, Mark Twain's opinions, his persona, and his image were as iconic in New York City as Broadway.

Despite the extent to which Twain satisfied his appetite for spectacle and acclaim through his New York performances, it is also the case that he returned to New York in times of grief and loss.[3] After his initial triumphant return to the United States in 1900, Twain settled in New York and constructed a barrier about himself, defining the scope of his privacy by aligning it with the city limits. In response to a request from drama critic William Winter to lecture out of town, Twain wrote: "The situation is this. When I came home a year ago I saw that in self-protection I must draw a line, establish a frontier, & never pass over it. I did; I made my frontier the boundaries of New York City" (MTP, 1901). In an interesting use of the language of frontier space, Twain implies that everything beyond the border of New York City is a kind of wilderness—a view not uncommon among New Yorkers. And, in a playful letter to the editor of *Harper's Weekly*, Twain asks that copies of his soon to be published obituary be sent to him for editing: "My address is New York City. I have no other than [*sic*] is permanent and non transient" (MTP, 1902). Toward the end of his life, Twain imagined New York as a refuge, a safe port, and everything beyond as a threat to his independence, which became particularly true after the death of Livy in 1904. Twain retreated to New York, where he lived in his home at 21 Fifth Avenue—grieving, raging, recuperating—for the next four years. Repeatedly, during this period, Twain was photographed giving interviews in bed, an eccentric gesture of self-determination that is a kind of metonym for his relationship to the city at this time: New York was at once a private sanctuary and a theatrical venue.[4] In this collusion of public and private, the aging Mark Twain explored the equally liminal spaces between life and death, between free will and fate, and between the artificial entity "Mark Twain" and the human remains of Sam Clemens.

Of course, Twain's relationship to New York City was no love affair: he

3. After declaring bankruptcy in 1894, Twain and Livy briefly considered moving to New York City before they settled on the world tour. Twain wrote to Henry Huttleston Rogers: "Moreover, Mrs. Clemens is not strong enough to walk the distances that lie between the horse-car lines. Therefore we have been obliged to give up the New York idea, and we don't want to live elsewhere in America—certainly not in Hartford, in the circumstances" (*MTHHR*, 119).

4. Linda Haverty Rugg, *Picturing Ourselves: Photography and Autobiography* (Chicago: University Press of Chicago, 1997). Rugg suggests that these bedroom photographs are at once ironized "deathbed" masks and playful performances through which Twain staged his own exposure before (and detachment from) the public.

was consistently critical of the corrupt atmosphere in New York, ranging from the gangster politics of Boss Tweed to the imperialist agenda of New York's Teddy Roosevelt; he complained about the city's rabble, its cabbies, its littered streets, and the bad manners of its citizenry. Nonetheless, New York City—as much as Hannibal, Elmira, or Hartford—was Mark Twain's home. Although Twain never rendered New York in the way that he continually resurrected Hannibal or illustrated London, New York City nonetheless informed Twain's fiction, his politics, and even his reflections on the human condition—or, more narrowly, what contemporary critics might call the problem of identity in an urban, industrial, and multicultural landscape.

## "LITTLE SAMMY" AND THE
## STREETS OF NEW YORK

Critical studies of the life of Mark Twain often begin, as James Cox famously preferred, not with the birth of Mark Twain on November 30, 1835, but with "Samuel Clemens' discovery of his pseudonym 'Mark Twain.'"[5] While it is true that biographers have also critically examined Clemens's early childhood and familial relations, many have moved rapidly toward what appear to be the more formative years in Twain's life: his experience on the Mississippi, his years as a reporter out West, his relations with the Langdons, and his emerging identity as an artist.[6] Even Jeffrey Steinbrink's compelling and focused study of Twain between 1867 and 1871 begins at the point that Twain's professional ambitions and creative powers are in the process of being defined.[7] Most biographers, understandably, do little more than mention Twain's anomalous encounter with New York City at the age of seventeen. There are only four extant letters from this period, and the portrait of the young Sam Clemens that emerges from them is at times unsavory. However, although Twain's first time in New York was little more than an extended visit, it would fuel his creative "machine" for years to come. These letters record the brief period when Clemens's sense of audi-

5. Cox, *The Fate of Humor* (Columbia: University of Missouri Press, 2002), 3.

6. See for example, Philip Fanning, *Mark Twain and Orion Clemens: Brothers, Partners, Strangers* (Tuscaloosa: Fire Ant Books, 2006).

7. Steinbrink, *Getting to Be Mark Twain* (Berkeley: University of California Press, 1991).

ence was more or less limited to family and friends, and his sense of self was still uncomplicated by celebrity.[8]

Clemens describes for his sister and his mother his precarious situation in the city while also extolling his independence and courage. He confidently assures Pamela, "If my letters do not come often, you need not bother yourself about me; for if you have a brother nearly eighteen years of age, who is not able to take care of himself a few miles from home, such a brother is not worth one's thoughts"; nonetheless, he also conjures the possibility of trouble: "and if I don't manage to take care of No. 1, be assured you will never know it. I am not afraid, however; I shall ask favors from no one" (*L1*, 17). Clemens's fears were not without merit. Not only was Lower Manhattan home to ruthless gangs and criminal enterprises, it was also infamous for its street life and its slums. Clemens lived in rooms he would later describe as "villainous" (*MTA*, 287). After a short walk crosstown, Clemens would arrive at John Gray's printing house, where he worked alongside two hundred other printers. From the windows of the fifth floor of Gray's establishment Twain could see, he reported to his mother, the "shipping beyond the Battery" where "the 'forest of masts,' with all sorts of flags flying, is no mean sight. You have everything in the shape of water craft . . . but packed so closely together for miles, that when close to them you can scarcely distinguish one from the other" (*L1*, 10). Despite the often cavalier pose he struck, Twain could still sound lost in the crowd, on the streets, and in the workplace—even the magnificent view of the harbor seems to have been a bit overwhelming.

These letters aspire to be a part of an emerging genre of urban writing, where the writer, often an urbane sophisticate, regales his audience with sensational accounts of city streets, theaters, taverns, and docks as well as the characters who inhabit them. In one such midcentury tract, Matthew Hale Smith explains, "Whoever writes of New York truly, will do so in lines of light and gloom. Though this city is not so large as London, life is here more intense; crime is more vivid and daring; the votaries of fashion and pleasure are more passionate and open." In *Lights and Shadows of New York*

---

8. For the sake of clarity and to distinguish the "innocent" Clemens from his later professional persona, I will refer to Twain as "Clemens" during his first New York sojourn from 1853 to 1854.

*Life; Or, Sights and Sensations of the Great City,* written in 1872, James Mc-
Cabe Jr. warns his readers, "No matter how clever he may consider himself,
no respectable man is a match for the villains and sharpers of New York,
and he voluntarily brings upon himself all the consequences that will follow his entrance into the haunts of the criminal and disreputable classes.
The city is full of danger."[9] Writing to his family (and assuming that Orion
will publish his letters for the local readership in Hannibal) Clemens negotiates his desire to strike a worldly pose before the hometown audience
while also, perhaps less intentionally, expressing to his immediate family
feelings of vulnerability and loneliness.

Nothing in Clemens's previous experiences could have prepared him for
the city he encountered at midcentury. With its population shifting dramatically, New York was also redefining the industrial and economic practices of the country. Clemens arrived in New York looking for work as a
journeyman printer. What he discovered was a printing industry emerging
from the mercantile economy of the eighteenth century into the market
economy of the nineteenth. Apprentices, whose instruction and well-being
had formerly been the responsibility of a master-craftsman, would soon be
replaced by wage-earning workers, whose well-being was as negotiable as
their pay. Caught between the innovation and the mechanization of this
changing economy, Clemens was both wonderstruck and fearful. Bruce
Michelson argues that Twain's response to the technologies being developed
by the printing industry was prescient, anticipating the cultural, intellectual, and aesthetic possibilities of our current digital age in both its profligate
representations of the self and its liberation of texts, words, and knowledge.
Years later, according to Michelson, Mark Twain the "veteran author and
businessman" would see in the Paige Typesetter "the complete mechanical
tradesman . . . obedient, reliable, tireless, deathless; no days off, no pay, no
membership in fractious unions."[10]

In 1853, however, Sam Clemens was not yet the name brand "Mark
Twain" and was still too vulnerable to the forces that turn workers into machines—or that replace them altogether—not to be somewhat cautious

---

9. Smith, *Sunshine and Shadow in New York* (Hartford: J. B. Burr and Co., 1869), 706; Mc-
Cabe, *Lights and Shadows of New York Life* (New York: Farrar, Straus and Giroux, 1970), 15.
10. Michelson, *Printer's Devil: Mark Twain and the American Publishing Revolution* (Berkeley:
University of California Press, 2006), 12.

about industrial progress. In one of his early letters to his mother Twain sounds alternately proud of the volume and diversity of his work and overwhelmed by his insignificance within the production process: "The price I get is 23 cents; but I did very well to get a place at all, for there are thirty or forty—yes fifty good printers in the city with no work at all" (*L1*, 9). In his autobiography Twain would link the money his father spent to "rent" a slave, "For a girl of fifteen he paid twelve dollars a year," to the wages of his own house servants: "But times have changed. We pay our German nursemaid $155 a year, Irish housemaid $150; Irish laundress, $150; negro woman, a cook, $240; young negro man, to wait on door and table, $360; Irish coachman, $600 a year" (*MTA*, 10). Sam Clemens, emerging as he had from a home where bodies were rented, bought, and sold, could not help but register an irony that he would more fully articulate later in life: there are unsettling similarities between the worker and the slave. Of course, in Twain's "times have changed" there is a note of payback; he inverts his experiences as a seventeen-year-old printer by claiming the rights of the boss and returning to their proper place the Irish and African American workers with whom he competed as a young New Yorker.

In his first letter to his mother, Clemens sounds uneasy about the variety of ethnic people in New York, particularly the Irish, and about his own servile position as a wage-earning worker. He describes the journals for which he sets type: "The Knickerbocker, 'New York Recorder,' 'Choral Advocate,' 'Jewish Chronicle,' 'Littell's Living Age,' [and the] 'Irish _____,' and a half dozen other papers" (*L1*, 9). The editors of Twain's letters suggest that the journal in question was the "'Irish American,' a political and religious manuscript," and that the ellipsis could have represented the nativist view of either Twain or Orion: "either of them might have regarded the conjunction of 'American' with 'Irish' as a sort of blasphemy" (*L1*, 11n4). Twain's small-town desire, as embodied by the gesture of eliding "American" in the title of the Irish journal, might have been to prevent American identity from being corrupted by foreign influences. By setting the print for this publication, however, he indirectly became a vehicle for an emerging multiethnic America. Additionally, the diversity of these journals points toward a larger reality in Clemens's life. In 1853 most printers in New York were native-born white men, although with the influx of foreign printers catering to specific ethnic communities this dominance would soon shift. After the December 1853 fires that severely damaged the printing houses of Harper Brothers and George F. Coolege and Brothers (*L1*, 45), Twain would be thrown back on the streets looking for work, competing with any number of equally qualified printers, some of whom could no doubt be had for a cheaper rate.

In addition to the increase in domestic immigrants such as Twain, mid-century New York was also transformed culturally, politically, and economically by an unprecedented number of foreign immigrants. According to Edwin Burroughs and Mike Wallace, "In 1854 alone, setting a record that would last for decades, the United States accepted 428,000 immigrants. Of that number roughly 319,000 (75%) descended upon Manhattan—more than the entire population of the city in 1840!"[11] By the 1850s three-quarters of the approximately two million Irish to flee the potato famine would head to America, most of them entering New York. By midcentury, New York was home to the third largest German-speaking population in the world, and even after the draft riot of 1860 it was also home to a thriving African American working class.[12] In addition, the religious majority of white Anglo-Saxon Protestants was challenged by the rise in competing religious institutions. Not only would the Jesuits establish Fordham University "as a base in New York City," but also, as Burroughs and Wallace report, "with the arrival of thousands of German or Yiddish-speaking Jews, the number of synagogues rose rapidly, reaching a total of 27 by 1860."[13] As these early letters reflect, New York City seemed to Sam Clemens like a terrifying, wonderful Babel, in which his own currency was not wholly secured by his race, religion, or class.

In the letters he wrote home, Clemens repeatedly represents himself as a victim of the changing demographics of New York. "Little Sammy" quite literally struggles to maintain his footing on the streets of this heterogeneous and—seen through the eyes of Hannibal, Missouri—heretical city. While his letters record a number of responses to New York, he pays particular attention to the racial and ethnic mélange that confronted him. On the way

11. Burroughs and Wallace, *Gotham: A History of New York City to 1898* (Oxford: Oxford University Press, 1999), 736.

12. Ric Burns and James Sanders, *New York: An Illustrated History* (New York: Knopf, 2003), 88.

13. Burroughs and Wallace, *Gotham*, 749–50.

from his lodgings on Duane street to Gray's establishment on Cliff Street, Twain would have passed through the notorious Five Points slum, home to a wide variety of brothels, taverns, and various dens of iniquity, many of which were staffed by, and catered to, a mixed-race clientele. In addition, Twain would have walked within blocks of the first official congregation of African American Presbyterians and past the bohemian haunts of Walt Whitman.[14] The vision of whites and blacks living, working, and even sinning together in the same neighborhood where black ministers were advocating for the civil rights of black Americans elicited from Clemens a darkly comic, racist backlash:

> Of all commodities, manufactures—or whatever you please to call it—in New York, trundle-bed trash—children I mean—take the lead. Why, from Cliff street, up Frankfort to Nassau street, six or seven squares—my road to dinner—I think I could count two hundred brats. Niggers, mulattoes, quadroons, Chinese, and some the Lord no doubt originally intended to be white, but the dirt on whose faces leaves one uncertain as to that fact, block up the little, narrow street; and to wade through this mass of human vermin, would raise the ire of the most patient person that ever lived. (*L1*, 110)

This response to the children who run wild on the streets of New York would reappear in *The Prince and the Pauper* when Prince Edward is "followed by a delighted and noisy swarm of human vermin" (*P&P*, 25). Like the Prince, the young Clemens was repulsed by his necessary association with the rabble; however, as is equally true of Tom Canty, Clemens evinced a sense of superiority that may be little more than self-delusion, a product of his Missouri upbringing and his white heritage. Despite the distance suggested by the derisive language of this letter, at seventeen Clemens was not far from the "trundle-bed trash" he waded through, and it would take very little to put him on the street, one more "commodity" produced by the industrial machinery of New York.

---

14. Ibid., 855, 707. Twain lived within a few blocks of the First Colored Presbyterian Church, later Shiloh Church, whose minister, Henry Highland Garnet, was a vocal advocate of black immigration to Africa. In 1853 Twain lived on the same block on Duane Street where Walt Whitman also lived during one of his residencies in lower Manhattan.

In his autobiography Twain describes Hannibal as a place where poverty did not erode social status: "everybody was poor, but didn't know it . . . and there were grades of society—people of good family, people of unclassified family, people of no family. Everybody knew everybody, and was affable to everybody, and nobody put on any visible airs; yet the class lines were quite clearly drawn" (*MTA*, 120). The poverty Clemens experienced in New York was of a far different flavor; not only did it erase the distinctions insured by caste and family, it effectively undermined white privilege by covering white skin with the grime and dirt of the city. This dirt surfaces again in *Innocents Abroad* where Twain represents Civita Vecchia as "the finest example of dirt, vermin and ignorance" (*IA*, 185) and describes a Constantinople where "everywhere there is dirt, everywhere there are fleas, everywhere there are lean, broken-hearted dogs every alley is thronged with people" (*IA*, 297). Of Jerusalem he wrote: "It seems to me that all the races and colors and tongues of the earth must be represented among the fourteen thousand souls that dwell in Jerusalem. Rags, wretchedness, poverty and dirt. . . . Lepers, cripples, the blind, and the idiotic assail you on every hand" (*IA*, 418). The alleys of Jerusalem might as well be Broadway, a confusion of race, tribe, and language. Twain's hostility to the beggars of Italy and the Holy Land is a version of his earlier hostility to the street children who likewise "assail" him. Twain's satiric portraits of the poor in *Innocents Abroad* have always seemed capricious and unnecessarily cruel. Placed alongside these early letters home, however, the poverty of the Holy Land takes on a more intimate connection. Twain's virulent response to beggars, street people, and freaks of all forms reflects something more than a lack of sympathy or an overly delicate palate; instead, these portraits are as defensive as they are offensive, a strategy of self-protection and self-definition that began in New York City.

Establishing his relationship to this mob of children became a psychological imperative for Clemens, part of the process of distinguishing himself as a white adult within this shifting ethnic morass. In order to get his meals, Twain had to cross Broadway, which even by 1853 had acquired an iconic status in American culture. In 1852 the *New York Times* rhapsodized about the appeal of Broadway: "The more noise, the more confusion, the greater the crowd, the better the lookers on and the crowders seem to like it . . . the din, this driving, this omnibus-thunder, this squeezing, this jamming, crowding, and at times smashing, is the exhilarating music which charms the multitude and draws its thousands within the whirl."[15] This paean could almost have been written by Walt Whitman; the charm was lost, however, on Sam Clemens, the white country boy for whom Broadway felt like an urban minefield. Although Clemens seems at times to have been drawn to the excitement of the streets, he was equally fearful about being identified with the crowd who inhabited this space. He represented this anxiety as a physical vulnerability:

> In going to and from my meals, I go by way of Broadway—and to cross Broadway is the rub—but once across, it is the rub for two or three squares. My plan—and how I could choose another, when there is no other—is to get into the crowd; and when I get in, I am borne, and rubbed, and crowded along, and need scarcely trouble myself about using my own legs; and when I get out, it seems like I had been pulled to pieces and very badly put together again. (*L1,* 10)

More than enough has been made of Twain's divided self, and scores of possible locations have been mapped—both psychological and geographic—as the locus of this division. To this number we can add Broadway as a candidate for the birthplace of "Mark Twain." In this first letter to his mother, Clemens describes himself—albeit playfully—as having been violently dismantled, "pulled to pieces" on the streets of New York. The bedlam created by this throng of children was read by the young Clemens as a mass of fragmented and confused identities, racial and ethnic, to the point that the humanity of the individuals disappears. Clemens represents these multicolored, multiethnic creatures as robbing him of his agency, carrying him along against his will until he becomes damaged goods, a byproduct of the urban landscape.

Mark Twain in his later life was an acute observer of crowds and mobs and of the psychology that they manifest. From the simplistic acquiescence of congregations like his mother's, to the voyeuristic longings of the loafers in Bricksville, to the violent appetite of lynch mobs, Twain understood the form and function of mobs in America. In this letter, the young Sam pro-

---

15. "Anti-Broadway Railroad Meeting," *New York Times,* September 8, 1852.

duces a comic version of Poe's "The Man of the Crowd." Unlike Poe's narrator, however, Clemens is more harried than obsessed by life on the street. Yet the underlying worry—that there is no secure boundary between the civilized gaze of the observer and the moral chaos of the mob—is the same. In "The Man of the Crowd" Poe conjures an urban nightmare in which his narrator descends into the street only to become neurotically engaged in a search for identity, initially for that of the man he pursues and eventually for his own. Poe's narrator is effectively lost in or by the crowd. Clemens re-presents this fear in somewhat comic terms as a daily ritual of self-destruction; he throws himself into the crowd on Broadway and emerges fragmented and distorted, "very badly put together again." Yet he emerges nonetheless. The crowded streets of New York assault Sam Clemens, but out of that experience will emerge the pieced together, somewhat artificial, and self-consciously constructed "Mark Twain."

## THE BORNEO TWINS AND THE PERFORMANCE OF RACE

Clemens's first letter home depicts other bodies, besides his own, that are fragmented and divided. In these sometimes playful representations of being broken or torn to pieces, Clemens initiates what will become a life-long contemplation on the nature of race and the problem of human identity, which often manifests itself in a fascination with twins and doubles. Clemens describes to his mother "a curiosity" he witnessed at a New York sideshow: "Two beings, about like common people, with the exception of their faces, which are more like the phiz of an orang-outang, than human. They are white, though, like other people." The editors of Twain's letters speculate that these performers were likely Hiram and Barney Davis, whom P. T. Barnum exhibited as Plutano and Waino, "The Borneo Twins."[16] Twain continues: "they are supposed to be a cross between man and orang-outang; one is the best natured being in the world, while the other would

16. The editors also note that, in an 1853 editorial, "Horace Greeley's New York *Tribune* inveighed against the custom whereby 'Broadway is never without one or more damnable monsters on exhibition'" (*L1*, 6). The Davis brothers were extremely short in stature, and they were also mentally handicapped. In the 1850s they began performing feats of strength for a number of sideshows, and by the 1880s they were working for P. T. Barnum.

tear a stranger to pieces, if he did but touch him" (*L1*, 4). Once again Sam Clemens—himself a stranger in the city—has imagined being physically assaulted in a particularly animalistic way.

An inescapable result of this shifting worldview for Clemens was the destabilization of racial identity, with whiteness no longer testifying to one's humanity or guaranteeing one's safety. In the case of the Borneo twins, race exists as a category beyond pigmentation. For while Clemens describes these men as having the physiognomy of an ape, he is nonetheless forced to admit that they are "white, though, like other people." Despite the supremacist assumption that equates whiteness with common humanity, we can hear in this passage the erosion of whiteness as a stable category for Clemens—a sea change that will eventually allow the adult Mark Twain to represent race as little more than a series of cultural markers. Although it's likely that these performers were Caucasian, their physiognomy suggests to Clemens some other racial status or identity. He seems unsure of what it means to be "white" even as he attempts to resolve the twins' problematic racial status with the comparative, "like other people." If the twins from Borneo are "white, though, like other people," perhaps Jim can be "white inside," just as Roxana's racial status in *Pudd'nhead Wilson* will be a "fiction of law and custom" and not a biological fact. If, in Clemens's imagination, his is the unified "body" torn to pieces by the savage twin, what is left behind are the fragments of a fallen racial identity: faces, colors, language, and bodies. In his letters home the young Sam is attempting—sometimes "very badly"—to put the pieces together again. In these letters, Clemens projects two different versions of an adulterated humanity: one that is mechanical, (commodities and pieces), and one that is bestial (vermin and primates). Clemens's attraction to these New York City entertainers, whom he characterizes conversely as circus monkeys and caged white men, marks one of his earliest explorations of racial identity as a performance. In his later writing, Twain complicates these performances: Roxy's minstrel-show speech marks her as black, despite the claims of her white skin; Mark Twain's white suit testifies uneasily to the purity of his own racial identity, while his texts, on the other hand, appear to be the product of miscegenation: "I was as uplifted and reassured by it [Howells's review of *Roughing It*] as a mother who has given birth to a white baby when she was awfully afraid it was going to be mulatto" (*MTHL1*, 10–11).

If the Borneo twins unsettled Clemens's assumptions about race, the sight of free blacks in New York antagonized him. In relating his journey to his mother, a frequent audience for his racial musings, Clemens wrote, "When I saw the Court House in Syracuse, it called to mind the time when it was surrounded with chains and companies of soldiers, to prevent the rescue of McReynolds' nigger by the infernal abolitionists. I reckon I had better black my face, for in these Eastern States niggers are considerably better than white people" (*L1,* 4). This passage, and specifically the promise to "black" his face, has received more critical attention than any other part of the early New York correspondence. Often critics seem intent on finding some reading that will mitigate Clemens's otherwise racist language. He may be, for example, trying to entertain his mother through a comic hyperbole, which is an ongoing dynamic between them. This assault on perceived black privilege allows Clemens to affirm his mother's belief in the spiritual and cultural value of a "mild domestic slavery" against the relative chaos of eastern liberalism, while also humorously picturing himself as a black-faced minstrel (*MTA,* 30). Philip Fanning has recently suggested that the nastiness of Clemens's response to African Americans in the East may reflect his desire to distinguish himself from the increasingly abolitionist Orion.[17] By playing the role of good southern boy, Clemens would ingratiate himself with his neighbors and affirm the dominant values of the Clemens household, with the added benefit of undermining his older brother. In this scenario, Sam Clemens is like Huck Finn trying to work his way into the home of Aunt Sally: "anybody hurt?; No'm. Killed a Nigger" (*HF,* 279). He appears to sling the epithet—"niggers are considerably better off"—as a strategy to gain entry to a community and a home—both nominally his own—in which he feels alien. Not only is this reading psychologically plausible, casting Twain in an Oedipal role of pleasing the mother and thwarting the father (or at least the father figure), it also deflects the racist intention of the language, making it part of a more complicated personal and cultural performance.

The critical vocabulary of performance, however, has its limits. It necessarily suggests an ironic detachment between the actor and the identity he or she assumes. In the case of Mark Twain's writing, this distance can create a buffer between the icon and the author. If, for example, Twain's use of the minstrel-show mask is primarily strategic and performative, then Mark

17. Fanning, *Mark Twain and Orion Clemens.*

Twain, the white-suited emblem of racial tolerance, can remain more or less untainted by this early expression of racist humor. If, on the other hand, these letters are something more than performative, then Sam Clemens's racism becomes less an idea than a practice. When critics take up this particular letter, the focus is often on the symbolic vehicle of minstrelsy rather than on the racist politics that may lie beneath the metaphor. Eric Lott, for example, accurately positions Clemens's attraction to minstrelsy within a larger cultural performance being enacted by working-class white men. According to Lott, "These subterranean links between black and lower-class white men called forth in the minstrel show, as in Mark Twain's work, interracial recognitions and identifications no less than the imperative to disavow them."[18] The crosscurrents Lott describes are evident in these early pieces, as Clemens unconsciously linked his anxiety about work, about his lack of control and status, and about the frightening possibility of being marked—by poverty and by accident—as, in essence, black. Yet, as the language of the letter suggests, Sam Clemens was far from being the patron of African Americans and their causes that he would someday be. And if, as Randall Knoper suggests, "Mark Twain" is the product of a masculine culture of performance being articulated in the saloons and burlesque houses of New York and San Francisco, the young Sam Clemens was at this point still too vulnerable to the streets of New York to fully embrace a bohemian pose or the politics that would attend it.[19] Twain's use of the tropes and images of minstrelsy eventually allowed him to perform his working-class attitudes about racial identity, as Lott argues, "with a sort of rowdy, wisecracking wonder."[20] It is equally the case that Twain's affinity for black people—he declares, almost defensively in his autobiography: "The Black face is as welcome to me now as it was then"—would become a sign of his

18. Lott, "Mr. Clemens and Jim Crow: Twain, Race, and Blackface" in *The Cambridge Companion to Mark Twain,* ed. Forrest G. Robinson (Cambridge: Cambridge University Press, 1995), 130.

19. Knoper, *Acting Naturally: Mark Twain in the Culture of Performance* (Berkeley: University of California Press, 1995). Knoper characterizes the late-night fraternal world of Twain's Bohemia as being both literally and metaphorically intoxicated by an association with the racial and sexual "Other." Twain's "in-the-know" status within the black community—a fallacy he will satirize in "A True Story"—eventually becomes part of an identity that he will both perform and market, and it will allow him to distance himself from those aspects of white bourgeois culture that he finds oppressive.

20. Lott, "Mr. Clemens and Jim Crow," 142.

transgressive masculinity, part of what Knoper sees as an assault on middle-class decorum and normative behavior.

However, Sam Clemens in 1853 was not yet the complicated amal-gam—part secular prophet and part industrial machine—that he even-tually would become. While he was in New York City his attitudes about African Americans were unambiguously racist, as is evidenced in the less metaphoric line that precedes the reference to blackening his face. When Clemens recalls "the rescue of McReynolds' nigger by the infernal aboli-tionists," he is not only performing the racist assumptions of his culture or negotiating anxieties about being white; he is also—and more signif-icantly—expressing an unmediated hostility to the racial and ethnic "Other" and to blacks in particular.[21] Clemens is directly affirming the cultural order of the white South against the mongrel politics of the East. Once again Clemens represents himself as the victim of a chaotic urban landscape; in Syracuse "niggers" are rescued and white boys seem aban-doned.

Certainly, the gesture of blackening his face carries with it a number of intricate associations, foremost among them being the minstrel-show mask; however, given the specific context of this letter, the potential blackness of Clemens's face also points toward the dirty faces of the children he en-countered on Broadway. Sam Clemens's loathing for the homeless children of New York City—the "human vermin" who had collapsed the boundaries between black and white—was wholly reactionary and personal, not a performance so much as an instinctual reflex. If Clemens could keep "McReynolds' nigger" in his place, then perhaps he could also keep at bay the crowd of dirty children whose racial and ethnic status was so disrup-tive. So, while Clemens's promise to blacken his face was a performative ges-ture of self-denial, anxiety, and cultural flux, it was also something more di-rect and less mediated. In *Jokes and Their Relation to the Unconscious,* a treatise informed by Twain's comic performances in Vienna in 1895, Sig-

21. On October 1, 1851, William "Jerry" Henry, an escaped Missouri slave, working as a cooper in Syracuse, N.Y., was arrested under the Fugitive Slave Law and taken into custody. In an effort coordinated by local and national antislavery organizations, citizens stormed the jail where Henry was being held and freed him. The event became a celebrated and notori-ous example for southerners like the young Sam Clemens of the social anarchy at the heart of abolition.

mund Freud represents the joke as a substitute for actual violence.[22] Although still a metaphoric vehicle, the joke has a primary function, which is to hit its target. The young Sam's suggestion that he blacken his face is a joke with a serious, hostile aim: to undermine the freedom of black people and to mock the whites who work on their behalf.

The chaos of the streets of New York, represented for Clemens by the mob of dirty children and by the confused racial status of the Borneo twins, led him toward his first true expression of cosmopolitan life: hatred and loathing. What we hear in Clemens's letters are the ugly sounds of a world-view under attack, which consequently gives rise to his reactionary feelings of indignation and race pride. Clemens's racism was a psychological response to the city as well as a political ideology. Walter Mignolo has suggested that "cosmopolitanism is a set of projects towards planetary conviviality," meaning that in a world where we are all, at some time or place, "Others," survival depends on some degree of mutual acceptance.[23] The seventeen-year-old Clemens was still a long way from convivial; oddly enough, however, these letters mark the beginning of his journey toward a less colonial, less "serious" politics.

## HUCK, PAP, AND THE TRAUMA OF RACISM

Clemens's virulent response to African Americans in New York City constitutes a traumatic memory, as powerful as the often sepia-tinted recollections the adult Mark Twain narrated in his *Autobiography*. These early letters constitute a kind of ur-text in which we hear the voice of Pap Finn in all his cruelty and self-pity, as well as the longings of his lonesome, fearful son. Certainly Pap Finn emerges from a number of biographical and cultural sources, but he is more than simply the product of Twain's observations of racism; he is also the product of Twain's early feelings of racism. Pap is a self-critique, Twain's response to the white boy who, in a crowd of seemingly privileged dark faces, longs to push them off the street and out of American public space:

22. Freud, *Jokes and Their Relation to the Unconscious*, ed. James Strachey and Angela Richards (New York: Penguin, 1976).
23. Mignolo, "The Many Faces of Cosmo-polis: Border Thinking and Critical Cosmopolitanism," in *Cosmopolitanism*, ed. Carol Breckenridge et al., 157.

There was a free nigger there, from Ohio; a mulatter, most as white as a white man. He had the whitest shirt on you ever see, too, and the shiniest hat; and there ain't a man in the town that's got as fine clothes as what he had; and he had a gold watch and chain, and a silver-headed cane. . . . And what do you think? they said he was a p'fesor in a college, and could talk all kinds of languages, and knowed everything. And that ain't the wust. They said he could *vote,* when he was at home. Well, that let me out. Thinks I, what is the country a-coming to? . . . And to see the cool way of that nigger—why, he wouldn't give me the road if I hadn't shoved him out o' the way. I says to the people, why ain't this nigger put up at auction and sold?— that's what I want to know. (*HF,* 34)

Encoded within the "cool way" of Pap Finn's black professor, dressed not in the costume of the minstrel but in the trappings of a Fifth Avenue gentleman (white shirt, top hat, gold watch, and silver-headed cane) is Clemens's adolescent response to the changing status of racial and ethnic minorities in New York City.[24] The adult Mark Twain inverts the early threat to blacken his face by clothing the fictional professor in whiteness, a costume that appears to erase his black identity altogether. And unlike the awkward Sam Clemens, who is barely able to walk across Broadway, the professor commands the street with a self-assurance that eludes the distinctly uncool Sam. In his essays "On Cosmopolitanism" and "On Forgiveness," Jacques Derrida explores the impossible (yet politically expedient) idea of the "city of refuge." Derrida's city is a space where what he terms "hospitality" dictates that the newly arrived "Other" remains free, unassimilated and unharassed by the citizens of the city. In response to the rise of immigrants and refugees in both France and Britain in recent decades, Derrida suggests that the urban space evokes both violence and violation, and that it likewise demands an absolute and unconditional acceptance of what we may find unacceptable, even unforgivable. In the twinned motions of pushing the black Professor off the street and retreating from the political process—"I drawed out. I says I'll never vote again" (*HF,* 34)—Twain's Pap Finn embodies a profound

24. It may be that Twain was specifically referring to Dr. John C. Mitchell, a black professor from Wilberforce College in Ohio. However, my interest here is less in the surface details of the character than in his metaphoric value and cultural resonance.

rejection of the "city of refuge." Pap will not share the street with a black man, and in refusing to do so, he drops out of an emerging, pluralistic American society.[25]

In the person of this educated, confident, and seemingly urbane African American man, Mark Twain, the mature writer, connects his teenage anxieties to the fears of rural white America. Pap angrily protests the professor's transgressions into white domains; while Huck—less violent in his response to black self-confidence, perhaps, but as worried—complains, "Give a nigger an inch and he'll take an ell." The anxiety that inspires so much hostility toward the progress of blacks (in education, in politics, in economics, and even in something as seemingly minor as clothing) equates black success with white failure. While visiting Philadelphia later in 1853, Clemens wrote to Orion: "I would like amazingly to see a good old fashioned negro" (L1, 29). We can infer that encounters with free African Americans—living versions of the fictionalized professor—excited in Clemens this nostalgia for subservient, comforting black faces, a nostalgia that at the end of the nineteenth century and start of the twentieth would become mythologized in representations of "The Lost Cause" of the Confederacy.

Pap's insistence that the professor be sold at auction imaginatively returns "McReynolds' runaway slave" to his bondage, and it recovers for Pap the status and privilege he will lose when the war ends and African Americans are enfranchised. Mark Twain, the cosmopolitan writer who gave birth to Pap, knew that—to echo both Yeats and Achebe—"things fall apart," that the political order that made possible his nostalgic memories of Missouri must collapse for some kind of just equilibrium to be achieved. He also knew, through personal insight and experience, that this radical realignment—the political version of Pap falling "head over heels"—would be marked by white rage and paranoia. Pap Finn expresses the outrage of white men who fear their own marginalization in this shifting American landscape, imaginatively equating the fact that the black professor can vote with his own loss of citizenship, "Well, that let me out."

Twain also invests Pap Finn with some of the attributes of the urban poor.

25. Jacque Derrida, *On Cosmopolitanism and Forgiveness,* trans. Mark Dooley and Michael Hughes (London and New York: Routledge, 2001).

Covered in mud and dirt, drunk and sleeping in the street, Pap Finn comes to represent for Mark Twain a nightmare version of urban poverty and the racism it propagates: "He had been drunk over in town, and laid in the gutter all night, and he was a sight to look at. A body would a thought he was Adam, he was just all mud" (*HF,* 33).[26] Dirt, as an emblem of degrading poverty, savagery, and corruption, replaces pigmentation for Twain as the mark of original sin. In Jerusalem, Twain arrives at the tomb of Adam, where he discovers the earth from which all mankind was made: "formed of the dirt procured in this very spot." Pap Finn, as another Adam, competes for the moral claim to be the "the father of the human race" (*IA,* 423). The dirt on the faces of the street children and the muddied exterior of Pap Finn are another form of blackness, a racial signifier that emerges from poverty and ignorance, one that particularly threatened to leave its mark on the seventeen-year-old Samuel Clemens. This urban blackness, less a pigmentation than a moral stain, evoked the racist impulses he recorded in his letters and that the adult Twain fictionalized years later in the rantings of Pap Finn. The memories of African Americans in rural Missouri—Uncle Dan'l, Sandy, the chained slaves about to be sold downriver—elicited from Mark Twain feelings of sympathy and guilt. "All the negros were friends of ours" Twain remembers of his childhood, claiming that "the black face" is still welcome to him (*MTOA,* 115); nonetheless, this generous-seeming synecdoche points back to a primal fragmentation of black identity into parts and pieces. In *Huckleberry Finn,* Mark Twain re-creates a time and, more important, a place when black faces inspired much darker impulses.

Twain drew again upon the emotional content of his life as a runaway teenager in New York in his pairing of Huck and Pap: Huck Finn, like one of the Borneo twins, is "the best natured being in the world," and his dark twin is Pap, who would "tear a stranger to pieces if he did but look at him" (*L1,* 4). Although Huck Finn has often been represented as a child of nature, he is more accurately a child of the streets whose survival skills seem to have been honed as much by his deep acquaintance with people—"I never seen

26. The streets of midcentury New York are a fitting home for Pap Finn, who is frequently associated with hogs, gutters, and dirt. Burroughs and Wallace report that in 1849 the city engaged in a campaign to rid lower Manhattan of the "estimated twenty thousand swine" being kept in tenement houses, cellars, and garrets. Cows and pigs were butchered in local slaughterhouses, "usually draining excess blood to the gutters"; horses deposited tons of manure into the streets (*Gotham,* 786–87).

Jacob Riis's photograph "Street Arabs in Sleeping Quarters" suggests the
scenes of poverty and decay that Twain would have encountered at midcentury.
Newspaper accounts from the period describe children sleeping in barrels
(like Twain's fictional Huck Finn) located near the docks of lower Manhattan.
(Courtesy Library of Congress)

anybody but lied"—as by his experiences in the backwoods of Missouri (*HF*,
1). In 1853 Twain lived in a city of tens of thousands of homeless children,
many of them sleeping in the streets, alleys, or doorways of lower Manhattan; these children survived as pickpockets, newsboys, beggars, and prostitutes.[27] According to the research of Timothy Gilfolye, these children also

27. Estimates of the number of homeless children in midcentury New York range from
15,000–20,000 to an outside figure of 40,000. "Children on their own were of necessity
members of the criminal and mendicant classes; if they were employed, they were de facto
enslaved. They slept on the docks, in cellars and basements, in alleys and doorways. . . . They
burrowed into the empty and derelict spaces, not that there were many in a city where adults
fought for sheltered hallways and cellar corners. Being small and beneath notice gave them
the mobility as well as the status of rats" (Luc Sante, *Low Life* [New York: Vintage Books,
1991], 306). Huck Finn's habit of sleeping in a sugar hogshead may be a reflection of this
New York landscape.

occupied the cultural imagination of the time. They were variously represented as "'rats,' 'gamins,' 'Arabs,' 'urchins' and 'guttersnipes,' . . . the replacement of community, familial and even spiritual bonds with the rootless individualism of the nomad." Yet they also excited a certain admiration in New Yorkers. Minister and child advocate Charles Loring Brace described these children as "sharp, ready, lighthearted, quick to understand and quick to act, generous and impulsive and with an air of being well used to 'steer their own canoe' through whatever rapids and whirlpools."[28] Brace seems to be describing the birthplace of Huckleberry Finn. Clemens's letters to his mother evince little sympathy for these children; however, as something of a runaway himself, he understood their tenuous lives, their frighteningly independent circumstances, and their loneliness.

In his letters from New York and Philadelphia, Clemens occasionally lets slip—between the descriptions of his own bravado—a longing for family. He asks repeatedly for information about how to reach his mother and, like many young people far from home, asks for someone to write to him, "I want you to write as soon as I tell you where to direct your letter. I would let you know now, if I knew myself. I may perhaps be here a week longer; but I cannot tell. When you write tell me the whereabouts of the family" (L1, 13). As Michael Kiskis has recently argued, the "whereabouts of the family"—its constancy or its transience—is one of the issues that inspired *Huck Finn*. According to Kiskis, Twain's experience of fatherhood gave him a new appreciation for the vulnerability of children and caused him to reflect on not only the lives of his own children but also the vulnerability of all children in a world that seemed intent upon harming them.[29] Mark Twain's affection for Huckleberry Finn reflects both the protective impulses of the father and the memory of his nomadic life in New York. Twain invests Huck with street smarts and with a willingness to question the norms of the adult world that is crucial to his emblematic status as a liberatory figure. Like the young Clemens, Huck's vocabulary is racist, just as his worldview is supremacist; however, a radical change in circumstances forces on

28. Gilfoyle, "Street-Rats and Gutter-Snipes: Child Pickpockets and Street Culture in New York City, 1850–1900," *Journal of Social History* 4 (Summer 2004): 853; Brace, *The Dangerous Classes of New York, and Twenty Years' Work among Them* (New York: Wynkoop and Hallenbeck, 1872), 344.

29. Kiskis, "Mark Twain, Quarry Farm, and the Cult of Domesticity," lecture, N.E.H Landmark Institute, The Mark Twain House, Hartford, Conn., July 2007.

Huck a new way of seeing. The inversions of race and color that mark Clemens's descriptions of the Borneo twins ultimately surface in Huck's contradictory responses to Jim, whom he comes to see as "white on the inside." Huck's search for a new racial category, fraught as it is with racist assumptions, reflects back upon the confusion of young Sam, and it will become a type for other of Twain's children who resist the normative expectations of the world they inherit: Tom Canty and his dreams of a new life; Roxy and her criminal transgression of the color line; even Susy and her original prayer, "that there may be a God and a Heaven—or something better" (*MTOA*, 29).

## PRINCES, PAUPERS, AND THE PROBLEM OF REFORM

*The Prince and the Pauper* is a narrative inversion of *Adventures of Huckleberry Finn:* opposing the deterministic world of Huck are the transcendent possibilities of Tom Canty's reign and Prince Edward's enlightenment. Where Huck's story ends with a flight into unknown territories, Tom and Prince Edward return to their previous identities and restore the order of the kingdom. *The Prince and the Pauper,* no less than its double *Huck Finn,* reflects Clemens's early experiences in New York City, as well as his own increasing wealth and prominence. Although Twain had visited London by the time he wrote *The Prince and the Pauper,* as Peter Messent notes in this volume, he did not tour or make much comment on the poverty of that city. London informs the setting of the novel through Twain's portraits of the city's famed landmarks: London Bridge, Buckingham Palace, the architecture of Old London, and so on. The ethical and political themes of the novel echo Twain's responses to poverty in New York, just as Tom Canty's rapturous descriptions of wealth and fame mirror Twain's feelings of miraculous good fortune in the 1870s and 1880s.

When Twain wrote both *Huck Finn* and *The Prince and the Pauper,* he was living in Hartford in a magnificent home, a "petted prince" who was nonetheless haunted by his close association with poverty. Prince Edward embodies this complex biographical inheritance. As Twain's little Prince wanders the streets of London, he is pursued by crowds, threatened with violence, and treated with disdain. Like the teenage Sam Clemens, Edward is stung by his own insignificance in the urban landscape: "the ragged but real Prince of Wales" is repeatedly humiliated and threatened by crowds who fail to recognize him, "they began to taunt him and mock him purposely to goad him into a higher and still more entertaining fury. Tears of mortification sprung to his eyes" (*P&P,* 80). Both Clemens and his fictional heir, Prince Edward, are mortified by their proximity to the poor: "he was no longer a petted prince in a palace, with the adoring eyes of a nation upon him, but a pauper, an outcast, clothed in rags, a prisoner in a den fit only for beasts, and consorting with beggars and thieves" (*P&P,* 72).

Edward's individual identity is more or less absorbed by the crowd and erased by the shabbiness of his appearance. Exchanging clothes with Tom Canty has the same effect that blackening his face would have had for Twain in the nineteenth century: Edward is enslaved by his new identity and rendered a commodity within the Canty household. As in *Connecticut Yankee* and *Pudd'nhead Wilson,* Twain explores the structures of race in America by effacing and dissolving the pigmentation of his characters into a uniform and universal whiteness; instead of signifying race through color, the functions of racial distinction and discrimination are accomplished by clothes, by speech, and by class. The discrete category of race exists nonetheless. In *The Prince and the Pauper,* for example, the tropes and structures of slavery dominate Edward's time on the street: Miles Hendon is whipped at a post; servitude is—like the honorifics Edward dispenses—inherited and permanent, and a farmer turned beggar is branded as a slave: "A SLAVE! Do ye understand that word! An English SLAVE!—that is he that stands before ye. I have run from my master, and when I am found—the heavy curse of heaven fall on the law and the land that hath commanded it! I shall hang" (*P&P,* 151). Twain's narrative is less interested in the history of English slavery than in the ironic condition of the white slave. As in the case of Roxy and Tom Driscoll, whose blackness is in many ways fictitious, Edward is the potential slave of a legal and cultural system that would lynch him—despite his birthright— as readily as it would some poor beggar. The urban space—whether it be New York City in the nineteenth century or London in the sixteenth—erodes individual identity; Edward's royal pedigree is no more a bulwark against the ideology that dominates in the city than is Sam Clemens's white skin.

The connection Twain makes in *The Prince and the Pauper* between poverty and racism (that is, the presentation of suffering as a common denomi-

nator between poor whites and enslaved blacks) would seem to indicate that
Twain's initial squeamishness around the urban poor had evolved over time.
And to some extent it had. At moments in the novel Edward is outraged by
the conditions in which his people live and the injustices that his own court
has generated. Yet much of this sympathy, like Twain's, is reserved for the
rural poor and the deserving outcast: for the displaced farmer, whose name,
Yokel, indicates his rural origins; for the "tradesman's apprentice" who finds
a hawk, takes it home, and is sentenced to hang as a result; and especially
for the Baptist women who are burned at the stake. Mark Twain repeatedly
expressed his outrage at the tyranny of the rich over the poor and the powerful over the weak; however, he was often viscerally repulsed by the actual sight, smell, and face of urban poverty.

Mark Twain's own journey into prosperity did little to alter his conflict-
ed response to the poor. When Twain returned to New York City in 1867,
he walked the streets with a great deal more confidence. Not only was he a
relatively successful journalist, he was an experienced urbanite, having
lived and worked in San Francisco for several years. Nonetheless, in his
1867 letters to the *Alta California,* Twain's ambivalence about the plight of
tenement dwellers is evident in his description of a cholera epidemic that
he seems both to dread and to invoke: "The city is said to contain over a
million inhabitants now, and half of them are packed away in these holes
and dens and cellars of tenement houses, where unimaginable dirt is the
rule and cleanliness is a miracle—would be a miracle, I mean, but they don't
have it. They are going to have all these tenement houses all white-washed
inside, but that will hardly save the occupants when the cholera comes. It
will be here soon, and it will sweep those sinks of corruption like a confla-
gration" (*MTTMB,* 235). Here Twain counters the 1853 gesture of blackening his face with the broad stroke of whitewashing the dirt of the city; however, in this case the dirt—the pigment of poverty—will remain unaltered
and perhaps unalterable by any attempt at reform.

Mark Twain did, like Prince Edward, condemn the legal system and cultural practices that created places like Offal Court and the Five Points slum.
He remained, nonetheless, unsure about the moral status—or for that matter, even the humanity—of the people who inhabited them. The Ruffler's
gang, for example, appears to Prince Edward not as whole persons but as
body parts and assorted costumes; this disarray of human elements forms

a complete portrait of degradation from "sore faced babes" to "old and wrinkled hags":

> A bright fire was burning in the middle of the floor, at the other end of the barn; and around it, and lit weirdly up by the red glare, lolled and sprawled the motliest company of tattered gutter-scum and ruffians, of both sexes, he had ever read or dreamed of. There were huge, stalwart men, brown with exposure, long-haired, and clothed in fantastic rags; there were middle-sized youths, of truculent countenance, and similarly clad; there were blind mendicants, with patched or bandaged eyes; crippled ones, with wooden legs and crutches; there was a villain-looking peddler with his pack; a knife-grinder, a tinker, and a barber-surgeon, with the implements of their trades; some of the females were hardly grown girls, some were at prime, some were old and wrinkled hags, and all were loud, brazen, foul-mouthed; and all soiled and slatternly; there were three sore-faced babies; there were a couple of starveling curs, with strings around their necks, whose office was to lead the blind. (*P&P,* 145–46)

Edward's nightmare vision of the "motliest company . . . he had ever read or dreamed of" mirrors Clemens's amazement at the strange mixture of children in the street: "some the Lord no doubt originally intended to be white, but the dirt on whose faces leaves one uncertain as to that fact." The Ruffler's gang defies categorization: while some of its members are tradesmen, their ambitions are criminal; although their ages range from infancy to the elderly, they all seem bound in a uniform state of decay; the women appear as course as men, and the men seem to be only a step above beasts. Covering them all is Twain's ubiquitous emblem of city life: dirt. What began in 1853 as a highly specific racial signifier—the blackened face—has become in the dirty faces of Pap Finn, John Canty, and the motley gang that surrounds him a symbol of the human race and, even more specifically, a sign of what effect the urban landscape has on the categories that organize identity. In Twain's fictional cities race, class, gender, and occupation dissolve into both social and moral confusion. Although *The Prince and the Pauper* ultimately empowers King Edward to redeem his people and reform the laws that oppress them (to "clean up the city"), such progress will be as short-lived as Edward's reign.

Unlike realist authors such as Dreiser or Crane who seem inspired by the urge to transform the depressed urban landscapes they represent, Twain is in many ways an ambivalent reformer, content to witness the horror of poverty but unsure about the efficacy of attempting change. In this highly visual novel—filled as it is with opulent accounts of the clothes, the food, and the residences of the palace—Twain devotes a great many words to describing the living conditions of the poor. In this way his novel seems to be part of a narrative practice established in sensational accounts such as *New York by Gaslight,* in which the author, George Foster, promises "[t]o penetrate beneath the thick veil of night and lay bare the fearful mysteries of darkness in the metropolis—the festivities of prostitution, the orgies of pauperism, the haunts of theft and murder, the scenes of drunkenness and beastly debauch, and all the sad realities that go to make up the lower stratum—the underground story—of life in New York!" In *The Prince and the Pauper,* Twain may even have been drawing upon Charles Dickens's *American Notes,* where Dickens describes the Five Points as a netherworld inhabited by a debased collection of blacks and whites, living in various states of moral and physical decay: "From every corner, as you glance about you in these dark retreats, some figure crawls half-awakened, as if the judgment-hour were near at hand, and every obscene grave were giving up its dead. Where dogs would howl to lie, women, and men, and boys slink off to sleep, forcing the dislodged rats to move away in quest of better lodgings."[30] Twain's novel engages in sensational and voyeuristic acts of seeing such as these; yet it claims to do so for a higher purpose.

In *Adventures of Huckleberry Finn,* Twain self-consciously insists upon a lack of moral agenda; yet in *The Prince and the Pauper* he appears intent upon transforming both the main characters and the society they inhabit. In his portrait of Offal Court and the Rufflers Gang, Twain accomplishes in prose what Jacob Riis will achieve eight years later in his photographs of New York's back alleys and side streets, places with names such as Bandits' Roost and Rag Pickers' Row. However, unlike the documentary work of Riis or the yellow journalism of Stephen Crane, Twain's novel does not finally convey a belief in the power of reform, any more than Twain believed that the dirt of

30. Foster, *New York by Gaslight and Other Urban Sketches* (Berkeley: University of California Press, 1990), 69; Dickens, *American Notes for General Circulation* (New York: Penguin Classics, 2001), 80.

the Five Points could be whitewashed. Despite its realist texture, the novel is a romance, set in a faraway land in a distant time. Long before Edward and Tom exchange their clothes, the events it describes are already part of an unredeemed history. Edward's commitment to justice and reform has failed before the novel begins. Instead of a narrative of social reform, Prince Edward's story is primarily a private memoir of courage and endurance. Not unlike the young Clemens, the Prince survives his time on the street as much as—if not more than—he learns from it. Edward's experience yields lessons that enrich him personally ("What does thou know of suffering and oppression? I and my people know, but not thou"), yet they fail to extend much beyond the personal (*P&P,* 289). He is able to improve the lot of some of the people he encounters on his journey; however, his reign, and by implication the effect of his exposure to poverty, has limited power.

Contemporary theories of the cosmopolitan take varying positions on the question of reform. On the one hand, a cosmopolitan worldview imagines that—while culture, nation, and race may organize in any number of ways—basic human needs must be met. Particular questions of how to meet these needs, however, raise the specter that also haunts a cosmopolitan political agenda. How can the needs of the poor be met without conceiving of that impoverishment in colonial, even imperial terms? The Prince has been transformed by his view of poverty and injustice on the streets of London; however, he has not made the human equation that health and wealth are utterly random, that "there but for the grace of God go I." Instead, Mark Twain's Prince Edward reclaims and asserts the "grace" that is his identity as an enlightened monarch. Twain's vision of urban poverty in London stops short of embracing a cosmopolitan, democratic political agenda.

## TOM CANTY AND THE
## TRANSCENDENCE OF ESCAPE

Shortly before Twain left New York in 1867 on the *Quaker City* excursion, he reflected on the fate of the poor during cholera epidemics in America's cities:

Only the poor, the criminally, sinfully, wickedly poor and destitute starvelings in the purlieus of the great cities suffered, died, and were hauled out to the Potter's field—the well-to-do were seldom attacked. It seems hard, but truly humiliation, hunger, persecution and death are the wages of poverty in the mighty cities of the land. No man can say aught against honest poverty. The books laud it; the instructors of the people praise it; all men glorify it and say it hath its reward here and will have it hereafter. Honest poverty is a gem even a King might feel proud to call his own, but I wish to sell out. I have sported that kind of jewelry long enough. I want some variety. (*MTTMB*, 236)

Although Twain expresses sympathy for the plight of the poor and disdain for the condescension of the rich, he represents the situation as inevitable, like disease itself:

It is no need to growl at the Government, state or municipal, about the pestilence-breeding tenement-houses, for they cannot help the matter much. They are doing all they can. They are making the landlords go to the expense of whitewashing the tenement-houses throughout, and when the landlord has done that he will gently raise the rent, and that will raise some of the tenants out, and then how much better off will they be? The cholera will follow them to the street. (*MTTMB*, 236)

Twain's wry portrait of himself as bejeweled with the gems of honest poverty is offset by the fatalism of his outlook. The most he can hope for is to escape a fate that will consume so many of his fellow New Yorkers, and wealth—not social or political reform—is the only inoculant. Twain has not simply lived among the poor; he's been one of them. In New York as a teenager he was susceptible to the same casual violence and hopeless suffering that pervaded his fictionalized London. (One element of Mark Twain's increasingly cosmopolitan identity was this conflation of many cities into one; for the cosmopolitan, all cities are the same. In a way that is similar to Eliot's perspective in *The Waste Land,* Twain finds the despair and alienation that is local to London also endemic to all modern urban spaces.) Twain, therefore, views poverty as inexorable and the charity it inspires as hollow. Edward's exposure to the realities of poverty, crime, and injustice provides a neat denouement: "The reign of Edward VI was a singularly merciful one for those harsh times. Now that we are taking leave of him, let us try to keep this in our minds, to his credit" (*P&P,* 289). Ultimately, however, Mark

Twain is less convinced by the philanthropy of Edward and more invested in the fate of his other hero, Tom Canty, whose escape from Offal court mirrors the trajectory of his own career.

Tom Canty lives in a state of loneliness that is a recurring theme in Twain's portraits of cities. Despite the many references to mobs and crowds, both in his early letters and in *The Prince and the Pauper* Twain was equally fascinated by the solitude, the "alone-ness" of urban life. Repeatedly in his letters to the *Alta California,* Twain represents himself as drifting around the "splendid desert" of New York (*MTTMB,* 259). Whereas Whitman's crowded New York makes possible the transcendental recognition of the "Self" in the Other, in Twain's New York the imagination needs space, specifically separation from those forces—often family and friends—that would constrain it. Twain, like his fictional characters, happily wandered the streets alone in search of some adventure: a glimpse of a real prince for Tom Canty, a story to send home for the seventeen-year-old Clemens, a glancing experience of celebrity for the thirty-six-year-old Mark Twain. The city became for Twain an experimental space, something like Emerson's "bare common," where Twain separates the "Me" from the "Not Me" and where "to be brothers, to be acquaintances, master and servant is then a trifle and a disturbance."[31] Tom Canty lives alone in a house filled with people, while he feeds his imagination with books and projects for himself an alternative identity: "For a long time his pain and hunger, and the swearing and fighting going on in the building kept him awake; but at last his thoughts drifted away to far, romantic lands, and he fell asleep in the company of jeweled and gilded princelings who lived in vast palaces, and had servants salaaming before them or flying to execute their orders. And then, as usual, he dreamed that *he* was a princeling himself" (*P&P,* 10).

In 1853, from his depressing lodgings in lower Manhattan, Clemens wrote to Pamela: "You ask where I spend my evenings. Where would you suppose, with a free printers' library containing more than 4,000 volumes within a quarter of a mile of me, and nobody at home to talk to?" (*L1,* 14). Likewise Clemens wrote his mother, "If books are not good company, where will I find it?" (*L1,* 10). Often cited as the adult Mark Twain's recommendation to read, the appeal sounds a great deal less precious and significantly

31. Ralph Waldo Emerson, "Nature," in *The Essential Writings of Ralph Waldo Emerson* (New York: Modern Library, 2000), 6.

more lonesome when placed in this urban—and adolescent—context. The books in the printer's library became "company" for Clemens, a substitute for the family he had left behind. Out of that reading emerged a new self, complete with a new set of desires. There is no record of the books Clemens read while in New York or their specific effect upon him. However, in Tom Canty we see a similarly lonely child, also in an urban setting, who is liberated by the process of reading, and who discovers in his books a magical alternative to his impoverished self.

New York City offered Sam Clemens a vision of opulence and luxury impossible to experience in the confines of Hannibal or even St. Louis. Early in his stay Clemens wandered uptown to the site of the Crystal Palace, which he described to Pamela: "From the gallery you have a glorious sight—the flags of the different countries represented, the lofty dome, glittering jewelry, gaudy tapestry, &c. with the busy crowds passing to and fro—tis a perfect fairy palace" (L1, 13).[32] Clemens arrived in a world far different from the slums of lower Manhattan, a place where crowds no longer threatened, where the flags of many nations did not undermine American identity, and where his imagination was free to construct an alternate reality, a "perfect fairy palace." Twain subsequently described several of his homes in these terms, particularly the Buffalo house given to him by his father-in-law, "the daintiest, darlingest, loveliest palace in America" (L4, 52). In Buckingham Palace, Tom Canty secures an ideal family complete with a loving father and refined and caring sisters. Tom Canty's catapult into wealth and prominence reflects Twain's own professional ambitions, while his acceptance within a royal family reproduces the effect of Twain's marriage. In his famed letter to Will Bowen shortly after his marriage, Twain characterized Livy as "my princess," and in a rapture he declared, "Before the gentle majesty of her purity all evil things & evil ways & evil deeds stand abashed. . . . She is the very most perfect gem of womankind that ever I saw in my life" (L4, 52). To Livy's parents he described himself as "Little Sammy in Fairyland" (L4, 66). The language of these letters characterizes Twain as both child and king. Having sold off the "gem" of honest poverty, he seems to have dis-

---

32. New York's Crystal Palace, built to rival its London counterpart, was the most magnificent structure in the city until it burned to the ground in 1858, "eighteen hundred tons of iron supporting fifteen thousand panes of translucent enameled glass that peaked in a 123-foot dome, the highest ever built in America" (Burroughs and Wallace, *Gotham,* 670).

covered a regal alternative in the "gem" Olivia Langdon. The palace—as home and fortress—became an emblem for Twain of both imaginative freedom and familial security.[33] In casting himself as a prince (Isabel Lyon later promoted him to "king") and his wife as a princess, Twain made wealth not simply a consequence of his success but a part of his domestic ideal and his imaginative self-conception. Without the princess, the gold, and the palace, Sam Clemens could not become his own fictional hero "Mark Twain."

And for Mark Twain the process of becoming American royalty begins and ends in New York City. Twain's letters to the *Alta California* reflect his urban ambitions: his desire to be one among the great names of New York (Henry Ward Beecher, Albert Bierstadt, William Cullen Bryant, Edwin Booth); to distinguish himself on the stage and on the street; and to separate himself from the fictional yokel and sidekick "Mr. Brown." In the midst of his 1867 residence in New York, Twain went back to Hannibal and St. Louis, towns that, despite having increased in population, appeared small: "the reality diminishes sizes and distances that have been lying on record in my memory so long." And the rural pace seemed slow: "They got into a perfect frenzy and talked of a railroad. . . . And behold, in the fullness of time—in ten or fifteen years—they built it" (*MTTMB*, 132, 145). By the late 1860s Twain's orientation had shifted East to the "ceaseless buzz, hurry, and bustle" of New York (*MTTMB*, 260). After this return trip to Hannibal, Twain no longer played to the hometown crowd, or even to the western audience he characterized as "friends." Instead, New York City became the standard against which his future achievements would be measured. Like a nineteenth-century Sinatra, Twain declared: "Make your mark in New York and you are a made man" (*MTTMB*, 176).

Tom Canty is just such a made man. He is Twain's ideal urban success story, a version of Emerson's self-reliant hero whose imaginative powers propel him into kingship: "vaulting at once into his throne." In an Emersonian moment of self-actualization, Tom's dream-self becomes a reality; his imagination "builds for itself a house, and beyond its house a world, and beyond its world a heaven."[34] And in this case heaven is Buckingham

---

33. Laura Skandera-Trombley, *Mark Twain in the Company of Women* (Philadelphia: University of Pennsylvania Press, 1994).

34. Emerson, "Nature," 37, 39.

Palace. Unlike the nihilistic aftermath of August Feldner's dreams, or the brutality of Hank Morgan's progressive ideals, or the romanticized violence of Tom Sawyer's fantasies, Tom Canty's imagination is powerful without being destructive. Through a collusion of random events and creative play, Tom transcends his inherited identity and redefines the world in which he lives.

Tom's escape from a life of poverty and abuse seems to be a triumph of the imagination over a historically and even a biologically prescribed fate. However, as his contradictory surname suggests—can't he, he can't—Tom's victory is both a self-realization and a fraud. Tom's education and his imaginative powers prepare him for the radical transformation he experiences; yet Tom does not, as Emerson would have it, effect this transformation himself. In fact, Tom inverts the Emersonian injunction to "Insist on yourself; never imitate"[35] by pretending to be another person entirely: "Did Tom Canty never feel troubled about the poor little rightful prince who had treated him so kindly[?] . . . Yes; his first royal days and nights were pretty well sprinkled with painful thoughts about the lost prince and sincere longings for his return and happy restoration to his native rights and splendors; but as time wore on and the prince did not come, Tom's mind became more and more occupied with his new and enchanting experiences, and by little and little the vanished monarch faded almost out of his thoughts; and finally when he did intrude upon them at intervals he was become an unwelcome spectre, for he made Tom feel guilty and ashamed" (P&P, 252).

Tom Canty's success is post-transcendental, illustrating Twain's belief in the limits of individual power and the illusion of an authentic identity. Unlike Emerson's woods, the city that emerges in Mark Twain's fiction does not empower "representative men" to transform history; instead, the city space makes it possible for individuals to traffic in identity and appearance. By shifting the moment of sublime awakening to an urban context, Twain makes his character less a heroic figure who plows his way through history (like Emerson's Jesus, or Plato, or Napoleon) than a con man who skims on its surface. Although Tom appears to be a good prince and would become a just king, his reign, like his identity, is illegitimate. While there is a

35. Emerson, "Self-Reliance" in Essential Writings, 150.

miraculous element in the circumstances that lead him to the throne, Tom's success carries with it—typical of Twain's other miracles and prayers—the darker consequence of Edward's alienation from his home, his birthright, and his own name.

The city as it emerges in *The Prince and the Pauper* appears to be a profoundly modernist, even postmodernist space. Crowds of people wander the streets unhinged from any sense of community or moral order, enjoying the pleasures of impersonation and the play of performance. Just as the end of *No. 44, The Mysterious Stranger* is populated by a series of doubles and dream selves, London becomes a confused space in which individual identity shifts, changes, and disappears in an instant: Edward is suddenly a pauper; Miles Hendon is unrecognizable to family and friends; and the pseudonymous identities of the gang of thieves—"The Ruffler," "Black Bess," "Yokel"—suggest that individuality has been replaced by caricature. The city as setting allows Twain to explore the instability of identity and conversely the permanence of human suffering.

What transforms Tom's future is not his own vision of a nobler self, nor is it the economic or political reforms of his newly enlightened twin, King Edward; it's his clothes. In one of the most recurring symbols of the vagaries of human experience, Twain uses the clothes of Tom Canty and Prince Edward to represent both the transcendental possibilities of urban life and the deterministic forces of poverty and race that often govern the streets of the city. By exchanging clothes, Tom Canty and Prince Edward effect the same radical change in identity and fate as Tom Driscoll and Chambers in *Pudd'nhead Wilson:* one boy becomes a prince, the other a pauper; one becomes a master, the other a slave. These sudden reversals in fortune represent the city as a space of almost miraculous transformations, a romantic world in which individuals—bound by no connections or obligations—can change identity as easily as changing their clothes. Yet the clothing of Tom and Edward also carries with it the absolute power to damn or to save, like white skin or wealth or the security of class: "In the ancient city of London, on a certain autumn day in the second quarter of the sixteenth century, a boy was born to a poor family of the name of Canty, who did not want him. On the same day another English child was born to a rich family of the name of Tudor, who did want him" (*P&P,* 1). Twain uses clothing as a metaphor to suggest that despite the apparent freedoms that the urban experience makes possible, the same random inequity of human experience abides.

Mark Twain's own fascination with clothing and costumes is legendary. As William Dean Howells recalls in his memoir, Twain had "a love of strong effect" that he demonstrated by "wearing a sealskin coat, with the fur out" or "in the white suit of complete serge which he wore in his last years, and in the Oxford gown which he put on for every possible occasion." Unlike the adolescent who made his first trips down Broadway at seventeen, Twain at thirty-six no longer feared the response of the crowd; he courted it. Howells wrote: "With his crest of dense red hair, and the wide sweep of his flaming mustache, Clemens was not discordantly clothed in that sealskin coat, which afterward, in spite of his own warmth in it, sent the cold chills through me when I once accompanied it down Broadway, and shared the immense publicity it won him."[36] While the seventeen-year-old Sam Clemens would occasionally strike a pose, he was still too defined by his white, American identity—and too frightened by the alternatives—to wear his race as a costume or use his name as a mask. However, by the mid-1860s, when he was about to launch his career on a national scale, Mark Twain walked the streets of New York with all the theatricality of a runway model. Having at this point invested in a fictionalized identity that would in time eclipse his former self, Mark Twain was as fascinated by the mutability of the human condition as he was once afraid of it. New York City functioned for Mark Twain the way "the territories" work for Huck. In the city Twain escaped the strictures of name, family, and even race; in New York he made for himself a new name, yearned for (and eventually discovered) an ideal family, and began to wear his race and his name as ironically as he did his white suit of clothes.

Like his creation Tom Canty, Twain enjoyed being on the street, so long as it was a theater where he was the star performer. By the late 1860s Mark Twain had achieved some measure of wealth and celebrity. Broadway no longer threatened his identity once it had become—as the streets of London do for Tom Canty—an intoxicating performance space. On the day of his coronation, the "splendidly arrayed" Tom Canty passes through throngs

36. Howells, *My Mark Twain* (New York: Dover, 1997), 4.

Here Mark Twain—world celebrity—engages in a bit of street "performance," as he attracts the attention of onlookers. (Courtesy Library of Congress)

of adoring people who line the gorgeously decorated streets: "'And all these wonders and these marvels are to welcome me—me!' murmured Tom Canty. The mock king's cheeks were flushed with excitement; his eyes were flashing; his senses swam in a delirium of pleasure" (*P&P,* 257). What Tom Canty discovers in his street performance is an artificial identity that feels more authentic than his own. Whoever the "me" refers to in this passage, it is a product of individual imagination and public affirmation, not unlike Twain's own persona.

## CONCLUSION: ALL THE WORLD'S A STAGE

In the experimental piece "What Is Man?" Mark Twain uses New York City as a setting to explore, among other moral conundrums, the counter-currents of egoism and empathy awakened when we encounter a beggar on the street. This Socratic exchange pairs an idealistic Young Man searching for proof that human beings are more than narcissistic machines with an

Old Man whose experience has proved otherwise. The Old Man describes a gentleman who gives his last quarter to "a gray and ragged old woman." He proves that behind this impulse of generosity—as is true for all other acts of heroism or nobility—there is self-interest: "It should make Wall Street ashamed of itself. On his way home his heart was joyful and it sang—profit on top of profit!"[37] The Old Man resembles Twain as he sat in bed in his Fifth Avenue brownstone and parried with young reporters. A kind of postmessianic figure, the Old Man seems glibly to concede that the poor will always be with us. If poverty, ignorance, and pain can be temporarily ameliorated, Twain insists that they cannot be eliminated. Paupers and princes may have the ability to transcend or transform their natures; however, these acts of transcendence appear to have limited political or historical power. Performance, then, seems to be one of the only consolations of Twain's cosmopolitan identity. In performance individuals can take advantage of the shifting conditions of the world, even if they cannot seriously affect those conditions. Performance for Twain appears to be a vehicle for escape, not a strategy for addressing many of the social and political ills that interested him as a young man and that obsessed him at the end of his life.

Yet Twain's involvement with the Children's Theater of New York may suggest otherwise. In 1907 Frederick Boyd Stevenson, a reporter for the *Brooklyn Eagle,* described the circumstances of his interview with Mark Twain: "He shifted his position a little in the big Venetian bed—where he receives some of his visitors and does much of his writing—took a good pull at his pipe and blew a cloud of smoke ceilingward. The night before the dramatization of his book the *Prince and the Pauper* had been presented at the Children's Theater of the Educational Alliance, where he had been host to a fashionable audience" (*Interviews,* 655). This tableau symbolizes many of the contradictions that surround Mark Twain's cosmopolitan identity, and it may even suggest that performance became for Twain something more than simply a personal plan of enrichment and escape. Here we see Twain engaged in a classic performance of his own, playing the part of the eccentric humorist who is willing to present himself unvarnished and un-

37. *The Complete Essays of Mark Twain,* ed. Charles Neider (Cambridge: Da Capo Press, 1991), 342, 343.

dressed. We also hear about the socialites who trailed behind Twain in his later years and with whom he had a sustained romance. Finally, there is the complicated adaptation of *The Prince and the Pauper* by The Children's Theater of the Jewish Educational Alliance: where a poor child who dreams of escaping his fate plays the part of a poor child who dreams of escaping his fate.

The Children's Theater Alliance was a reform project aimed at exposing the impoverished children of the East side, most of whom were immigrants, to the ideals of American citizenship through the vehicle of drama.[38] In this interview Twain claims that his involvement with the Children's Theater is "the most important work of my life" (*Interviews*, 658). He declares, "There is a great deal of the dramatic in the makeup of every human being. By the dramatic we can appeal to one's sympathies, to one's highest sentiments, to one's sense of justice and right and to one's ambition to progress" (*Interviews*, 656). No longer fleeing from the dark-skinned and foreign "human vermin" who originally frightened and harassed him, Twain was now engaged in a reform project that mirrored his own path to success: he encouraged these immigrant children to discover their true identities by playing a part. Certainly there was a colonial assumption at work; Twain imagined this effort as a way of creating new citizens. However, he also seemed convinced that these poor children were destined to replace and improve upon the American originals, and, in a circular exchange of performances, that "we" would eventually imitate "them": "We have good reason to emulate these people of the East Side. They are reading our history and learning the great questions of America that we do not know and are not learning, and they are learning them first hand and are doing their own thinking" (*Interviews*, 658).

In 1853 Sam Clemens resented the progress of blacks and immigrants, a fear that Mark Twain would incarnate in Pap Finn's paranoid response to the white shirt and top hat of an educated black man. Yet, by the end of his life, Twain seems to have been actively engaged in re-dressing—using the costume of American citizenry—the wrongs of history and even anticipating the look, feel, and sound of this newly imagined America. And

---

38. For further discussion of Twain and education, as well as The Children's Theater Alliance, see Joseph Csicsila, "The Child Learns by Doing," *Mark Twain Annual* 6 (2008): 36–51.

Twain located the site of this cultural redemption—the most important work of his life—in New York City.

In December 1900 at an elegant dinner sponsored by the St. Nicholas Club and held at Delmonico's, Twain was asked to respond to the toast, "The City of New York." In the midst of a comic assault on the corrupt politics and dirty streets of the city, Twain described its skyscrapers:

> In the daylight they are ugly. They are—well, too chimneyfied and too snaggy, like a mouth that needs attention from a dentist, like a cemetery that is all monuments and no gravestones. But at night, seen from the river where they are columns towering against the sky, all sparkling with light, they are fairylike. They are beauty more satisfactory to the soul and more enchanting than anything that man has dreamed of since the Arabian nights. We can't always have the beautiful aspect of things. Let us make the most of our sights that are beautiful and let the others go.[39]

Twain's New York's skyline appears savage (gaping mouths and gravestones) and magical (sparkling with light, a fairyland). In these architectural structures, Twain finds an honest representation of his own urban identity: a mixture of dark and light, cynicism and magic. The skyscrapers of New York are metaphors for the dark awakening that will occupy Twain's final years. No longer concerned with the truth of things, Twain was finally content to accept what beauty he could salvage in performance and "let the others go." Tom Canty's dream of a better life does not alter the course of history or improve the lives of the urban poor; just as Huck's personal independence fails to translate into a broader politics of liberty and justice for all. Nonetheless, New York City revealed to the young Clemens the possibility of radical self-transformation. In 1853 Sam Clemens wrote a final letter to Pamela from New York: "I've taken a liking to the abominable place . . . it is just as hard on my conscience to leave New York as it was easy to leave Hannibal" (L1, 16). While Twain's affection for small southern towns would wane over the course of his career, his fascination with New York—its values and its char-

---

39. *"New York," Plymouth Rock and the Pilgrims, and Other Speeches,* ed. Charles Neider (New York: Cooper Square Press, 2000), 191.

acters—grew and shaped his fiction. Twain would recall that at seventeen he lived in a city where blacks behaved like citizens, children ruled the streets, white men wore black faces, and a working-class apprentice wandered through libraries and a Crystal Palace dreaming of becoming a prince in the city.

# Sam Clemens and the
# Mississippi River Metropolis

BRUCE MICHELSON

**A**S Ann Ryan observes in her introduction to this book, "cosmopolitan" is a concept—or a hope, or a posture, or in any case a recurring and molting "keyword"—with histories meandering back to the Stoics and Cynics of the Greek Golden Age. If a dram of Cynicism has endured, through the ages, as one affiliated demeanor, the ghosts of Stoicism have been shooed away by something like their opposite: five-star, globalized Epicurean self-indulgence, flourishing on a scale that would have boggled poor, sickly Epicurus, who rarely got out of town. We can exploit "cosmopolitan" with either spin on it, for in our own times it seems stuck in a tussle between affluent connoisseurs and unregenerate humanitarians. What should it call to mind? Volunteers from CARE, Doctors without Borders, and other heroic NGOs, living and working rough with the oppressed and the forgotten? Pampered fashionistas, swaggering through photo shoots on some sugar-candy beach where dowdy indigenous people are not allowed to intrude? As with any "ism," the longer the pedigree the deeper the interpretive mess. With "cosmopolitan," however, troubles lurk not only in the conflicting ideological and moral implications of this potentially useful and important adjective but also in the tones of voice with which the word is commonly written and spoken. At the London School of Economics,

David Held is a leader of a determined set of scholars urging us to keep the word *cosmopolitan* on higher moral ground:

> Cosmopolitan values can be expressed formally in terms of a set of principles. . . . These are principles which can be universally shared, and can form the basis for the protection and nurturing of each person's equal significance in "the moral realm of all humanity." Eight principles are paramount. They are principles of: (1) equal worth and dignity; (2) active agency; (3) personal responsibility and accountability; (4) consent; (5) collective decision-making about public matters through voting procedures; (6) inclusiveness and subsidiarity; (7) avoidance of serious harm; and (8) sustainability. . . . While eight principles may seem like a daunting number, they are interrelated and together form a basis of a cosmopolitan orientation.[1]

Writing for broader audiences, Kwame Anthony Appiah uses *cosmopolitan* in a similar way, to signify a useful private or public commitment of money, apparatus, and energy across international borders to relieve human suffering. He means concrete efforts to promulgate and exemplify a universal ethic subtending all nations and peoples—the kind of cosmopolitanism exemplified in the global media, right now anyway, by people like Al Gore, Bono, Samantha Power, Andrew Kimbrell, and Jeffrey Sachs; and perhaps also by Greenpeace, UNESCO, and the World Bank, depending on which op-ed perspectives you accept about those organizations.

> [W]e cosmopolitans believe in universal truth, too, though we are less certain that we have it all already. It is not skepticism about the very idea of truth that guides us; it is realism about how hard the truth is to find. One truth we hold to, however, is that every human being has obligations to every other. Everybody matters: that is our central idea. And it sharply limits the scope of our tolerance.
>
> To say what, in principle, distinguishes the cosmopolitan from the counter-cosmopolitan, we plainly need to go beyond talk of truth and tolerance. One distinctively cosmopolitan commitment is to *pluralism*.

1. Held, "Principles of Cosmopolitan Order," in *The Political Philosophy of Cosmopolitanism,* ed. Gillian Grock and Harry Brighouse (Cambridge: Cambridge University Press, 2005), 12.

> Cosmopolitans think that there are many values worth living by and
> that you cannot live by all of them. So we hope and expect that differ-
> ent people and different societies will embody different values. (But
> they have to be values *worth* living by.)[2]

For cosmopolitanism of this sort, no sophistication of taste is required, no
platinum-level frequent flyer cards or special savvy about exotic treats and
pricey consumer goods. For basic membership, all you need to do is affirm
the worth of human beings everywhere and try to contribute, in some ef-
fectual way, to bettering conditions on the other side of an international and
cultural divide.

Even so, bulky alternative categories of "cosmopolitan" discourse must
also be reckoned with, for along with travel-magazine and wine-snob
screeds of personal delectation and luxurious adventure, there are academic modes of analysis and discrimination that are likewise bracingly global
and jaded, and ostensibly beyond the parochial taint of any one cultural perspective.

If we want to situate Mark Twain within a tradition or ideology of cosmopolitanism, this is a paradox in the way: though the ostensible objectives
of cosmopolitan discourse in the humanities are political and moral, the
tone and the process are imbued with connoisseurship. Thriving on dispu-
tation about methodology, this mode of critique pursues ideological and
intellectual sophistication largely as an end in itself: elite discriminations,
occasionally spiced up with categorical disdain. In a book subtitled *Cosmopolitanism Now,* for instance, a scholar in a university English department
disparages the bourgeois pretensions of most of his forebears and colleagues
in the same general enterprise—thumbs down for the lot, from a skybox
high up to our left:

> Whatever its merits, cosmopolitanism as a prolonged effort to ar-
> gue for the expertise and political responsibility of academic profes-
> sionals is a decidedly mainstream position, solidly in the convention-
> al liberal center of the American intellectual scene. It is not today, of
> course, meant openly to extol a salvational Europe threatened by for-

2. Appiah, *Cosmopolitanism: Ethics in a World of Strangers* (New York and London: W. W.
Norton, 2006), 144.

eign incursions like communism, Garveyism, Islam, or ethnic partic-
ularism. In it's [sic] more recent life, the concept is intended to assert
that the institutional being of American professionals allies them to
non-Western cultures. That is, being an intellectual means being worldly, transnational, or cosmopolitan.[3]

Take up a voice of scholastic po-mo worldliness, and massive accumula-
tions of other people's theorizing and practice can be brushed aside with
wonderful disregard for cultural and historical contingency. Stratospheric
scorn from another American English department:

> Humanism is an ideology of mystification and ascesis; it does not
> enrich or enlarge. In fact, it restricts desire by creating submissive man,
> by projecting into society through discourse and discipline a taboo
> upon power. Moreover, one can say that the discourse of humanism
> injects men and women into master-slave relations by assigning pow-
> er to a "naturalized" and "transcendent" elite; and as a result, in the
> name of the highest ethical and cultural values of the West, human-
> ism denies power to the oppressed. Civil rights, religious freedom, the
> critical intelligence, human nature—all of these and other images help
> cloak the power of discourse within an illusion of a just and stable so-
> ciety.[4]

Wow. The tone in evidence here recurs often in writings emanating from
academic programs aspiring to cutting-edge cosmopolitan perspectives.
Above the reach of specifics and ground-level fact, the prose soars like a
recreational hang glider, high on summer alpine thermals, on updrafts and
whooshes of clean thin air—the culture-critic as liberated and dissatisfied
master of all that he or she surveys.

These passages reflect an attitude that Amanda Anderson regards as almost inevitable in theoretical cosmopolitan discourse, even when such writing sets out to describe or critique cosmopolitan perspectives. The prose
affects a condition of impartiality, repose, and removal that is at once dis-

---

3. Timothy Brennan, *At Home in the World: Cosmopolitanism Now* (Cambridge: Harvard University Press, 1997), 23–24.
4. Paul Bové, *In the Wake of Theory* (Hanover and London: Wesleyan University Press,
1992), 132.

ingenuous and paradoxical—a condition that troubles my own words as I try to describe where we are. As Anderson sees it, to hold that a cogent cosmopolitan ethos can be constructed by rigorous reasoning alone is to privilege "a theoretical practice of critical detachment," a pretension that can be attacked on the basis of what is generally understood about the informative power of personal upbringing and firsthand cultural experience. She also asserts, however, that argumentation of an opposite sort—for the inherent impossibility of achieving an objective cosmopolitan perspective—can result in "acts of parodic distancing that illuminate and subvert defining matrices of power"—only another way of being aloof and cooler than everyone else in the room.[5]

So maybe there's no way out: the perspective of the cosmopolitan traveler, tourist, and aesthetic-ideological critic (as opposed to those who go out there not for the pristine snorkeling, the last authentic *ceviche,* and the opportunities for one-upmanship,[6] but rather for the benefit of others) gravitates toward the voice of the sabbatical savant, and with no genuine stake in, or any serious argument about, any given geographical or cultural context.

To sum up: about cosmopolitanism as a body of imaginative and literary perspectives, the available commentary is often complicated or compromised by postures and mentalities not unlike those being called into question. Even so, if we want to talk about the modern and contemporary self as transformed, or traumatized, by encounters with international and global otherness, and also about the difficulty of finding intellectual, emotional, and ideological byways through such trouble, then this is probably where we have to begin, with an accumulating, involuting discourse that critiques, usually from some (imaginary) loftier position, the moral and aesthetic responses of everyone else—other writers and artists; religious, cultural, and

5. Anderson, *The Powers of Distance: Cosmopolitanism and the Cultivation of Detachment* (Princeton: Princeton University Press, 2001), 27, 26.

6. Brennan, for example, on what he sees as the general failure of the American cultural studies enterprise: "Cultural studies in practice has actually stunted an internationalism of value by glorifying a specifically U.S. mass culture, by superimposing literary critical readings onto nonliterary texts and thereby giving a cramped literary criticism a second life and by conceiving nonwriting (mass-cultural practices and the media) as the extraliterary without confronting the force of the literary itself. The point should not be simply to expand what is studied but to give to the art forms of other peoples and nations the same authority and seriousness that the literary now enjoys" (*At Home in the World,* 312).

corporate big-league players on the global scene; and sometimes, if we're feeling frisky, entire nations and peoples.

As a traveler, humorist, satirist, and moralist about places far from the homes of his boyhood, Mark Twain never acquired credentials as an altruistic well-digger in remote villages; polemics in national magazines about atrocities on other continents were about as far as he went, in public, in the cause of international justice. Because we remember and value him more for his perceptions and moods as he moved through the world, we can ask a question about each episode of the life and each stage of the career, a question that interrogates his modernity, his relevance on this rapidly globalizing planet. The question is this: what commonalities and differences can we discern between the temperament that Sam Clemens or Mark Twain reveals in those moments—his voice and demeanor as a visitor to each new locale, the values that subtend his response—and a plausible, basic description of a modern cosmopolitan identity, meaning a way of seeing rather than of doing, a more or less sophisticated balance of tastes, discriminations, and moral judgments?

Whether feigned or authentic or just plain unavoidable, "cosmopolitan detachment" is not a phrase that calls Mark Twain to mind right away, though he does rate as one of America's first world-trotting superstars, and perhaps the very first indeed from the realms of literature and popular culture in the English-speaking nations. Exuberance, whimsy, despair, irreverence, moral indignation, even sentimentality—these qualities seem to fit with the life and the name; but in the Mark Twain we seem to know, and also in the Mark Twain that we perennially, as a culture, seem to want, there isn't much of the Gilded Age *flâneur,* strolling bemused in piazzas and boulevards; or the "world-besotted traveler," a phrase that Yeats pulled from a Latin epitaph about twenty years after Mark Twain's death, as the world they shared for a while was globalizing toward another disaster. Late in his life, though his personal and literary mood notoriously darkened, Mark Twain's passions about injustice at home and in other lands only intensified. And with regard to visitation and residence in fashionable and culturally vibrant locales, his credentials can rival those of other affluent wanderers in the *bel epoque,* fin de siècle, or whatever we want to call that swath of time. During the last thirty years of his career he unpacked for pampered stays in many exciting cities, leasing luxurious places in and around Vienna, Venice,

London, Munich, Paris, Menton, Berlin, Rome, Florence, and New York. The grandest house he owned was a show-off mansion, situated so as to impress the passersby on a main drag about a mile from downtown Hartford. In 1906, after his partial recovery from bankruptcy and the death of his wife, he moved into his final house, a modest and secluded place compared to Nook Farm, on rolling acreage close to the town of Redding, Connecticut, about twenty miles from Bridgeport, thirty or so from New Haven—picturesque suburban New England. A tally of top-class hotels where Mark Twain resided for pleasure and business during those years of touring and travel would fill pages, as would a list of exclusive downtown clubs and restaurants where he socialized, orated, and dined very well at other people's expense.

If we do go looking for signs of "detachment" in Mark Twain's accounts of big-city adventures, we can find plenty, though the signifiers we find might not be the ones we would prefer. In Mark Twain's writings about urban settings, one conspicuous feature is a shortage of attention to the particulars of life in the streets, to the vitality and challenge of these metropolitan contexts. In the latter half of *Life on the Mississippi,* half a dozen short chapters center on New Orleans, about which more later. In this same thick book, Mark Twain's engagement with St. Louis is also sparse—and in substance and spirit it aligns with his published writings about Chicago, Paris, New York, and London, and other dynamic and sprawling urban settings that Clemens came to know well. The pattern is familiar: anecdotes and reminiscences are set against a blurry metropolitan background; wisecracks are offered on the fly about locals and their social quirks in one busy place or another. Even in his bulkiest travel tomes, the chapters and embedded stories that are situated vividly in big-city contexts are rare. In *The Prince and the Pauper,* for example, the descriptive tour de force about London Bridge in the time of the Tudors only underscores Mark Twain's silence about the modern-day "Heart of the Empire" that he experienced firsthand, spectacles of noise, color, and human vitality compared to which the old London Bridge scene might rate as a sideshow. In *The Innocents Abroad* and *A Tramp Abroad,* the chapters on Paris, Geneva, Turin, and Rome are coaxed along by local guides and Baedeker handbooks, with more attention centered on old churches, ruins, tombs, and galleries than on the spontaneous and evolving life of the contemporary streets.

One obvious and stunning absence of this sort turns up in Mark Twain's most famous novel. In the middle of the night, Huck and Jim on their raft drift by the blazing lights of St. Louis on their way south on the river. But they don't indulge any natural curiosity and pull in to shore for a closer look; and no reason is given:

> The fifth night we passed St. Louis, and it was like the whole world lit up. In St. Petersburg they used to say there was twenty or thirty thousand people in St. Louis, but I never believed it till I see that wonderful spread of lights at two o'clock that still night. There warn't a sound there; everybody was asleep. (*HF,* 79)

So much for St. Louis—three sentences in chapter 12. These lines do provide a pinch of help, however, in arguing for the time of the novel's action—the later 1840s—as the city, with pomp about its own modernization and technological progress, had begun to brighten the downtown with a natural gas lighting project in November 1847.[7] But for thematic interest or interpretive importance, that's about it. Though neither of these village-raised travelers has ever seen such a great place before, there is no adventure, not even the briefest reconnaissance in that forest of riverboats and warehouses along the quays, a concentration of design, commerce, chaos, and power that should dazzle any small-town boy. Here's a city more than ten times larger than the village Huck knows, and offering, one might assume, terrific opportunities for a curious boy to explore and an accomplished storyteller like Mark Twain to cut loose—and we get nothing. Why not?

As for the city of New Orleans in *Huckleberry Finn,* its presence is even more oblique. Back in chapter 8, Jim has told Huck of Miss Watson's rumored plan to sell her slave down the river to New Orleans for $800, causing Jim to "run off" to Jackson's Island, and then to join Huck on the raft journey from there; later, in chapter 20, the younger of the two con artists, the one calling himself the Duke of Bridgewater, breaks into an unwatched village print shop and turns out a set of official-looking wanted posters,

---

7. James Cox, *Old and New St. Louis: A Concise History of the Metropolis of the West and Southwest, with a Review of Its Present Greatness and Immediate Prospects* (St. Louis: Central Biographical Publishing Co., 1894), 114.

identifying Jim as an escaped slave from a plantation near New Orleans. Ostensibly an alibi for Jim, as well as for Huck and his fellow travelers, this poster eventually provides the pretext for selling Jim to Silas Phelps, who aims to collect the fictitious reward mentioned on the handbill. That's all for New Orleans—and also for the metropolitan dimensions of Mark Twain's most famous work.

It is hard to avoid an inference that St. Louis was one Mississippi River attraction that Mark Twain decidedly did *not* want his young hero to explore. Pokeville, Bricksville, Pikeville—Huck and Jim never pull into places larger than these. Is there something vulnerable in Huck's temperament, or (for the craft of storytelling) something advantageously limited in his range of experience, that Mark Twain would not risk disrupting with even a brief encounter with metropolitan life? The journey with Jim is punctuated by trouble in small settlements—inhumane communities they sometimes are, but all of them on a human scale: no vertiginous plunges into multitudes, no scary episodes in labyrinths of streets that cannot be easily figured out. This pattern of metropolitan avoidance continues beyond the one novel: later in Huck's imaginary life, in the Tom-and-Huck potboilers that followed *Adventures,* the boys never try their luck in cities or even come close to doing so, not even on a flyover in a sci-fi hot air balloon, the intercontinental mode of transport in *Tom Sawyer Abroad.* The pattern is also echoed in Mark Twain's major fictions that don't involve Tom or Huck at all. Hadleyburg, Lakeside, Eseldorf, Dawson's Landing—such smaller, quieter settlements are clearly favored as contexts, suggesting Mark Twain's abiding aversion to the modern city as a site for human experience to be explored, and for his own imagination to thrive.

With only a little coercion of the facts, however, such authorial reluctance might be plumped up as another indicator of Mark Twain's cosmopolitan temperament. Baudelaire as *flâneur* in Paris; Nick Carraway at loose ends after work, drifting and dreaming his way up Broadway; Walter Benjamin meandering the *gallerias*, pondering a writing project about them that he never finishes—for urban wanderers like these, the metropolis is to be enjoyed and endured as a spectacle of impressions, some of them bordering on the hallucinatory and the surreal, but implicitly consoling as well, reassuring these footloose observers that they have no allegiance here and do not belong to the world they observe. Looked at as a group, these texts and authors can suggest a familiar and complex social and psychological condition associated with modern-style alienation, a feeling of vague relief blended with inchoate regret. The metropolis and its sights are cruised through and visited, yet the visitation is essentially solitary: the genuine life, the human relationships that matter—for the observer loose in the big city, such comforts are somewhere else. In a similar spirit, as a veteran of many cities before he reached his prime as a writer, Mark Twain maintained his own imaginative and affective distance. In the century since Clemens's death, some of the motives for that artistic alienation may have grown even more ubiquitous, with the triumph of the megalopolis. The limo from the airport goes straight to the theme-park tourist districts, with their rampart avenues of corporate opulence and flashy public venues designed by globe-trotting "starchitects." In contexts like these, suspicions can glow, like embers in the back of the mind, that reports of genuine difference between one "world-class" metropolitan downtown and the next are (in the words of somebody or other) greatly exaggerated.

To think more seriously about Mark Twain as showing some kind of cosmopolitan sensibility recognizable to us now, I want to review how Sam Clemens's direct experiences with the two largest cities in his own home region, experiences that unfolded over a span of about eight years while he was an adolescent and a young man, may have influenced, in lasting ways, his understanding of what a metropolis was, and what it could be—the enticements, challenges, and outright dangers that he encountered in these specific streets and along these moorages. I want to look speculatively at the dynamics of those early sojourns, how he first saw those new places and moved through them repeatedly; and who he was, and who he thought he wanted to be, as all this daily work and sporadic adventuring went on. As the primary source for the news stories that he set in movable type and printed off in those Hannibal shops, St. Louis, Missouri, with a population in the scores of thousands and growing at an amazing pace, offered him his opening encounters with any human assembly larger than a hamlet. Moreover, in the same year that Sam went there from Hannibal, St. Louis, eighty thousand strong in 1853, was enjoying swift progress in connecting itself to the older and bigger urban zones on the East Coast. These changes included enhancements in speed and efficiency that radically transformed commerce and culture in the central Mississippi valley, as well as the imaginative conception of distances from the Atlantic to the heartland. With "steam and lightning," St. Louis was a place binding itself to the other dominions of modernity.

About seven hundred miles south of Hannibal—and considerably farther via the boat-safe channels of the convoluting river—New Orleans, with a population at that time of about 120,000, was half again as large. Sam began to know that city about four years later, first as an apprentice steamboat pilot and then as a licensed captain in the closing years of the 1850s. In that profession, he laid over in New Orleans and St. Louis many times, usually for stints of less than a week,[8] before the Civil War closed down the river traffic and forced him out of this high-paying and glamorous employment. The unpleasant prospect of being conscripted, for his skills, into a new Federal navy of gunboats and troop transports sent him west, on the coattails of his elder brother Orion, to the gold-rush regions of Nevada. Sam's adventures in St. Louis and New Orleans were followed by his sojourn in and around Virginia City, after that by his months in San Francisco, and not long after that by the voyage to the Sandwich Islands as a correspondent. Then it was back to the East Coast and, soon after, the *Quaker City* tour to Europe and the Holy Land; then home again—and onward from there, years of crisscrossing piedmont, prairies, plains, oceans, and continents. To build an impression of how Sam Clemens's cosmopolitan imagination took shape, what can we see in a review of his opening encounters with the modern city, encounters in the vast river basin where he grew up?

It will help to pull together some relevant facts about those early years.[9] In May 1853, Sam Clemens was seventeen years old, with about five years of hands-on experience in print shops turning out hometown newspapers,

8. *L1* includes a remarkable compilation of arrival and departure dates for Mississippi River commercial steamboats on which Sam Clemens served as a cub pilot and a licensed pilot. See appendix B, 387–90.

9. Most of the facts in this summary come from Dixon Wecter, *Sam Clemens of Hannibal* (Boston: Houghton Mifflin, 1961), 200–265; Everett Emerson, *Mark Twain: A Literary Life* (Philadelphia: University of Pennsylvania Press, 1999), 1–10; and, most important, the marvelous annotations in *L1,* esp. 1–120. Some additional material on Clemens's formative years can be found in Bruce Michelson, *Printer's Devil: Mark Twain and the American Publishing Revolution* (Berkeley: University of California Press, 2006), 21–55.

each of them a weekly single-sheet four-pager, produced by sustained, focused attention, physical skill, and muscle—one sheet at a time, one side at a time, on a bed and platen press. At the age of twelve, Sam had begun as an apprentice at the *Missouri Courier,* situated in a Main Street shop owned and operated by a man named Joseph B. Ament. Older than Sam by a decade, Orion Clemens had taken a similar pathway into this trade; about two years younger than Sam, Henry Clemens would follow his brothers into these workrooms in due course. In 1851, Orion had returned to Hannibal after years of typesetting in St. Louis for the firm of Thomas Ustick, whose house produced work under contract for the mighty and automated *Evening News.* Although he had an up-close knowledge of the production revolution underway in that city—steam-powered type-revolving presses, electrotype, new machines for feeding sheets and folding them and cutting them—Orion had neither the resources for such new gear back home nor the population base there to justify a shift to modern apparatus. He had bought out one of the *Courier's* rivals, another struggling weekly called the *Hannibal Western Union,* folding it soon afterward into an additional half-starved paper he also bought cheap, the *Hannibal Journal;* and in 1852, Sam had quit the *Courier* to help his brother with the business, for their father had been dead for years, and the work of the boys was needed to help keep the family afloat. While Orion struggled with the *Journal,* eventually trying—in desperation, and with his usual disregard for pragmatics and actualities—to multiply the work by turning the *Journal* into a daily, Sam developed into a passable journeyman printer, as well as pro tem reporter, editor, and publisher of the *Journal* whenever Orion was out of the shop, on business trips and other excursions that sometimes kept him away for weeks.

Much of Sam's textual education in the wider world took place in these workrooms, where stories from elsewhere—chiefly from St. Louis sources, as Hannibal had no telegraph—were reset by his own hands, copy-edited, and printed off for the scattering of raggedly educated local readers. The *Journal* also filled space and collected meager revenue by publishing columns of advertisements for national weekly and monthly magazines, alluring and ominous little assertions, in each issue, that a new era in American media was running at (literally) full steam in the population centers. In Sam's childhood, the powered press, the electrotype process for duplicating chases of set movable type, along with the railroad, the telegraph, cheap paper,

and lowered postal rates, had transformed printing from a slow neighborhood craft into an efficient industry with regional and national reach:
there were long-distance news services now, and commonplace daily print
runs of tens of thousands of copies.[10] Serial publications, thick and handsome, could flow from metropolitan factories to villages like Hannibal
with a velocity, volume, and affordability unimaginable in the year of
Sam's birth.

For an ambitious kid brother, Hannibal's connection to that glamorous
upheaval was painfully remote. In 1853 most news of the nation and the
world arrived at the steamboat landing, days after the city papers had har-
vested the glory of informing their multitudes. And with automated high-
volume operations, metropolitan publishers were making money, while
Sam in Hannibal had no regular wages at all, and no prospects of doing any
better with the *Daily Journal*. Hannibal was too small to support its own
compliment of papers and print shops; Orion's insolvent enterprise was
sliding toward liquidation, and it was time to get out. In 1851, Sam's older
sister Pamela, married now to a businessman named William Moffett, had
set up housekeeping in a rented place in downtown St. Louis, about a dozen
blocks from the landings and the publishing centers. Family in the big town;
a place to sleep or assistance in finding one;[11] brighter opportunities for a
boy with ambition and technical skills; and a starting point for greater adventures farther away on the East Coast: Sam left home on a southbound
packet in the late spring of 1853. In St. Louis he found a job with Ustick,
where Orion had worked, but he also did stints in other local printing operations.[12] Apparently, however, his professional luck in his first big city did
not hold up, for on August 24 of that year Sam wrote to his mother that one

10. One useful source on the rapid development of high-speed printing presses for newspapers and mass-market magazines is Robert Hoe, *A Short History of the Printing Press and of
the Improvements in Printing Machinery from the Time of Gutenberg Up to the Present Day* (New
York: Hoe Company, 1902). For the contemporary and commensurate impact of new press
technology on book publishing, see John Tebbel, *A History of Book Publishing in the United
States*, vol. 1, *The Creation of an Industry, 1630–1865*, 2 vols. (New York: R. R. Bowker, 1972),
221. See also Michelson, *Printer's Devil*, 21–29.

11. The annotations for *L1* indicate that Sam probably stayed with the Moffetts in the neighborhood around Pine Street, but no firm evidence of where he actually slept, in these first
months in St. Louis, has been uncovered (*L1*, 2).

12. From the annotations in *L1*: "Clemens's principal job was as a typesetter for the St. Louis
*Evening News*, but he also worked on several other weekly journals published in the city" (2).

of his reasons for quitting the city was that he was currently unemployed (*L1*, 3). A few weeks later, on August 19, with enough cash to cover the most ambitious excursion of his young life, he was on his way to New York City.

But the fall of 1853 turned out to be a season of hard times for New York printers, and after about two months of short jobs at establishments in lower Manhattan, Sam moved on to Philadelphia, where he plied the trade until the middle of February 1854. After a week in Washington, D.C., he returned to New York, and by the spring of that year he was back in the Hannibal region. Then there were months in Muscatine, Iowa—working with Orion once again—followed by the longest of his sojourns in St. Louis, from August 1854 into June 1855 (*L1*, 44–46, 121, 122). After that, it was up the Mississippi River to Keokuk, Iowa, and neighboring towns; another two weeks in St. Louis in October; and then five months in Cincinnati, well into April 1857.

As we near the end of Mark Twain's career as a printer, we can speculate about his imaginative and psychological experience of looking at city life through the perspective of that kind of daily work. Setting movable type for a newspaper, a journeyman printer would find himself in daily, indirect, professional confrontation with life in the streets and neighborhoods around him, as well as with the world farther off. Literally with his hands as well as with his vigilance, he would engage the daily doings that most other citizens—in towns to which he himself felt no strong connection—were privileged to ponder or ignore as they choose. Down at the port, shipping tonnage had increased or slacked off; stories were coming in about another outbreak of violence among the rubes in some other county; the latest antics at city hall or at the nearby courthouses had their own backstories and implications—daily emulsions of probably forgettable fact and ephemeral editorial comment. In his work in St. Louis, Sam Clemens may have learned important lessons in how to imagine and negotiate the metropolis: the city as incessant, high-volume manufacturer of random and often pointless narrative. A newspaper printer must reckon with the life of a city in a peculiar way, especially if that city is not his own, as St. Louis and these others were never home for Sam Clemens. Mark Twain's decision to keep Huck and Jim out of the big towns might have roots in that kind of personal and professional experience.

On August 26, 1857, Sam boarded the *Paul Jones,* a steamboat leaving Cincinnati and bound for New Orleans. Apparently he had enough money in his pocket to get him started on a longer and more perilous journey he may have been contemplating. His ambition (as he recalled it many years later in his sometimes embellished autobiographical dictations) was to cross the Gulf of Mexico and join, somehow, in the Yankee adventuring underway in Latin America, and possibly travel up the vast and perilous Amazon (*MTA,* 2:289). But this turned out to be the fated trip on which Sam fell into a relationship with the pilot, Horace Bixby; when the *Paul Jones* reached New Orleans, Bixby agreed to accept Sam's payment of $500, in installments, for thorough training in a profession he had admired since childhood.[13] Months of apprenticeship would follow, an education taking Sam up and down the Mississippi, especially on the stretch between New Orleans and St. Louis. Acquiring his license in September 1859, Sam kept at this practice for about a year and a half longer, arriving in each city frequently and with money in his pocket—until the secession of the South and the American Civil War put Louisiana into the Confederacy, forced St. Louis and New Orleans into Union occupation—uneasy but generally quiet in the northern city; hostile in the Delta—and closed down the river for commercial navigation on the route he was qualified to navigate.

It matters that Sam's first metropolitan adventures unfolded in this condition of being on the move, camped out, and unsettled. He experienced three years of such oscillation, along with the crews of hundreds of other steamboats hauling cargo and passengers. At that time, in fact, the commercial flotilla on the Mississippi River was so large as to constitute an additional "city" for Sam to negotiate, a kinetic, rootless, mechanized population out in midstream and along the quays, many thousands more people than lived in the town where he had grown up. The Mississippi River realms where Sam spent most of his time between April 1857 and July 1861 (when he began the journey to the West) were sites of constant transition and trade. At the two embarkation points, he lived on land as a visitor with wages in his pocket, but never as an assimilated local. By necessity now, he was a per-

13. *L1,* 70–71, includes an annotation on various accounts of the first encounter with Bixby, the instructional agreement, the payments, and how Sam acquired the money to cover them.

petual outsider, taking up this new profession of boiler-powered motion
and drift. Only a year before Sam made this decision, or fell into it, the great
British art critic John Ruskin was lecturing and writing with curmudgeon-
ly alarm about the havoc, to any refined sensibility, of traveling at any pace
faster than a walk, and especially of journeys propelled by modern machines:

> I say, first, to be content with as little change as possible. If the atten-
> tion is awake, and the feelings in proper train, a turn of a country road,
> with a cottage beside it, which we have not seen before, is as much as
> we need for refreshment; if we hurry past it, and take two cottages at
> a time, it is already too much: hence, to any person who has all his
> senses about him, a quiet walk along not more than ten or twelve miles
> of road a day, is the most amusing of all travelling; and all travelling
> becomes dull in exact proportion to its rapidity. Going by railroad I do
> not consider as travelling at all; it is merely "being sent" to a place, and
> very little different from becoming a parcel; the next step to it would
> of course be telegraphic transport. . . .
>
> A man who really loves travelling would as soon consent to pack a
> day of such happiness into an hour of railroad, as one who loved eat-
> ing would agree, if it were possible, to concentrate his dinner into a
> pill.[14]

For Ruskin, all this too-easy moving around was messing up not only the
going but also the destination; and old and glorious European cities were
being toured to ruins before Sam could get there. As early as 1846, Ruskin
was complaining that the quaint quarters of major European cities were already being degraded, by the influence of rails and mass visiting, into trav-
esties of their former authentic selves:

> Care and observance, more mischievous in their misdirection than in-
> difference or scorn, have in many places given the medieval relics the
> aspect and associations of a kind of cabinet preservation, instead of

14. *The Works of John Ruskin*, ed. E. T. Cook and Alexander Wedderburn, 39 vols. (London:
George Allen; New York: Longmans, Green, 1903–1912), 5:370–71. The passage originally
occurred in vol. 3 of *Modern Painters* (London: Smith Elder and Co., 1856).

that air of majestic independence, or patient and stern endurance. . . . Nominal restoration has done tenfold worse, and has hopelessly destroyed what time, and storm, and anarchy, and impiety had spared. The picturesque material of a lower kind is fast departing—and for ever. There is not, as far as we know, one city scene in central Europe which has not suffered from some jarring point of modernisation. The railroad and the iron wheel have done their work, and the characters of Venice, Florence, and Rouen are yielding day by day to a lifeless extension of those of Paris and Birmingham. A few lustres more, and the modernisation will be complete . . . and here and there a solitary fragment of the old cities may exist by toleration, or rise strangely before the workmen who dig the new foundations, left like some isolated and tottering rock in the midst of sweeping sea.[15]

Poor Sam, born too late, and still too insolvent for the exquisite pleasures of aristocratic pilgrimage at a Medieval pace. But if Ruskin's observations can support a case that Sam's own travels up and down the Mississippi River were an experience in mechanical-engineered alienation, and another early reinforcement to his feeling of detachment from the modern metropolis, we can also recognize that his mode of travel to those places was also in a sense primordial, especially on the southward run. The motion was natural, geological, despite the technology and glamour associated at that time with steam-powered riverboats. They were state-of-the-art transportation, to be sure, and to command such a vessel could boost the prestige and spirits of almost any young American male with a capacity to dream. Even so, the rising muddy water that rolled south past Hannibal in the spring of 1853 could conceivably carry you almost effortlessly down to the confluence with the Illinois, and soon after to the mouth of the Missouri; past the commercial action at Leclede's Landing; to the confluence with the Kaskaskia and the mighty Ohio; past the Saint Francis, the Arkansas, the White, and the Big Black—and so on to the delta and the bayous of the Deep South. And steam boilers and paddle wheels were not absolutely necessary for riding this great flow. Before the advent of the Mississippi lock and dam system, an idle boy up north in Missouri could toss a dry length

15. "Samuel Prout," in *Works of John Ruskin*, ed. Cook and Wedderburn, 12:314–15.

of stove wood into that flood and reasonably imagine that it would drift all the way to the open exotic waters of the Gulf of Mexico. Adventure and the future lay downstream, off to your right as you faced east from the Hannibal shore; and all you had to do was find something to carry you—rowboat, canoe, a raft perhaps—and push away from those too-familiar shores and out into the current. This was travel of a simple, ancient sort, like predynastic Egyptians on the upper Nile, before the advent of oar and sail. Compared to such a drift, modern expeditions to cities on the Eastern Seaboard would entail a vigorous expenditure of energy and cash; though in the year of Sam's escape from home, American rail lines and steamships were cutting the required time dramatically—according to newspaper advertisements, it was now possible to do the trip from St. Louis to New York City in fewer than three days.[16]

In the spring and summer of 1853, when Sam Clemens began to move, what else was going on in the destination he chose first, the city of St. Louis? In less than half a century, the place had developed from a French and Spanish colonial village into certifiable sprawl. According to a census published in March of that year, the total population of 87,654 included 44,779 white males, 39,561 white females, 668 black male slaves, and 1,191 black female slaves. Also in this mix, and compounding the everyday big-city uncertainties about personal identity, social status, and moral and legal practices, there were· 630 men and 825 women who were both African American and free.[17] River traffic had created there the third busiest port in the United States, and in the spring of 1853 it was common for dozens of freight and passenger-hauling boats to be loading and unloading at dockside on a single afternoon.[18] The telegraph in that spring had reached the Illinois shore, less than a mile from town; soon after, an underwater wire coated in gutta-percha would cross the river, bringing wire service "intelli-

16. *New York Daily Times*, April 18, 1853, p. 6. Sam's trip to New York took him about five days. His journey, as reconstructed in the notes to his August 24, 1853, letter to his mother (*L1*, 5), included a steamboat up to Alton, Illinois, a rail link to Springfield and a stagecoach over to Bloomington, an Illinois Central rail line north to the twin towns of La Salle and Peru, and the brand new Chicago and Rock Island rail link, which took him east to the city of Chicago. From there, it was trains to Monroe, Michigan; a steamer across Lake Erie to Buffalo; a rail connection to Albany; and a Hudson River boat down to New York City.
17. Philadelphia *North American and United States Gazette*, February 18, 1853, p. 1.
18. Milwaukee *Daily Sentinel*, March 16, 1853, p. 1.

gence" straight into town without the minor inconvenience of ferrying over to retrieve it.[19]

St. Louis was new, and growing very quickly, and radiating pride in that newness and growth.[20] The reinvigoration of the downtown was on occasion a matter of necessity, as devastating fires in that neighborhood broke out several times in Sam's youth, the worst such incident being a blaze that destroyed most of a ten-block commercial district from Locust Street south to Market, and from Second Street eastward to the river—an area that included much of what is now the extensive waterfront park known as the Jefferson National Expansion Memorial, presided over by Eero Saarinen's soaring steel arch.[21] Over the three-year period from 1850 to the time of Sam's arrival, when the river threatened to change its course to the east side of Bloody Island (a sandbar known at that time as a place for settling disagreements with pistols), thereby silting up the St. Louis harbor, the city on its own initiative, and without significant state or federal help, had undertaken the construction of an earthen dike to fend off that disaster.[22] The city was committed to making its own luck. In April, across the river and about three miles north, the small Illinois town of Venice was being rocked by a feud over land rights, for rapid population and commercial growth in the region were transforming nearby real estate into a commodity to kill for.[23] Though there were outbreaks of epidemic disease, as there were in many large American settlements in those years, the summer casualty rate in St. Louis was no match—especially in that summer—for the devastation in New Orleans. The 1853 estimated death toll there, from the worst yellow fever epidemic in the city's history, eventually topped eight thousand—the number is only an estimate because with a quarter of the entire population struck by the disease at one time or another between June and December, civil order and official record

19. See William Hyde and Howard L. Conard, *Encyclopedia of the History of St. Louis* (New York: Southern History Co., 1899), 1630, 2231.

20. Less than a decade after the 1853 census cited above, the population of the city had grown, by some reports, to 160,000, thanks to a massive influx of people and extensions of the municipal borders. See Cox, *Old and New St. Louis,* 16.

21. Ibid.

22. Philadelphia *North American,* June 27, 1853, p. 1.

23. Washington, D.C., *Daily National Intelligencer,* April 15, 1853, p. 1.

keeping paid a price.[24] The story was lurid enough to make headlines for months in the St. Louis, Chicago, and East Coast newspapers,[25] a steady warning to one young typesetter to seek his work and adventure somewhere else.

Moreover, in America's fast-evolving conception of itself as a nation of race slavery, St. Louis, in the eyes of a young Missourian from upriver, could seem like a familiar anomaly, a setting with convoluted racial laws, where free African Americans could, with a government-issued license, live and work alongside people who were still in bondage.[26] The varieties of slavery visible there were of a sort that Sam Clemens may have recognized as more or less like practices back home, not the notorious "down the river" world of murderous labor that would threaten Jim in *Huckleberry Finn*. It is also worth noting that in 1853 *Uncle Tom's Cabin* was at the peak of its popularity and notoriety as an American publishing and cultural sensation, and Stowe's novel was doing New Orleans no more good with regard to its national and international reputation than was the yellow fever epidemic. The book includes two harrowing portraits of the New Orleans slave market, the largest in the United States; and dramatizations of the novel, not only in the North but also across the Atlantic in England and France, were centering on the horrors of that place and that trade.[27]

24. For a detailed and grim description of the epidemic, taken from contemporary records and reports, see Robert C. Reinders, *End of an Era: New Orleans, 1850–1860* (New Orleans: Pelican Press, 1964), 96–103.

25. While Sam was working as a printer on the East Coast, the New York papers, the *Chicago Daily Tribune,* and other major journals around the country were covering the epidemic luridly and regularly. See "The Fever in New Orleans," *Chicago Daily Tribune,* September 6, 1853, p. 3, and "Yellow Fever—More Details of the Desolate and Plague-Stricken City," *Chicago Daily Tribune,* September 12, 1853, p. 2. On September 5, the *Tribune* had reported that an entire day's receipts from the Crystal Palace Exposition in New York were being allocated for "relief of the New Orleans Sufferers" (p. 2). Late in the year, when news of an outbreak of cholera followed all the reports of the yellow fever scourge, New Orleans apparently went on the defensive about its reputation with regard to public health, and the *Tribune* reported that Louisiana journalists had grown "indignant at some exaggerated statements as to cholera here, furnished by a correspondent of certain New York papers" (December 14, 1853, p. 2).

26. On February 24–26, 1855, Sam wrote to the Muscatine *Tri-Weekly Journal* about a free African American girl named Chloe Ann Harris, who had "entered the State without a license, and was passing as a slave to avoid the consequences of this breach of the law" (*L1,* 51).

27. From a report titled "Uncle Tom on a French Stage": "The slave market in New Orleans was represented on a grand scale; an immense number of people as buyers, as well as slaves

There is no evidence, however, that *Uncle Tom's Cabin* was having an impact on Sam's imagination or values in his adolescent years, or that the novel was on his mind as he considered his options for places to make money and see more of the world. By 1857, he was apparently thinking of New Orleans primarily as a gateway, an embarkation point for international travel and exploits in places that railroad systems had not yet penetrated. The derring-do of the Tennessean named William Walker, a self-commissioned "General" and soldier of fortune much in the headlines in that year, may have piqued his imagination more strongly, at that time, than did either the content of *Uncle Tom's Cabin* or the financial success that one American writer was enjoying from it.[28] Walker was a proslavery rogue entrepreneur who regarded Latin American national sovereignty as a joke; like a conquistador he had barged into Nicaragua in 1855 with a small army of mercenaries. A couple of years earlier he had failed in a similar exploit, when he tried to grab Baja California away from Mexican control and set himself up there as head of his own nation. In Nicaragua he was having better luck, conquering the country in 1856 and winning diplomatic recognition from the United States government for his new regime, and American newspapers were playing him up as something of a swashbuckler. After this interlude of luck and glory, however, he had pushed too far, plotting war against four neighboring countries at once and jeopardizing, in the process, the shipping short cut across Nicaragua from the Gulf of Mexico to the Pacific Ocean, via the enormous freshwater lake and the rail line owned and operated by fellow American Cornelius Vanderbilt. That threat was the last straw for Vanderbilt and other Yankee moguls who had formerly backed Walker, and these were people with influence in Washington. In the spring of 1857, the newspapers that Sam was working for were carrying stories of Walker's struggle against rising opposition, bankrolled now from Wall Street. Surrendering for personal protection to American representatives in May, Walker made it home to New York as something of a hero. Three years later, however, with the Civil War looming, and with Washington's patience with him and his proslavery sentiments at an end, Walker went back south

---

for sale, was placed on the stage. It was a scene which produced as much affect upon the audience as any other" (*Chicago Daily Tribune,* March 7, 1853, p. 1).

28. The evidence seems clear that by the time Sam and Olivia Clemens were planning their great house in Hartford, Sam was pleased by the prospect of having Harriet Beecher Stowe as

for a similar escapade in Honduras, thereby arousing hostility in the bordering British colony. Overwhelmed and apprehended, Walker was turned over to Honduran authorities and shot by a firing squad in September 1860.[29] In April 1857, however, he still seemed like a man of destiny—and if you were dreaming of romance, riches, and power in the tropics, then the great city of New Orleans could be the portal to that kind of adventure.

By the time Sam was settling into his cadenced professional visits to New Orleans, however, his imagination had been tempered not only by the passage of additional years and by his sojourn in New York, Washington, and Philadelphia but also by the training he was undergoing for the pilot's license, a training in the technical, treacherous configurations and pathologies of the Mississippi River itself. When he had floated down to St. Louis for the first time, he had been a village boy with one marketable set of skills and only a village boy's knowledge of the power of great watercourses and the limits of human skill in exploiting them. He saw low-lying New Orleans with different eyes, and in paragraphs he wrote for *Life on the Mississippi* during and after a return trip downstream as an established author well into his forties—about twenty years after the apprenticeship with Bixby—we find evidence of that difference:

> The approaches to New Orleans were familiar; general aspects were unchanged. When one goes flying through London along a railway propped in the air on tall arches, he may inspect miles of upper bedrooms through the open windows, but the lower half of the houses is under his level and out of sight. Similarly, in high-river stage, in the New Orleans region, the water is up to the top of the enclosing levee-rim, the flat country behind it lies low—representing the bottom of a dish—and as the boat swims along, high on the flood, one looks down upon the houses and into the upper windows. There is nothing but that frail breastwork of earth between the people and destruction. (*LOM*, 422–23)

---

an immediate neighbor. But that was more than a dozen years after the period under consideration here.

29. For an overview of William Walker's exploits, see James M. McPherson, *Battle Cry of Freedom: The Civil War Era* (New York: Oxford University Press, 1988), 78–116.

After years of work as a printer, to become a licensed pilot required another professionally imperative alteration of consciousness, an alteration that may have carried over, in those years, to Sam's imaginative experience on-shore. As before, attention to details and minute discriminations were a matter of survival. Errors at the composing stones and proofing tables, or carelessness with a finished chase of movable type, could get a journeyman printer fired from a shop in hurry; on the river, informed awareness of every signifier on the water's surface could be a genuine matter of life and death. To know the Mississippi River in those years also meant understanding seasonal cycles and a slice of geological history: patterns of high water and low, gradual or catastrophic changes in the depth of the navigation channels, the configuration of the shore. The psychological and intellectual process of tourist travel was therefore inverted; this traveler had to pay considerably more attention to the minute business of going than to the destination:

> The world was new to me, and I had never seen anything like this at home. But as I have said, a day came when I began to cease from noting the glories and the charms which the moon and the sun and the twilight wrought upon the river's face; another day came when I ceased altogether to note them. Then, if that sunset scene had been repeated, I should have looked upon it without rapture, and should have commented upon it, inwardly, after this fashion: This sun means that we are going to have wind to-morrow; that floating log means that the river is rising, small thanks to it; that slanting mark on the water refers to a bluff reef which is going to kill somebody's steamboat one of these nights, if it keeps on stretching out like that; those tumbling "boils" show a dissolving bar and a changing channel there; the lines and circles in the slick water over yonder are a warning that that troublesome place is shoaling up dangerously; that silver streak in the shadow of the forest is the 'break' from a new snag, and he has located himself in the very best place he could have found to fish for steamboats; that tall dead tree, with a single living branch, is not going to last long, and then how is a body ever going to get through this blind place at night without the friendly old landmark.
>
> No, the romance and the beauty were all gone from the river. All the value any feature of it had for me now was the amount of usefulness it could furnish toward compassing the safe piloting of a steamboat. (*LOM*, 119–20)

For a working pilot, an arrival down in New Orleans or back in St. Louis may have been something of an anticlimax, an emotional letdown after the challenge and the tension of the journey; so perhaps it is not surprising that Mark Twain's writings from those years and afterward show no special attention to either place, or any keen affection for them. Possibly the climate itself played a role in keeping him aloof, for both of the great cities on his route were characteristically and notoriously hot and humid in the summers; and later in life, as Sam acquired wealth and a measure of geographic independence, he and Olivia would typically "summer" like Eastern aristocrats, on breezy heights above the swelter of nearby towns.

Unlike St. Louis, however, New Orleans seemed to Sam Clemens a contingent sort of place, insecure in its very setting, like some of those navigation channels in the river. It was also a city with a more burdensome past, a southern city where the initial vitality of settlement had fallen, in his view, into quiescence, where aboveground communities of the dead rivaled in grandeur and general interest the neighborhoods of the living. Again, *Life on the Mississippi* provides more guidance than do Sam's letters and journals from the piloting years as to what he noticed, early on and also later, and in what spirit he observed and recollected:

> The city itself had not changed—to the eye. It had greatly increased in spread and population, but the look of the town was not altered. The dust, waste-paper-littered, was still deep in the streets; the deep, trough-like gutters alongside the curb-stones were still half full of reposeful water with a dusty surface; the sidewalks were still—in the sugar and bacon region—incumbered [sic] by casks and barrels and hogsheads; the great blocks of austerely plain commercial houses were as dusty-looking as ever.

> Canal Street was finer, and more attractive and stirring than formerly, with its drifting crowds of people, its several processions of hurrying street-cars, and—toward evening—its broad second-story verandas crowded with gentlemen and ladies clothed according to the latest mode.

> Not that there is any "architecture" in Canal Street: to speak in broad, general terms, there is no architecture in New Orleans, except in the cemeteries. It seems a strange thing to say of a wealthy, far-seeing, and energetic city of a quarter of a million inhabitants, but it is true. There is a huge granite U.S. Custom-house—costly enough,

genuine enough, but as a decoration it is inferior to a gasometer. It looks like a state prison. But it was built before the war. Architecture in America may be said to have been born since the war. New Orleans, I believe, has had the good luck—and in a sense the bad luck—to have had no great fire in late years. It must be so. If the opposite had been the case, I think one would be able to tell the "burnt district" by the radical improvement in its architecture over the old forms. (*LOM,* 423–24)

Back in 1857, however, New Orleans had taken one of the most important steps in its cultural history, with regard to assuring its own festive strangeness to outsiders; for in that year the annual Carnival for Mardi Gras was formally established and organized.[30] When Sam wrote to his sister Pamela on March 9 and 11, 1859, he described himself as stumbling on the wild pageant, a defining civic event that was still officially in its infancy:

> At the corner of Good-Children and Tchoupitoulas streets, I beheld an apparition!—and my first impulse was to dodge behind a lamp-post. It was a woman—a hay-stack of curtain calico, ten feet high— sweeping majestically down the middle of the street (for what pavement in the world could accommodate hoops of such vast proportions?) Next I saw a girl of eighteen, mounted on a fine horse, and dressed as a Spanish Cavalier, with long rapier, flowing curls, blue satin doublet and half-breeches, trimmed with broad white lace . . . And then I saw a hundred men, women and children in fine, fancy, splendid, ugly, coarse, ridiculous, grotesque, laughable costumes, and the truth flashed upon me—"This is Mardi Gras!" (*L1,* 88)

Though Sam keeps up in this fashion for several more pages, he never reports or implies a wish to join in the frolic, never seems to step out imaginatively from the protection of that lamp post; his concluding line, "Cer-

---

30. The official founding of the Mystic Krewe of Comus, and the formulation of plans for its first parade, took place at a saloon on Royal Street on January 10, 1857. See Martin Siegel, *New Orleans: A Chronological and Documentary History, 1539–1970* (Dobbs Ferry, N.Y.: Oceana Publications, 1975), 31.

tainly New Orleans seldom does things by halves," is appropriate for a *flâneur,* gazing curiously and dispassionately at street spectacles he doesn't belong to, taking in the diverting and inconsequential strangeness of these throngs of festive others. He has no urge to plunge into the civic ruckus, like the enthralled and befuddled Clifford Pyncheon in *The House of the Seven Gables;* no yearning to become perilously one with the town—for to a young visitor from up north, this practice was replete with strangeness that extended deeper than the color and the noise. Mardi Gras in New Orleans was, and remains, a spectacular (and lucrative) rendition of a folk practice with roots in the cultures of Roman Catholic southern Europe; and New Orleans on Fat Tuesday was affirming itself as a Catholic stronghold at the mouth of the Mississippi. To someone with Sam's Protestant upbringing in austere Hannibal, that historical and cultural difference may have compounded and confirmed his sense of disconnection from what he was watching.

With a smaller population of French, Spanish, Mexican, and Irish ancestry, St. Louis was also a cathedral city; and Sam at this time in his life— as a young printer and as a man on the riverboats—was periodically reporting his affiliation with Presbyterian churches.[31] In one of his 1855 letters from St. Louis to Orion Clemens and Charles Wilson (this was a correspondent's report for the Muscatine *Tri-Weekly Journal*) we find this flickering malediction, concerning some expansions in the metropolitan print industry:

> A new evening paper is about to be started here, to be called the Evening Mirror. I do not know who are to be its editors. A new Catholic paper (bad luck to it) is also soon to be established, for the purpose of keeping the Know Nothing organ straight. (*L1,* 47)

About these Know Nothings of St. Louis, there is nothing negative from Sam in this letter, although that cohort of anti-Irish, anti-Catholic nativists was large and ugly enough to trigger a newsworthy street riot on April 5, 1852,

31. In a letter to Orion Clemens and Charles Wilson at the Muscatine *Tri-Weekly Journal* (February 16, 1855), he refers to "the handsome sum our preacher collected in church last Sunday to obtain food and raiment for the poor, ignorant heathen in some far off part of the world" (*L1,* 47).

and a bloodier outbreak on August 7, 1854, a multinight melee that killed
ten people and injured thirty others.[32] This uglier trouble started about a
month after Sam had returned to the city for his longest stay, and he was
there to see it firsthand, and even to do some participating. Back in the city
more than three decades later, gathering material to fatten up *Life on the Mississippi,* he remembered briefly those violent nights of religious bigotry and
ethnic hate. But centering on his own few hours of involvement in a peace-
keeping effort, his reminiscence is cool, ambivalent, even comic—in fact
not strikingly different in tone from his self-portrait as a bystander at that
first Mardi Gras parade:

> We saw some of the fightings and killings; and by and by we went one
> night to an armory where two hundred young men had met, upon call,
> to be armed and go forth against the rioters, under command of a mil-
> itary man. We drilled till about ten o'clock at night; then news came
> that the mob were in great force in the lower end of the town, and were
> sweeping everything before them. Our column moved at once. It was
> a very hot night, and my musket was very heavy. We marched and
> marched; and the nearer we approached the seat of war, the hotter I
> grew and the thirstier I got. I was behind my friend; so, finally, I asked
> him to hold my musket while I dropped out and got a drink. Then I
> branched off and went home. (*LOM,* 507)[33]

Remarks and evasions like these—from a teenager's letter to a big brother's
small-town paper, and from a middle-aged author's rambling reminiscence
thirty years after that—cannot, in themselves, loom large in a moral portrait of the artist that Sam Clemens became. Even so, shaped in these early years of heartland urban experience, a pattern of response to cities elsewhere does echo down through the career. In the European travel books
*The Innocents Abroad* and *A Tramp Abroad,* Mark Twain often wrote skepti-
cally of styles, stories, and practices associated with the Church of Rome
and its crowds of followers; and there are no indications that Sam Clemens, in the first four decades of his life, entered a Catholic shrine as any-

32. Cox, *Old and New St. Louis,* 19.
33. In *L1,* the annotations speculate that Clemens may have been back in St. Louis as early as July 8, 1857 (see p. 46).

thing other than a curious tourist, an outsider seeking not spiritual consolations but a widening of his historical, aesthetic, and essentially secular
worldly experience, embellishment of his own claims to cosmopolitan
savvy. From the Protestant outpost of Hannibal, Missouri, Mark Twain had
his first up-close experiences with Roman Catholicism, as a force in the cultures of North America, in the neighborhood of a foursquare stone church
of modest proportions, carrying a ponderous name, the Basilica of St. Louis,
King—the very first cathedral in North America west of the Mississippi—
on a hillock at the east end of Walnut Street, only a short walk from where
the arch stands now; and also around that much grander, three-spired
wooden edifice named for the same crusader king, the landmark on the
northwest side of Jackson Square on Chartres Street in New Orleans and,
like its namesake church up in Missouri, only a few dozen yards from the
Mississippi shore.

Did Sam Clemens regard such realms invariably as places of otherness,
cities he could visit often, yet never really call his own? There are indications that through much of his life he saw them in just that way. Moreover, if these early experiences schooled him in the craft of cosmopolitan
detachment, Mark Twain may also have learned in those years something
of the solace that can go along with that condition. For detachment or
alienation of that kind can also bring a measure of psychological repose:
not belonging, and knowing it, can be a kind of escape, at least for a while,
from the endemic strangeness and pathos of paying out money (as Sam
so often had to pay in those years and long after) to sleep in hired bed-
rooms, to face breakfast and supper as a client euphemized and pandered
to as a "guest"; to be hosted in so many American and worldwide cities
as a commodity and a curiosity—never as family, and only rarely as a true
friend.

In his later life, Mark Twain's lecture tours and personal expeditions took
him to St. Louis several times more, his last visit being the 1902 gala return
to his Missouri homeland, replete with an entourage of press, with interviews and photo ops—a pilgrimage of a modern, consecrated cosmopolitan. From the Hannibal portion of that same journey, one photograph shows
him standing uneasily and alone in front of the old family house; another
image shows him standing at the local depot, waiting for an outbound train,
an old man apart from the crowd once more, anxious for the next escape,

or perhaps resigned to it—either way, homelessly at home. As for New Orleans and the American Deep South: after the upward spiral to national and international fame, and after the 1882 river excursions to gather facts and fresh impressions to fill out *Life on the Mississippi,* Mark Twain never went back again.[34]

---

34. The last prewar journey to New Orleans that Twain wrote of was an excursion with his mother in February and March 1861; see *L1,* 118–19. For a useful interactive map of Mark Twain's American lecture tours, see Steve Railton's "Mark Twain in His Times" (http://etext .virginia.edu/railton/onstage/maps/tourmapsf.html).

# Mark Twain, San Francisco's Comic *Flâneur*

JAMES E. CARON

**AFTER** Halley's Comet became visible again in the fall of 1909 on one of its trips past Earth, Sam Clemens imagined God saying, "Here are those unaccountable freaks [Halley's comet and Mark Twain]. They came in together; they must go out together" (*MFMT*, 279). Clemens thus linked his life near its end with one of the most famous phenomena in the solar system, but the association would have served equally well to suggest the meteoric rise of his career as a professional writer. Like a comet streaking through the night sky, Mark Twain in the 1860s established his ascendancy in San Francisco's periodicals, where the brilliance of his comic qualities let him outshine all competitors.

Though Sam Clemens achieved fame and notoriety at an astonishing pace during his sojourns in both Nevada and California, "meteoric rise" becomes doubly apt when describing his career while he resided in San Francisco. The city's growth from a sleepy village with two hotels and eight hundred inhabitants to a West Coast metropolis had also happened in gaudy fashion, suddenly and brilliantly, once gold was discovered at John Sutter's ranch in 1848. When prospectors discovered silver in the Nevada territory

Revised from James E. Caron, *Mark Twain, Unsanctified Newspaper Reporter* (Columbia: University of Missouri Press, 2008).

in 1859, thirteen thousand new inhabitants poured into San Francisco to more than double its population and assessed value. After the gold and silver seekers came a third wave, entire families wishing to escape the Civil War. By the time of Clemens's stay in the city, from May 1864 to December 1866, San Francisco had become the premier financial and cultural center west of St. Louis, rivaling New York City and Boston as it boasted 41 churches, 105 schools, 12 daily papers, and 231 dealers in whiskey. Though Clemens had literally come from nowhere, from the hinterlands of the Nevada Territory, to rule the rough-and-tumble journalism of the Comstock with his Mark Twain pseudonym while at the *Virginia City Territorial Enterprise,* in San Francisco he followed that feat with one even more dramatic. He established a national reputation by wrangling the pseudonym out of its primary association with newspapers and placing it squarely into the world of literary periodicals on both coasts. When he left San Francisco, Sam Clemens's success had been financial as well as literary, and with his contract to write travel letters for the *Alta California* securely in hand, his path toward even greater successes would prove to be sure, though perhaps elliptical.[1]

A brief retracing of Mark Twain's meteoric career in San Francisco reveals important developments in the writer Sam Clemens that correspond with two distinct employments. The first was a brief stint with a newspaper, the *San Francisco Morning Call,* which Clemens would remember as "soulless drudgery" but which nevertheless provided a workshop for writing satire. Mark Twain's appearance in a literary periodical, the *Californian,* delineates a second phase. The material in the *Californian* represents the first concerted effort by Clemens to be a *feuilletoniste,* a freelance professional writer for literary periodicals. In what follows, I will first suggest how the *Call* experience sharpened satiric skills and then present examples of Clemens employing burlesque and parody in his *Californian* articles to create two new

---

1. Mick Sinclair, *San Francisco: A Cultural and Literary History* (New York: Interlink Books, 2004), and Gunther Barth, *Instant Cities: Urbanization and the Rise of San Francisco and Denver* (New York: Oxford University Press, 1975), detail the suddenness of San Francisco's emergence as an urban space. Statistics about San Francisco are taken from Franklin Walker, *San Francisco's Literary Frontier* (New York: Alfred A. Knopf, 1939), 6, 90, 97–98. Sam Clemens's comic stature in the Nevada newspapers was expressed in Fitzhugh Ludlow's nickname for Mark Twain, the "Washoe Giant" ("A Good-Bye Article," *Golden Era,* November 22, 1863, p. 5). Much of the financial success came from Clemens's lecture "Our Fellow Savages of the Sandwich Islands."

comic roles for his alter ego, Mark Twain: a literary critic who employs a Bohemian aesthetic and a literary *flâneur* who wanders the city to chronicle its
events and portray its inhabitants. San Francisco thus functioned as a prov-
ing ground for Sam Clemens using Mark Twain as a literary vehicle to express an incipient comic vision of the world.

   Clemens began work as the new local reporter for the *San Francisco Morning Call* on Monday, May 30, one week after he arrived in San Francisco. He
landed the job despite having left Virginia City, Nevada, with his comic reputation eclipsed by community disapproval of aborted duels. The challenges resulted from recriminations over a sketch and an editorial that joked
about the Sanitary Fund drive on the Comstock. The *Call's* editors considered Clemens to be a reliable reporter despite what his detractors had to say
in the wake of the imbroglio (*CofC*, 16).[2] Working for the *Call* proved to be
a mixed blessing. The editors had hired Sam Clemens to be a reporter rather
than to joke as Mark Twain, for throughout the four months that Clemens
labored for the *Call*—during which time some fifty-four hundred local
items were published—no comic sketches signed "Mark Twain" were printed in the newspaper.[3] Without the freedom editor in chief Joe Goodman
had granted him at the *Enterprise,* Clemens cramped down hard on his Mark
Twain style of journalism. His job plain and simple was reporting local
events. News gathering focused on three areas—the Police Court, the District Court, and the theaters—but his efforts overall had to be wide ranging to fill his daily quota of words. In 1906, Clemens remembered those
full-time efforts: "After having been hard at work from nine or ten in the
morning until eleven at night scraping material together, I took the pen and
spread this muck out in words and phrases and made it cover as much
acreage as I could. It was fearful drudgery, soulless drudgery, and almost
destitute of interest" (*CofC*, 282).[4] Clemens went on to say that his lack of

---

2. Clemens had written a series of letters for the *Call* in the latter half of 1863. For more
on the Sanitary Fund saga, see Effie Mona Mack, *Mark Twain in Nevada* (New York: Charles
Scribner's Sons, 1947), and Paul Fatout, *Mark Twain in Virginia City* (Bloomington: Indiana
University Press, 1964).

3. Edgar Branch compiled a list of items from the *Call* and attributed them to Clemens after reviewing the fifty-four hundred local items for the pertinent period. Branch's list contains
less than 10 percent of those items, and he reprints fewer than half. See *CofC*, 289–300.

4. From an autobiographical dictation, June 13, 1906, originally printed in *Mark Twain in
Eruption,* ed. Bernard DeVoto (New York: Harper and Brothers, 1940), 254–60.

interest became apparent to the senior editor, who one day politely fired him. George E. Barnes, the editor who did the firing, states that Clemens admitted his "reportorial shortcomings" and that the parting was friendly, occurring "when it was found necessary to make the local department more efficient."[5]

Nevertheless, Edgar Branch's meticulously documented presentation of Clemens's work in the *Call* demonstrates that the earlier and obviously comic version of Mark Twain in Nevada could not be completely repressed, even under the strictures placed upon him as a member of the *Call's* staff.[6] A substantial number of the *Call* items written by Clemens in 1864 illustrate how Mark Twain, already saturated by the ridicule of personal abuse routinely employed along the Comstock, could convey social satire. Sam Clemens thus first began to develop a comic vision while living in San Francisco, not merely discovering the laughable in individuals and everyday incidents, his métier in Nevada, but also measuring the foibles and vices of humanity as well as the shortcomings of social institutions. Dispatches from the Nevada territorial legislature early in 1864 had shown Clemens experimenting with the brashness of Mark Twain in a political setting. That setting provided topics necessarily important enough to allow the routine of lampoon and witty personal ridicule to be harnessed in service to social satire. The *Call* material from the summer of 1864 offers for the first time a body of Mark Twain material that depicts the satirist's world of knaves and fools rather than only the humorist's cast of eccentric characters.

This satirist's world was not a deliberate creation of a Dickensian order but rather emerged from the daily pressure of providing copy for the *Call* when Sam Clemens's regular beat included the courts and jails of San Francisco. Routinely writing up the courts, especially the Police Court, with its cases of assault and battery, drunk and disorderly, swindling, larceny, and immorality—this repetition provided the impetus for Sam Clemens's traversals past mere lampoons and buffoonery and toward satire. His sustained view in San Francisco of the damned human race and its flawed institutions

5. Barnes, "Mark Twain as He Was Known during His Stay on the Pacific Slope" (*San Francisco Morning Call,* April 17, 1887, p. 1).

6. For this "Washoe" version of Mark Twain see Caron, *Unsanctified Newspaper Reporter,* 85–160.

necessarily developed Clemens into what Bernard DeVoto called "the purposeful satirist."[7]

In the *Call* material, Clemens in piecemeal fashion develops several themes, among them an advocacy for the working class. He targets businesses refusing to pay a reasonable wage or the government effectively committing the same offense by paying its employees in debased paper money. He also frequently highlights the related topic of shady business practices that defraud workers. Other targets for Mark Twain's satire include the manifest inefficiencies of bureaucracy; the manifold shortcomings of the judicial system; and the venality, corruption, and absurdity of politics.

Clemens creates satiric effects in his reporting for the *Call* by liberally sprinkling comic phrasing or comic commentary throughout a news item. He employs a variety of tones, such as sarcasm. Speakers at rallies for the Democratic Party he characterizes as "feeble" or "troubled with Alcatraz on the brain," a reference to the occasional imprisonment of people judged to be so publicly disloyal to the war effort that their speech amounts to treason (*CofC*, 214–15). Bland understatement appears in "Extraordinary Enterprise" (*CofC*, 64), in which Mark Twain wonders about quail served a mere six hours after the season for hunting them has opened and pretends to worry that the hunter will "wear himself out" with his enterprise. The description of Mary Kane, a habitué of the jail, strikes a harsher cord: "drunk as a loon, [this] accomplished old gin-barrel [has] a full cargo aboard by this time [and] will probably clear for her native land in the County Jail today . · . , with her noble heart preserved in spirits, as usual" (*CofC*, 146). Clemens winds up his account of a naive man swindled by con men in an ambiguous fashion. The con men "deserve to be severely punished, but perhaps the merchant ought to be allowed to go free, as this was his first offence in being so criminally green" (*CofC*, 162). Feigned astonishment accompanies a comment on a witness who said that "Providence provided her with invisible wings" when escaping an assailant: "Judging by the woman's appearance, and her known character and antecedents, this interference of Providence in her behalf was remarkable, to say the least, and must have been a surprise to her" (*CofC*, 161).

7. DeVoto, *Mark Twain's America* (Boston: Houghton Mifflin, 1967), 164.

Occasionally, such comic phrasing accumulates and creates a barrage of ridicule from which a satiric analysis takes shape. This more sustained effort occurs in "What Goes with the Money?" (*CofC*, 454–55), which vigorously attacks mining companies for consistently hiding the state of their financial soundness, to the detriment of stockholders, and calls for an honest company to step forward and voluntarily publish a monthly statement. Another clear example of a news item shaped by satiric intent is "A Small Piece of Spite," published on September 6, 1864. This item attacks the coroner's office for refusing to maintain a regular means of providing reporters with information. The caricature of the coroner's assistant nearly transforms the report into a comic sketch. The "slate" refers to a routine means of disseminating information, a chalkboard, which has been withdrawn—apparently after someone added a false entry as a practical joke[8]—thus inspiring the following diatribe:

> You ask one of [the coroner's assistants] a dozen questions calculated to throw more light on a meager entry in the slate, and he invariably answers, *"Don't know"*—as if the grand aim of his poor existence was not to know anything, and to come as near accomplishing his mission as his opportunities would permit. . . . What do you suppose the people would ever know about how their interests were being attended to if the employees in all public offices were such unmitigated ignoramuses as these? One of the fellows said to us yesterday, "We have taken away the slate; we are not going to give you any more information; the reporters have got too sharp—by George, they know more'n we do!" God help the reporter that don't! (*CofC*, 236)

Clemens enjoyed this item enough to brag about it in a September 25, 1864, letter home to Jane Clemens and Pamela Moffet as "the wickedest article I ever wrote in my life" (*L1*, 311–14).

Clemens may have bragged about so slight a satiric effort because much of his writing during the summer of 1864 was dissatisfying. Indeed, much of his existence that summer was apparently dissatisfying. Trying to rent rooms in which he could sleep during the day after working all night, Clemens in the first four months of living in San Francisco tried two hotels and

---

8. Ivan Benson *Mark Twain's Western Years* (Stanford: Stanford University Press, 1938), 115.

five lodging houses.[9] This forced wandering no doubt contributed to Clemens's asking *Call* editor George Barnes to put him on a day shift, even though it meant a cut in pay at a time when Clemens had little money. *Roughing It* pictures Mark Twain at this time becoming "very adept at 'slinking'" (*RI,* 428–29). Much later, Clemens presented himself as having been in such despair during this period that he put a gun to his head. Although this scenario in my view is fictional, Clemens in the summer of 1864 apparently did apply to the federal government to return to the river as a pilot. Abandoning his writing career for piloting on the river was the metaphoric gun Sam Clemens held to Mark Twain's head. The drudgery of writing for the *Call,* combined with the poverty of a Bohemian existence, drove Clemens into this personal and professional nadir.[10]

Drudgery that it was, the experience with the *San Francisco Morning Call* nevertheless had operated as a workshop for Sam Clemens, providing him with the raw material for continuing to develop the weapons of a satirist that he had first used effectively when reporting on the Nevada Territorial legislature. Despite the *Call* experience deemphasizing Mark Twain's "Washoe" humor of personal raillery, comic invective remained a large part of Clemens's stock in trade as he continued to develop his comic alter ego.

Though Sam Clemens nearly gave up his career as a professional writer while living in San Francisco, the remarkable aspect of his residence there was not that he decided to continue, but that he decided to shift his career focus from newspaper dailies to literary weeklies. Concentrating his best efforts on writing sketches for the world of literary weeklies committed Clemens to a professional writing career much more ambitious than newspaper reporting. Writing for the literary weeklies also committed Clemens to an implied audience different from newspaper readers, one whose aesthetic taste differed because its gender and economic status were typically differ-

9. Walker, *Literary Frontier,* 189.

10. Albert Bigelow Paine, *Mark Twain, a Biography,* 4 vols. (New York: Harper and Brothers, 1912), 1:291, mentions the suicide attempt. Also see *L1,* 325n6. For the story on returning to piloting, see *Early Tales and Sketches, 1851–1864,* volume 1, ed. Edgar M. Branch and Robert H. Hirst (Berkeley: University of California Press, 1969), 28. Though many people over the years, starting with Paine, believed the near-suicide tale, the incident is too similar to the many dramatic exaggerations Clemens was fond of making as he "remembered" the past when dictating his autobiography.

ent. The story of Sam Clemens in San Francisco, therefore, becomes the story of how he reworked "Washoe Mark Twain" of Nevada to fit this more literary ambition.

Aiming consistently for the middle-class and more feminine audience that literary weeklies represented rather than "the boys" for whom the *Enterprise* staff wrote, Clemens took his cues from two writers who had already demonstrated their literary abilities, who could claim to be *feuilletonistes* rather than mere reporters, Francis Bret Harte and Charles Henry Webb. Clemens met Harte first and, despite later animosity, developed a much closer relationship with him while in San Francisco than with Webb. The offices of the *Call* were housed in three stories of the same building that held the San Francisco branch of the United States Mint, where Bret Harte worked as secretary to the superintendent.[11] Shortly after Clemens started work for the newspaper, the editor George Barnes introduced the two men. Harte in May 1864 was the best known of a group of young writers in San Francisco and the star contributor to the newest literary venture on the Pacific Coast, the weekly *Californian*. This literary periodical was the pet project of Charles Henry Webb, also a highly regarded writer and a transplant from New York City's Bohemia. In addition to regular appearances in two daily newspapers, Webb had been a frequent contributor as "Inigo" to the *Golden Era,* the premier periodical publication for literature on the Pacific slope. Webb intended for the *Californian* to surpass the *Golden Era* in that distinction. The *Californian's* first issue had come out two days before Clemens's arrival in San Francisco.

Meeting Bret Harte proved to be pivotal for Sam Clemens in his development as a professional writer. Harte as editor for the *Californian* in late August or September 1864 offered Clemens fifty dollars a month for biweekly articles. In addition, Harte apparently read Mark Twain material and offered editorial advice.[12] Perhaps most important, as the cynosure of a notable group of writers, Harte provided a model for literary aspiration. Of the six writers besides Harte and Clemens that Franklin Walker identifies as producing "the best literature of the Far-Western frontier"—Ina Cool-

---

11. Details from Margaret Duckett, *Mark Twain and Bret Harte* (Norman: University of Oklahoma Press, 1964).

12. Walker, *Literary Frontier,* 190.

brith, Prentice Mulford, Henry George, Charles Warren Stoddard, Ambrose Bierce, and Joaquin Miller—only George was not associated with the frequent gatherings in Harte's office. Margaret Duckett states that Clemens "spent much time" in the office.[13] A compelling topic for discussion among Harte and his friends throughout the summer of 1864 would very likely have been the progress of the *Californian*. Harte and his coterie of writers offered Sam Clemens opportunities to participate in literary discussions in what amounted to a San Francisco–style salon atmosphere; those opportunities must have developed his ambition to write earnestly for literary weeklies. No doubt the literary atmosphere impressed Clemens by showing him vistas beyond his newspaper fame in the Nevada Territory. No doubt Harte soon introduced Clemens to Charles Webb, whose East Coast literary credentials added to the sense that San Francisco offered possibilities for writing not just for a living but also with artistic purpose.

Between October 1864 and April 1866, two dozen sketches signed Mark Twain appeared in the *Californian*. Most of these comic pieces came in two distinct time frames. The first ran from early October to early December 1864, the second from early May to early July 1865. Bret Harte solicited the first batch soon after he took over the editorship while Charles Webb vacationed.[14] During the early part of the summer of 1864, when writing for the *Call* dominated Clemens's working efforts, his reportorial voice had become more satiric in intent—and ironic, sarcastic, or caustic in tone. The opportunity to publish regularly in the *Californian* provided Clemens the freedom to experiment with Mark Twain as a comic character while continuing in new and more literary ways the satiric efforts associated with the *Call*.

Clemens's satiric impulse in the *Californian* material accentuated cultural issues by overwhelmingly concerning itself with writing, literature, and

13. Duckett, *Twain and Harte*, 22, 23. See also Walker, *Literary Frontier*, 88.

14. Duckett, *Twain and Harte*, 24. While reporting for the *Call*, Clemens noted the change in editorship, saying that Webb would "rest a while on the shores of Lake Tahoe" (*CofC*, 63). Webb resumed the editor's duties from November 1864 until April 15, 1865. Harte was editor again until the end of the year, when Webb once more resumed those duties. A comparison of the dates of editorship with the publication dates of Mark Twain material shows that the overwhelming majority of the sketches were printed when Harte was in the editor's chair. "Charles Henry Webb," in *American Authors, 1600–1900: A Biographical Dictionary of American Literature,* ed. Stanley J. Kunitz and Howard Haycroft (New York: H. W. Wilson, 1938), 789.

As this 1956 Old Crow Whiskey ad suggests, the friendships Twain cultivated in San Francisco during the 1870s became part of the mythology that surrounded the author. Here Twain is represented—at the Hartford home, well after the end of their relationship—supposedly celebrating "Bret Harte's completion of one of his finest stories." (Used by permission of Beam Global Spirits & Wine)

aesthetics. Clemens treated these subjects with his favorite comic tactic, burlesquing the usual way that periodicals—newspapers as well as literary weeklies—covered them. Mark Twain makes fun of common features in periodicals such as "Answers to Correspondents" columns or invites laughter at specific fads, such as the craze for conundrums.

The burlesque approach Clemens used to score satiric points against the bad writing so often found in popular literature comically expressed the *Californian's* serious literary aspirations. The emphasis in the *Californian* on literary topics linked the journal to high-culture East Coast publications. Making satiric attacks on inferior literature in a burlesque style had been fashionable in New York City at least since the early 1860s when the well-known comic writer Charles Farrar Browne had published burlesques of popular types of novels in *Vanity Fair,* sometimes signed "Artemus Ward" and sometimes not. That New York comic periodical had been a fertile ground for burlesquing the serialized novels that defined the story papers and routinely occupied significant space in so many literary periodicals like *Harper's Monthly* and the *Golden Era.* Other burlesques by Fitzhugh Ludlow, George Arnold ("McArone"), and Robert Newall ("Orpheus C. Kerr") complemented Browne's efforts during *Vanity Fair's* brief existence.

This efflorescence of comic mockery was far from an isolated phenomenon. The burlesquing impulse had been indulged onstage at the New York Olympic theater since the late 1830s, mostly at the expense of famous operas, and reached a climax during the 1850s at Burton's Chambers Street theater due to the writing and acting of John Brougham. Minstrel shows were scripted primarily with burlesque. The first famous comic writer in California, George Derby, had written numerous burlesques signed "John Phoenix," published as a book in 1855. Thus burlesque had been rife in antebellum popular culture, a ready tool for a writer who wished to deflate pretension, laugh at the latest sensation, or display familiarity with well-known material. The irreverent attitude that underlies burlesque and parody as well as the application of those comic tactics to all manner of art—including dramatic, musical, and literary productions—are the identifying characteristics for many of the significant comic writers who followed the Old Southwest writers.[15]

---

15. Browne in 1858 had also published three installments of "Our Novel," which bur-

The most immediate models encouraging Clemens to employ literary burlesque were the founders of the *Californian,* Bret Harte and Charles Webb. Despite Harte's early personal reputation as a dandy with a remote bearing or his later literary reputation as a writer with a penchant for Victorian sentiment and morality, he also possessed a satiric eye able to spot conventional hypocrisies as well as bad writing. Famous before he met Clemens for his liberal views on Native Americans and for his poetic efforts on behalf of the Union cause, Bret Harte would achieve his first national reputation by publishing a book of condensed burlesque novels originally appearing in the *Californian* between July 1865 and June 1866. Despite obvious differences in their sensibilities, Harte would have been nevertheless disposed to encourage satire and burlesque from the former *Call* reporter.

Similarly, Charles Webb's literary credentials meant that when Sam Clemens wrote for the *Californian,* he knew he had the most sympathetic of editors reviewing his Mark Twain sketches.[16] Webb already had a reputation as a wit before he came to California, initially established by his work for the *New York Times.* Following his arrival in California in April 1863, that reputation had been augmented by several efforts: his weekly letter for the *Sacramento Union* as "John Paul," a column for the *San Francisco Evening Bulletin,* and a series of comic sketches called "Things," written for the *Golden Era* and signed "Inigo." In addition, he had a dramatic hit, *Arrah-no-poke* (1865), a parody of Dion Boucicault's runaway stage success, *Arrah-na-pogue.* After leaving California, Webb would write parodies of two famous novels: *Liffith Lank* (1866), which mocked Charles Reade's controversial *Griffith Gaunt;* and *St. Twel'mo* (1868), which made fun of Augusta Wilson's

---

lesqued popular romance novels, in his column "City Facts and Fancies" (*Cleveland Plain Dealer,* March 16, 22, 29, 1858). For more on burlesques from American writers, see Walter Blair, "Burlesques in Nineteenth-Century American Humor," *American Literature* 2 (1930): 236–47. For the burlesque on the popular stage, see George Kummer, "The Americanization of Burlesque, 1840–1860," in *Popular Literature in America: A Symposium in Honor of Lyon N. Richardson,* ed. James C. Austin and Donald A. Koch (Bowling Green: Bowling Green University Press, 1972), 146–54. For minstrel burlesques of opera, see William J. Mahar, *Behind the Burnt Cork Mask: Early Blackface Minstrelsy and Antebellum American Culture* (Urbana: University of Illinois Press, 1999), chap. 3. In his second chapter Mahar discusses burlesques of rhetorical forms such as speeches and lectures. Derby's book was titled *Phoenixiana; or, Sketches and Burlesques* (New York: D. Appleton, 1855).

16. For Harte's early career, see Gary Scharnhorst, *Bret Harte* (New York: Twayne, 1992), and Duckett, *Twain and Harte,* 3–45. For Webb, see "Charles Henry Webb," in *American Authors,* ed. Kunitz and Haycroft.

popular *St. Elmo*. Mark Twain's appearance in the *Californian* as a comic literary critic shows the particular influence on Clemens of Harte and Webb as well as the broad influence of the vogue for burlesque.

"Lucretia Smith's Soldier" (*ETS2*, 128–33) illustrates these influences by burlesquing sentimental novels via the condensed novel form. Clemens creates comic drama by juxtaposing contingent reality with the sentimental wishes of the vain and selfish heroine, Lucretia. He neatly captures this clash by mixing slang into a rhetoric of sentimentality. Lucretia's bookish ideas about the glory of war and the satisfaction of nursing her wounded lover are shattered by a mistaken identification. This wake-up-call effect would be used by Clemens against foolish sentiment throughout *The Innocents Abroad* and in "Old Times on the Mississippi." "Lucretia Smith's Soldier" was very popular on both coasts: reprinted in New York and California periodicals, it became the first big hit signed "Mark Twain" in the literary weeklies.

The heart of Clemens's efforts to give Mark Twain the voice of a satiric literary critic can be found in six *Californian* pieces, all with the title "Answers to Correspondents," which appeared from June 3 to July 8, 1865.[17] The series parodies its main target, the column devoted to answering any sort of question from all manner of correspondents, mocking the genre it pretends to be. Because the *Golden Era* prominently featured such a column, Mark Twain's "Answers to Correspondents" not only implicitly ridicules questionable taste in literary weeklies in general but also invites laughter at the *Californian*'s rival. Carrying out this agenda allowed Clemens to assume different roles by creating multiple items in each column. Mark Twain can therefore in one item be an acerbic literary editor, railing at bad writing, while in another he is a sarcastic meta-critic, ridiculing bad theater criticism.

In order to create his mock column, Mark Twain maintains an unhelpful attitude at odds with the conventional answers-to-correspondents, advice-giving columnist. This unhelpful Mark Twain in the guise of a witty literary critic stands ready to excoriate, ridiculing the questions as often as he an-

---

17. The *Californian* (February 25, 1865, p. 3) mentions "Josh Billings" (Henry Wheeler Shaw) conducting an "Advice to Correspondents" column for the *New York Sunday Mercury*. Possibly the idea for the Mark Twain series was suggested to Clemens and/or Harte by this example.

swers them, or giving advice in a down-to-earth manner bordering on the rude and condescending. He mercilessly targets the correspondents, who are capable of asking about the difference between geometry and conchology (*ETS2*, 203–4). By dispensing sarcastic advice to young lovers about their romances or to a yahoo about how to behave in public places like the theater, Mark Twain openly proclaims the inanity of his correspondents so that his attempts to "help" promote proper behavior display a cranky Lord Chesterfield, at best. By the end of the series, in an item entitled "Student of Etiquette," Mark Twain has explicitly named his biggest satiric target by wondering at the foolishness of editors "gravely" answering the seemingly endless stream of "foolish," "unnecessary," and "absurd" questions (*ETS2*, 229).

Over and over again, Clemens uses Mark Twain to attack the root of these ridiculous questions: people's foolish beliefs. In "St. Clair Higgins, Los Angeles," Mark Twain goes behind sentimental language and fiction to target the unrealistic attitudes supporting them:

> "My life is a failure; I have adored, wildly, madly, and she whom I love has turned coldly from me and shed her affections upon another; what would you advise me to do?" You should shed your affections on another, also—or on several, if there are enough to go around. Also, do everything you can to make your former flame unhappy. There is an absurd idea disseminated in novels, that the happier a girl is with another man, the happier it makes the old lover she has blighted. Don't allow yourself to believe any such nonsense as that. The more cause that girl finds to regret that she did not marry you, the more comfortable you will feel over it. It isn't poetical, but it is mighty sound doctrine. (*ETS2*, 183–84)

In other examples where Clemens's talent for ridicule has shifted from the personal emphasis found in his Nevada phase to attacks on issues and attitudes, Mark Twain makes fun of conventional and genteel sentiments mindlessly and endlessly reiterated, such as praising small children (*ETS2*, 204–6), or people's self-righteousness concerning morality and patriotism (*ETS2*, 189–90, 200–202). Such pieces reveal a new depth to the satiric attacks of Mark Twain, reaching past literary practices for the cultural values that underpin them. The most specific target for Mark Twain during this period was Albert Evans, who wrote for the *Alta California*, sometimes under the comic pseudonym "Fitz Smythe." Clemens persistently ridiculed Evans because he represented exactly what Mark Twain as a comic literary critic had been attacking in the *Californian* articles: conventional thinking expressed in conventional writing.[18]

The attitude about the aesthetics of writing that Mark Twain expressed in the *Californian* sketches invited laughter at the usual genteel methods of composing poetry and fiction. The burlesque poems and satiric commentaries on periodical writing showed by negative example what constituted a literary standard for Sam Clemens during his stay in San Francisco. Mark Twain promotes a more direct and plainer way of phrasing than was often found in popular writings, particularly in the blood-and-thunder adventure tales or romances that dominated popular story papers. More direct, plainer phrasing could be particularly important when expressing strong emotion, holding out the possibility of a vigorous style of writing neither inundated by bathos nor overly inflated by grandiloquence. The *Californian* exemplified good writing for Clemens. He made the judgment clear in a notice written while working for the *Call*, characterizing the journal as a "sterling literary weekly [and] the best paper in its particular department ever issued on this coast" (*CofC*, 63).

In mounting his attacks both during and after his regular contributions to the *Californian*, Clemens not only used Mark Twain to exercise his satiric abilities on the topic of aesthetics but also conducted that exercise from an unconventional perspective loosely defined in the 1850s and 1860s as "Bohemianism." Clemens's flat purse and multiple lodgings during the summer of 1864 suggest the lifestyle of an impecunious and artistic Bohemian, and he also fit the profile in his aesthetics. Two of Mark Twain reviews of popular performers demonstrate how that aesthetic did not fit the conventional mold established by standard, high-culture ideas about artistic en-

18. Clemens attacked Evans often; see for example, *ETS2*, 338–39, 345–46, 348, 350–52, 355–58, 510. The *Californian* had also frequently ridiculed Evans in a regular feature called "The Lion's Mouth," designed to roar at humbugs. The feature offered comments on extracts from other periodicals, often with a superior tone and especially when belles lettres was the topic, and it contributed to the weekly's Bohemian iconoclasm. Evans was targeted as late as April 6, 1867, when "The Unhappy Fitz Smythe" appeared, which called him "the imbecile humorist of the Pacific Coast" and a "born fool." The piece also recalled how often Mark Twain had ridiculed Evans.

deavor. "A Voice for Setchell" (*ETS2,* 172–73) discusses Dan Setchell, a well-known stage comedian who had come to San Francisco in April 1865 and had been playing to enthusiastic houses for weeks when Clemens wrote his short notice praising the actor's comic abilities. The second piece appeared in the *San Francisco Dramatic Chronicle* with the title "Enthusiastic Eloquence" (*ETS2,* 235). In it, Mark Twain compares three different banjo players with the famous concert pianist Louis Gottschalk—and Gottschalk loses. To carry his message of Bohemian alignment against conventional aesthetics, Mark Twain presents comically exaggerated images of gentility: "The piano may do for love-sick girls who lace themselves to skeletons, and lunch on chalk, pickles, and slate pencils. But give me the banjo" (*ETS2,* 235). Genuine music like the playing of Tommy Bree had the same effect as the comic performances of Dan Setchell, providing "more real pleasure" than all the operas and tragedies combined (*ETS2,* 172). Favorably comparing Setchell's "funny personations and extempore speeches" to operas and tragedies again signals a preference for what conventional society would call a low-culture taste over symbols of a high-culture taste, just as did the comparison of banjo to piano.

In both reviews, a perceived sense of vitality provides the chief reason for elevating what society normally considered low. That vitality, however, threatens a standard decorum. Mark Twain associates the piano with fainting girls and insubstantial food. Even Gottschalk's acclaimed ability does not escape comparison with such feeble parlor fare. In contrast, the "glory-beaming banjo" gives a listener goose bumps, and Mark Twain links its effects with hot whiskey punch, strychnine, and measles. The danger of this power becomes even more comically explicit in a suggestion to smash pianos in favor of banjos. Similarly, Mark Twain implicates Setchell's performance style in metaphoric assaults on genteel aesthetics and decorum. The laughter Setchell elicits happens "naturally and unconfinedly," and thus resembles an urge to smash parlor pianos. Finally, Clemens through his Mark Twain alter ego completes his Bohemian stance on what constitutes good music and theater by endorsing Setchell's abilities despite the cavils of the prominent critics. He votes down the conventional taste of such critics because the audiences laughed "extravagantly." Though such natural and genuine laughter is out of place in and even threatening to the gentility of parlor aesthetics, Clemens reads it as a sign of excellence in comic literature. "That kind of criticism can always be relied upon as sound, and not only sound but honest" (*E1S2*, 173).

Sam Clemens's affinity for Bohemian aesthetics, then, comes in several forms. Mark Twain scoffing at the sentimental pretensions and melodramatic sensationalism of Albert Evans as Fitz Smythe represents Sam Clemens's sense of the complacency of well-established newspapers and the small-mindedness of some reporters. The satiric inversion of the mock "Advice to Correspondents" column in the *Californian* resulted in a sarcastic and cranky Mark Twain dispensing refreshingly candid advice that ridiculed literary genres and their implied genteel attitudes. Mark Twain's advocacy of a less-than-genteel aesthetic developed the satirical possibilities of Mark Twain commenting on social values as well as a new role for his alter ego: a Bohemian critic.

This Bohemian rebellion provided an aesthetic base from which Sam Clemens in San Francisco worked to become a *feuilletoniste*. In the process, Clemens developed another role for Mark Twain similar to the Bohemian critic: a comic version of the *flâneur*, a figure embodying a literary journalism that characterized the most sophisticated of periodical correspondents. The *flâneur* relies upon a reporter's habit of close observation as he strolls about town, taking in what he observes in order to explicate it for the literary periodicals. Though a *feuilletoniste* in *flâneur* mode must cater to a market, he also conveys the image of an artist with an unconventional Bohemian attitude. Beginning in the 1840s, *bohemian* and *flâneur* both connoted an artist, with Balzac as the key to this linkage.[19]

Charles Webb was undoubtedly the best model of a comic writer in a *flâneur* mode with whom Sam Clemens would have been familiar. Webb wrote a series of articles as "Inigo" for the *Golden Era* called "Things" that ran from late July 1863 until May 1864, when he transferred the column to the pages of his literary weekly, the *Californian*. The Inigo persona must have been riveting to Clemens in its sarcastic presentation of the so-called respectable social world. The cheeky familiarity with which Webb discussed

19. Priscilla Parkhurst Ferguson, "The *Flâneur* on and off the Streets of Paris," in *The Flâneur*, ed. Keith Tester (London: Routledge, 1994), 22–42 (29).

any topic, the column's conversational tone, and Webb's willingness to mix high and low diction were all worthy of study for clues about how to adapt a successful "Washoe" style to something more literary.

Freelancing as a *feuilletoniste* not only meant the freedom to be satiric *à la Bohème;* it also meant that Mark Twain could operate as a comic *flâneur* when he reports on the city scene. Clemens, however, did not simply adapt Mark Twain to the specifications of a comic *flâneur* like Webb's Inigo. In his version, Mark Twain also parodies *flânerie.* Clemens manufactured his parodic *flânerie* by overturning the priority of the spectator's gaze, the keen observation, that informs the serious *flâneur.* Rather than maintaining an artist's distance from the object of his gaze, Clemens retooled the comic *flâneur* so that Mark Twain somehow becomes laughably entangled in what he was supposed merely to observe and report. Clemens was famous and infamous in the Nevada Territory for creating a comic figure embodied within the represented scene who nevertheless functioned as alter ego, which led to charges about chronic lying. Mark Twain was, for his Nevada detractors, too much in the scene. After Clemens finished his stint with the *Call* and began his association with the *Californian,* in some sketches he presented Mark Twain trying to render the scene as would that most sophisticated reporter, a *flâneur.* Failing to fulfill the role, Mark Twain embodies a humorously inept parody.

Because Mark Twain appears within the narration as a character, his comic *flânerie* can dramatize an ironic outcome. For example, in "Early Rising, As Regards Excursions to the Cliff House," Mark Twain and a companion arrange a dawn departure in an open buggy for the Cliff House, a well-known restaurant and hotel overlooking the Pacific Ocean. The plan includes a "road unencumbered by carriages, and free from wind and dust; a bracing atmosphere; the gorgeous spectacle of the sun in the dawn of his glory; the fresh perfume of flowers still damp with dew; a solitary drive on the beach while its smoothness was yet unmarred by wheel or hoof, and a vision of white sails glinting in the morning light far out at sea" (*ETS2,* 26). The excursion should be pleasurable. Moreover, the account of the trip would refresh the reader vicariously, possibly even inspire him or her to undertake the journey. However, with the exception of a road unencumbered by carriages, nothing goes right for Mark Twain and his companion.

The road beckons, free of other carriages, because nothing has risen yet,

The original Cliff House epitomizes the intriguing aspects of the urban landscape that fueled Mark Twain's *flâneur* role. (Courtesy of the San Francisco Public Library)

including the sun. The air slaps the travelers awake more than braces them, with the very cold wind blowing hard from an ocean that Mark Twain imagines dotted with icebergs. The fresh perfume of flowers cannot compete with the smell of the horse blankets required to keep warm. The wind blows dust onto Mark Twain and his companion, and Mark Twain feels especially favored in this regard, receiving a "three-cornered" bit of gravel in the eye. So much for an exhilarating ride at dawn.

When they arrive at the Cliff House, no picturesque view enchants them. Rather, Mark Twain speaks of a "ghastly picture of fog, and damp, and frosty surf, and dreary solitude." The charming and sportive seals on the rocks have a "discordant [bark], writhing and squirming like exaggerated maggots" (*ETS2*, 28). So foul is Mark Twain's mood that the cheerful demeanor of the barkeeper at the Cliff House causes the excursionists to leave immediately for the Ocean House. When a cold fireplace greets them upon arrival, Mark Twain "sought surcease of sorrow in soothing blasphemy." Only "red-hot" coffee and the gloom of the man who brings it can thaw out the men and brighten their mood. The irony of feeling better because a bad mood engulfs someone else epitomizes the comic results of the excursion. As an exercise in acquiring romanticized sentiments about the healthfulness of drives into the country and the beauty of the natural world, the excursion turns out to be a laughable disaster. Two epigraphs to frame the experience adorn the sketch. One is Franklin's famous saying from *Poor Richard's Almanac*: "Early to bed and early to rise makes a man healthy, wealthy, and wise." Mark Twain in the end cannot endorse a ride to the Cliff House, and his narrative clearly shows that starting at the crack of dawn displays manifest foolishness. The whole piece therefore confirms the second epigraph, attributed to George Washington: "I don't see it." Putting the refutation of Franklin's wisdom into slang associated with poker and into the mouth of George Washington encapsulates the comic strategy of narrating the excursion: a vulgar practicality trumps not just a romantic sentimentality about interaction with the natural world but also the respectable practicality of the ultimate bourgeois role model, Ben Franklin.

In other sketches, the would-be *flâneur* does not simply embody an ironic outcome. Instead, no outcome exists because the reporter fails entirely to cover the event. "'Mark Twain' on the Launch of the Steamer *Capital*" unfolds in this way. As in similar examples, the event to be explicated by the *flâneur* has stirred the community. Several thousand spectators have turned out to witness the actual launch of the new steamboat, the *Capital*. As he plans to cover the event, Mark Twain directly presents the *flâneur's* role of moving significantly beyond the mere reporting of events: "the papers would teem with the inevitable old platitudinal trash which this sort of people have compelled to do duty on every occasion like this since Noah launched his ark—but I aspire to higher things. I wanted to write a report which should astonish and delight the whole intellectual world—which should dissect, analyze, and utterly exhaust the subject—which would serve for a model in this species of literature for all time to come" (*ETS2*, 362).

Mark Twain here elaborates the difference between the plodding reporter of events and the poetic, philosophic explicator of events and makes an explicit declaration of his intention to fulfill the exalted role of the *flâneur*. To accomplish this end, Mark Twain has secured the services of an expert on steamer launchings, Mr. Muff Nickerson. Mark Twain manages to arrive at the scene, onboard another steamer in the bay, with a good view of the *Cap-*

*ital* in its launching scaffold. However, when someone notes the existence of a bar belowdecks and invites Mark Twain and Muff Nickerson to take a drink, they agree. A series of yarns follows that culminates in Nickerson's tale, told in his vernacular style, about a pianist working for a traveling panoramist who constantly plays music inappropriate to the morally uplifting pictures. As the story concludes, someone comes into the bar declaring the launch a splendid success. Mark Twain has missed the event, despite being there. Ready to be the *flâneur extraordinaire,* instead he cannot even reach the level of the lowly reporter.

Clemens in San Francisco used Mark Twain at times like a comic *flâneur* in the mold of Charles Webb's Inigo—a satiric cultural critic who can also project a quirky and humorous personality. Mark Twain as comic *flâneur,* however, does not necessarily stroll about town to observe and explicate. Mark Twain exhibits more purpose in his urban travels than a stroll suggests. He prowls the city for noteworthy items. The need for copy curtails leisure. Mark Twain nevertheless does explicate what he observes, with an intention of providing a greater significance to the scene. Moreover, the characteristic phrasing of Mark Twain renders the scene vividly—though the resulting perspective is comic. In all this, "comic *flâneur*" aptly describes an important role for Mark Twain that Clemens developed in San Francisco.

"Comic *flâneur*" also insinuates the way Clemens parodies the *flâneur.* The biggest laugh Mark Twain garners from the comic *flâneur* role comes from his thwarted intention to provide greater significance for the quotidian scene or the special event, even in comic terms. By being unable to provide the explication expected of the *flâneur,* by being unable to attend the special event or by failing to pay attention to the event once present, Mark Twain embodies the idea that no greater significance exists for either daily events or the special occasions punctuating their routine—other than taking pleasure in them. The pleasure of simply being present, the pleasure of simply narrating, may be the comic "message" of the stories that do not happen, such as "'Mark Twain' and the Launch of the Steamer *Capital.*" In those instances, Mark Twain parodies the *flâneur.* When the event does not happen for his readers, Mark Twain nevertheless tells them all about it. Apparently locked into his reportorial need for copy to fill his column, Mark Twain as parodic *flâneur* instead comically symbolizes an individual most liberated from the strictures of business schedules, and liberated also from the moral imperative of satire. In his failures to find meaning in the urban scene and explicate it, Mark Twain when he parodies the *flâneur* escapes the need for meaning by adhering only to the desire for the fun of travel and talk. Not even a Bohemian morality, but pleasure, defines this version of Mark Twain.

Sam Clemens did not create a San Francisco Mark Twain the way he fashioned his "Washoe" version, adopting Comstock customs and habits for his alter ego in a comic version of local color. The Mark Twain elaborated in San Francisco does not twine itself into the local urban scene so much as use the city as a backdrop for comic excursions and its periodical writers as targets for scoring satiric points.[20] Nevertheless, San Francisco impressed Mark Twain, stamping the comic figure with its literary culture. One of the remarkable features of the city that created Mark Twain's meteoric rise to cosmopolitan status was its swift recognition of genuine literary talent. The early establishment of a literary periodical, the *Golden Era,* provided a focal point for this endemic talent. Founded by Rollin Daggett and J. MacDonough Foard in 1852, the *Golden Era* quickly became popular among the mining camps because of its shrewd mixture of local items with materials selected from other publications. In 1860 Daggett and Foard sold the journal to James Brooks and Joe Lawrence, Lawrence becoming the editor in chief. He kept the friendly tone of the "Correspondents' Column" and the other local departments, such as mining and agricultural intelligence, that had made the *Era* indispensable in the rural districts. To this foundation, Lawrence added enough literary tone to make the *Era* important in San Francisco too—theater reviews, town gossip, and literary contributors and commentators.

By 1864, when Sam Clemens arrived on the bayside scene, the first flowering of artistic ability was apparent, not only in the publication of local talent in the *Golden Era* but also in San Francisco's easy assimilation of lesser

20. Patrick D. Morrow discusses Mark Twain during his stay in San Francisco within a local color context in "Bret Harte, Mark Twain, and the San Francisco Circle " in *A Literary History of the American West,* ed. Max Westbrook (Fort Worth: Texas Christian University Press, 1987), 339–58. Focusing on *Roughing It,* Gary Scharnhorst declares that Clemens "fudges or obscures many of the specific details normally associated with local-color realism" ("Mark Twain, Bret Harte, and the Literary Construction of San Francisco," in *San Francisco in Fiction: Essays in a Regional Literature,* ed. David Fine and Paul Skenazy [Albuquerque: University of New Mexico Press, 1995], 21–33 [24]).

and greater East Coast talent when individuals traveled west: Ada Clare, Fitzhugh Ludlow, Robert Newall, Frances Fuller Fane, Adah Mencken, Charles Farrar Browne, and Charles Webb. The very fact that Charles Webb felt that a market existed for a second literary weekly as well as the fact that a local literary star, Bret Harte, agreed to contribute to the enterprise signals this flush time of ability and aspiration. Reaching for literary excellence within a cosmopolitan atmosphere that assumed the importance of artistic endeavor, Harte and Webb inspired Sam Clemens to redouble his efforts to be a successful comic writer. San Francisco would have other moments of literary fame, next with Harte's *Overland Monthly* and then with turn-of-the-century notables that included Frank Norris and Jack London, down to, perhaps most famously, the Beat Poets of the 1950s. Mark Twain, for a short and memorable time, however, took his place in the city's first literary harvest.

# Taming the Bohemian
## Mark Twain in Buffalo

JOSEPH B. MCCULLOUGH

**MOVEMENT,** travel, and wanderlust were fundamental parts of Mark Twain's makeup. He enjoyed depicting himself as a vagabond or a bohemian, an air-born plant without roots, restlessly moving from place to place as circumstances dictated. It is not surprising, then, that travel informs a large part of his literary output, from the quasi-autobiographical travel narratives such as *The Innocents Abroad; or, The New Pilgrim's Progress* (1969), *Roughing It* (1872), *A Tramp Abroad* (1880), *Life on the Mississippi* (1883), and *Following the Equator: A Journey around the World* (1897), to his fictional works such as *Adventures of Huckleberry Finn* (1885) and *A Connecticut Yankee in King Arthur's Court* (1889), to name only a few. It is against this backdrop of Twain's penchant for an itinerant lifestyle that his "settling" in Buffalo, New York—where he co-owned, edited, and produced sketches for the *Buffalo Express* from 1869 to 1871 and began his life as a husband and father—is significant. The time he spent in Buffalo was pivotal in Twain's career. It marked his final attempt at the daily grind of full-time journalism and

Portions of this essay originally appeared in the introduction to *Mark Twain at the "Buffalo Express,"* ed. Joseph B. McCullough and Janice McIntire-Strasburg (DeKalb: Northern Illinois University Press, 1999), xiii–xlvii.

looked forward to his move to Hartford, Connecticut, where he became a man of letters.

In many ways, the years between 1869 and 1871 were the best of times and the worst of times for Mark Twain.[1] Prior to 1869, he had spent fully half of his life traveling both east and west as a typesetter, journalist, riverboat pilot, prospector, and finally travel writer and platform lecturer. While living in San Francisco in 1866, he arranged with his friend Colonel John McComb, the editor of the San Francisco *Alta California,* to produce a series of weekly letters describing his journey to New York, then later his tour of Europe, Egypt, and Palestine on the steamship *Quaker City.* For compensation, he received his passage for the excursion to the Holy Land and twenty dollars for each of his fifty "Holy Land Excursion Letters."[2] A signal moment of his travels occurred in June 1867 when he boarded the *Quaker City* for the first transatlantic excursion undertaken strictly for pleasure to Europe and the Holy Land, organized by Henry Ward Beecher, influential pastor of the Plymouth (Congregational) church in Brooklyn. Although disappointed that Beecher had withdrawn just before sailing (Twain would meet him in Brooklyn in January 1868, soon after the conclusion of the 163-day voyage), Twain made a number of acquaintances, two of whom would figure prominently in his life: Mary Mason Fairbanks ("Mother Fairbanks"), who was to become a close friend and trusted adviser for the next thirty-two years, and eighteen-year-old Charles Jervis Langdon, from Elmira, New York, who showed Twain a picture of his sister, Olivia, who would become Twain's wife more than two years later, following a robust courtship.

When the ship returned to New York in November, Twain went to Washington, D.C., where he served for a few weeks as a private secretary to William Stewart, the Republican senator from Nevada, while also acting as a correspondent for the *Virginia City Territorial Enterprise,* the San Francisco *Alta California,* and the *New York Tribune.* He received a number of offers from book publishers but finally contracted with Elisha Bliss at the Ameri-

---

1. For convenience, I have used the name Mark Twain rather than Samuel Clemens throughout (except when directly citing other scholars), instead of awkwardly shifting between the two.

2. Susan McFatter, "San Francisco *Alta California,*" in *The Mark Twain Encyclopedia,* ed. J. R. LeMaster and James D. Wilson (New York and London: Garland Publishing Co., 1993), 652.

can Publishing Company, a subscription firm in Hartford, Connecticut, to complete a manuscript based on his *Alta California* letters and such new material as he deemed necessary. This manuscript would become *The Innocents Abroad.* When he returned to New York, he was invited to dinner with Charles Langdon and his family, and there he met Olivia Langdon for the first time. He paid a long postponed visit to the Langdon family at Elmira in August 1868, after which he embarked upon a campaign of letter writing and personal reformation to deserve, earn, and win her hand in marriage, during which he made decisions that would profoundly alter his life. Olivia provisionally accepted his proposal by Thanksgiving of 1868, and the engagement became official on February 4, 1869. With his formal acceptance as Olivia's future husband, Twain urgently felt the need for a settled, permanent position in life, something he did not believe could result from the support of his pen alone.

In his insightful study, *Getting to Be Mark Twain,* Jeffrey Steinbrink explores the formative changes in Twain's life between 1868 and 1871 and convincingly argues what while other moments in his life were perhaps more catastrophic, or more dominated by triumph or despair, it was during these years that his life took the shape it was essentially to hold until its close:

> During this period Clemens came East—for good, as it turned out— acquired international renown and the beginnings of a considerable fortune with the best-seller *The Innocents Abroad,* courted and married Olivia Langdon, and determined to *settle,* first as a newspaper editor in Buffalo and then, more lastingly, as a professional writer of books in Hartford. Each of these accomplishments represented a profound change of circumstance and, potentially, of outlook in the former Wild Humorist of the Pacific Slope. Even in a life as charged with fortuity and calamity as Clemens's, this span of just three years is remarkable for its compression of crucial choices and turns of fate. By the time it drew to a close in the fall of 1871, with the move to Hartford, the most fundamental of his lifelong evolutions had run its course, providing, in place of the volatility and incoherence of his extended adolescence, the relative stability that informed the great middle period of his career.[3]

3. Steinbrink, *Getting to Be Mark Twain* (Berkeley: University of California Press, 1991), xvi.

During his courtship of Olivia, Twain looked forward to a life of stability and domestic tranquillity, and his letters to her often indicate a desire to end his traveling days and to settle into a permanent home where he could provide them both with the comfort and security that she was enjoying at the Langdon residence in Elmira. But, as Tom Quirk observes in *Mark Twain and Human Nature,* domestic bliss would not curb Twain's itinerant impulse, even though he assured his bride-to-be otherwise. It might be expected that his courtship of Olivia would be conducted on the run and largely through correspondence (numbering more than two hundred letters), as he was lecturing in several states and writing her continually from one to another.[4] Often, he would try to convince her, as well as her family, that he was ready to give up his bohemian lifestyle. On January 24, 1869, for example, he wrote:

> Wherefore I now speak to you standing in the presence of God. And I say what I have been I am not now; that I am striving & shall still strive to reach the highest altitude of worth, the highest Christian excellence; that I know of *nothing* in my past career that I would conceal from your parents, howsoever I might blush to speak the words; & that is my *strong conviction* that, married to you, I would never desire to roam again while I lived. . . . Your father & mother are overlooking one thing, Livy—that I have been a wanderer from necessity, three-fourths of my time—a wanderer from choice only one-fourth. . . . Wandering is not a *habit* with me—for that word implies an enslaved fondness for the thing. And I could most freely take an oath that all fondness for roaming is dead within me. . . . Wandering is *not* my habit, nor my proclivity. Does a man, five years a galley-slave, get in a habit of it & yearn to be a galley-slave always? Does a horse in a tread-mill get infatuated with his profession & long to continue in it? . . . And being pushed from pillar to post & compelled so long to roam, against my will, is it reasonable to think that I am really fond of it & wedded to it? I think not. (*L3,* 74–75)

It is worth noting, however, that despite his protestations, he indeed managed to travel a great deal after his marriage, and indeed for the rest of his

---

4. Quirk, *Mark Twain and Human Nature* (Columbia: University of Missouri Press, 2007), 60.

life. As Quirk observes, in the 1870s alone, when we lump together the time spent in separate excursions abroad, we find that Clemens lived nearly three full years outside the country—pitching his several tents in Germany, France, Bermuda, Switzerland, Ireland, the Netherlands, Italy, Belgium, and, most often, England. It became almost routine for the family to spend the summer months in Elmira, New York, and he frequently embarked on lecture tours in the United States. Although there were often practical professional reasons for his travels—to secure British copyright for his books, to make money lecturing, to acquire literary material, and so forth—and while he often complained about the aggravation of the lecture circuit, "the fact remains that if, as he implied in *Roughing It,* the perfecting influences of civilization counseled stasis, not movement, then Mark Twain was far from civilized."[5] Even while Twain was attempting to reassure his fiancée that he planned to curb his nomadic tendencies, she would probably not have been convinced had she attended one of his favorite lectures, "The American Vandal Abroad," which he was delivering on a lecture tour while he was writing to her. He chose this topic in order to generate publicity for his forthcoming book, *The Innocents Abroad,* which was issued in July 1869.

> I am to speak of the American Vandal this evening, but I wish to say in advance that I do not use this term in derision or apply it as a reproach, but use it because it is convenient; and duly and properly modified, it best describes the roving, independent, free-and-easy character of that class of traveling Americans who are *not* elaborately educated, cultivated, and refined, and gilded and filigreed with the ineffable graces of the first society. The best class of our countrymen who go abroad keep us well posted about their doings in foreign lands, but their brethren vandals cannot sing their own praises or publish their adventures. . . . If there is a moral to this lecture it is an injunction to all Vandals to *travel.* I am glad the American Vandal *goes* abroad. It does him good. It makes a better man of him. It rubs out a multitude of his old unworthy biases and prejudices. It aids his religion, for it enlarges his charity and his benevolence, it broadens his views of men and

5. Ibid. See *Mark Twain at the "Buffalo Express,"* ed. McCullough and McIntire-Strasburg, for a complete reprinting of Twain's signed sketches, as well as unsigned editorials and items from a "People and Things" column, sometimes written in collaboration with Joseph Larned, with arguments and evidence for attribution.

things; it deepens his generosity and his compassion for the failings and shortcomings of his fellow creatures. . . . Cast into trouble and misfortune in strange lands and being mercifully cared for by those he never saw before, he begins to learn that best lesson of all—that one which culminates in the conviction that God puts *something* good and something lovable in every man his hands create—that the world is *not* a cold, harsh, cruel, prison-house, stocked with all manner of selfishness and hate and wickedness. It *liberalizes* the Vandal to travel. You never saw a bigoted, opinionated, stubborn, narrow-minded, self-conceited, *almighty mean man* in your life but he had stuck in one place ever since he was born and thought God had made the world and dyspepsia and bile for *his* especial comfort and satisfaction. So I say, *by all means* let the American Vandal go on traveling, and let no man discourage him.[6]

In addition to pleading his case to Livy that he was prepared to give up his bohemian lifestyle, Twain felt that he must convince her parents that he was not only fit to marry their daughter but also able to support her. As Justin Kaplan suggests in *Mr. Clemens and Mark Twain,* when it came to the matter of reliable "references," he argued that only five people at the most had ever known him at all well and that he felt in entire sympathy with only two of them. One of them was his dead brother Henry; the other was Livy. Furthermore, when the letters of reference began to come in, they were shockingly bad and "came within an ace of breaking off my marriage" (*L3,* 290). But, as Kaplan goes on to argue, even before the appalling reports came in, Twain had felt restive and resentful under the Langdons' scrutiny. On November 28, 1868, in his first letter to Livy after their formal engagement he declared:

> I do love, love, *love* you, Livy. My whole being is permeated, is renewed, is leavened with this love, & with every breath I draw its noble influence to make me a better man. And I shall yet be *worthy* of your priceless love . . . Livy, I could not tell your honored father & mother how deeply I felt for them, & how heartless it seemed in me to come, under cover of their trusting, generous hospitality, & try to

6. *Mark Twain's Speeches,* ed. Albert Bigelow Paine (New York: Harper and Brothers, 1910), 21, 29–30.

steal away the sun out of their domestic firmament & rob their fireside heaven of its angel . . . I could not tell them how grateful I was, & how I loved them for pausing to listen to my appeals when they could have upbraided me for my treachery & turned me out of doors in deserved disgrace. I call these things by their rightful names, Livy, because I *know* I ought to have spoken of them long before I spoke to you—& yet there was nothing criminal in my *intent,* Livy—nothing wilfully & deliberately underhanded & dishonorable—I could say it in the high court of Heaven. (*L2,* 290)

But Twain did decide to make his case directly to Olivia's parents that he was a different man now from the one his references depicted. On February 13, 1869, he wrote Livy's mother:

I could refer you to fifty friends, but they could only tell you (& very vaguely, too,) what I *have* been—just as a forester might talk learnedly of a bush he had once known well, unwilling that it had stretched its branches upward & become a tree, since *he* saw it. It is a bold figure, but not altogether an unapt one. For those friends of mine, who certainly knew little enough of me in the years that are gone, know nothing of me *now.* For instance, they knew me as a profane swearer; as a man of convivial ways & not adverse to social drinking; as a man without religion; in a word, as a "wild" young man—though never a dishonorable one, in the trite acceptation of that word. But now I never swear; I never taste wine or spirits upon *any* occasion whatsoever; I am orderly, & my conduct is above reproach in a worldly sense; and finally, I now claim that I am a Christian. I claim it, & it only remains to be seen if my bearing shall show that I am justly it, & it only remains to be seen if my bearing shall show that I am justly entitled to so name myself. . . . I do not wish to marry Miss Langdon for her wealth, & she knows that perfectly well. As far as I'm concerned, Mr. Langdon can cut her off with a shilling—or the half of it. To use a homely phrase, I have paddled my own canoe since I was thirteen, *wholly* without encouragement or assistance from any one, & am fully competent to so paddle it the rest of the voyage, & take a passenger along, beside. While I have health & strength, & the high hope & confidence that God gave me in my nature, I will look to it that we always have a comfortable living, & that is all (of a purely worldly nature,) that either of us will care a great deal about. Neither of us are much afflicted with a mania for money-making, I fancy. (*L3*, 90–91)

To be sure, each of Twain's attempts to characterize himself as a transformed and reformed man was less a statement of fact than an indication of a struggle that he was undergoing in an attempt to reconcile what he desired to do with his natural impulses. Twain was most often suspicious of an ability to reform one's basic inclinations or nature for any length of time. While he would attempt to curtail his drinking and smoking, at least in front of the family, for example, he returned to these "vices" time and time again. In many of his writings, notably in *Roughing It*, chapter 33 of which is sometimes reprinted under the title "Fruits of Our Reform," he undercuts the ecstasies of the renunciation of various vices—smoking, drinking and gambling in particular—by having his characters renew their old ways once a crisis has passed, vowing "to say no more about 'reform' and examples to the rising generation'" (*RI*, 219).

Twain's representations of his acceptance of Christian values in his correspondence with Livy and her family did not suggest the complexity of his beliefs or the struggle that he was in fact already having with religion. On the religious excursion recounted in *The Innocents Abroad*, for example, he found the devout ceremonies of the "pilgrims" too frequent and too sanctimonious and was more comfortable associating with the "sinners," as he called his card-playing, smoking, and drinking companions. It is within the context of Twain's religious thought that we can only guess at Livy's response to one of the most curious "love letters"—if one can so characterize it—that he wrote to her, dated January 8, 1870:

> I have been reading some new arguments to prove that the world is very old, & that the six days of creation were six immensely long periods. For instance, according to Genesis, the *stars* were made when the world was, yet this writer mentions the significant fact that there are stars within reach of our telescopes whose light requires 50,000 years to traverse the wastes of space & come to our earth. And so, if we made a tour through space ourselves, might we not, in some remote era of the future, meet & greet the first lagging rays of stars that started on their weary visit to us a million years ago? . . .
>
> How insignificant we are, with our pigmy little world!—an atom

glinting with the uncounted myriads of other atom worlds in a broad
shaft of light streaming from God's countenance—& yet prating com-
placently of our speck as the Great World. . . . Did Christ live 33 years
in each of the millions & millions of worlds that hold their majestic
courses above our heads? Or was *our* small globe the favored one of all?
Does one apple in a vast orchard think as much of itself as we do? . . .
Do the pismires argue upon vexed questions of pismire theology—&
do they climb a molehill & look abroad over the grand universe of an
acre of ground & say "Great is God, who created all things for Us?"
    I do not see how astronomers can help feeling exquisitely insignif-
icant, for every new page in the Book of heavens they open reveals to
them more & more that the world we are so proud of is to the universe of careening globes as is one mosquito to the winged & hoofed
flocks & herds that darken the air & populate the plains & forests of
all the earth. If you killed the mosquito could it be missed? Verily,
What is Man, that he should be considered of God? (*LLMT,* 134–35)

The concerns expressed in this letter were to command Twain's attention for
the rest of his life. Over the years he wrestled with their implication in many
works, both humorous and serious. Many of the pieces he published; others he failed to complete or held back because he felt them too radical for
publication. Close to the same time that he wrote this letter to Olivia, he
also privately wrote another piece, "God of the Bible vs. God of the Present
Day," which reflects a concept of the Creator that Twain would hold well
into the 1890s. Like the letter it also introduces the theme that would continue to fascinate him for the rest of his life, namely, the almost unimaginable magnitude of the universe as revealed by science.[7] What is particularly interesting about these letters is that Twain was already showing a
philosophical depth and seriousness very much at odds with his reputation
as "The Wild Humorist of the Pacific Slope."

    In his quest for acceptance by Olivia's parents, in the end, as Justin Kap-
lan suggests, Twain's "refusal to deny his past was rewarded by Jervis Langdon's bluff declaration of faith. 'What kind of people are these? Haven't you

---

7. *The Bible According to Mark Twain: Writings on Heaven, Eden, and the Flood,* ed. Howard G.
Baetzhold and Joseph B. McCullough (Athens: University of Georgia Press, 1995), offers a useful collection of Twain's religious writings, including unpublished pieces from this period.

a friend in the world?' Langdon asked after reading the letters [testifying to Twain's character]. 'Apparently not,' was the answer. As Clemens remembered the episode in his autobiography, Langdon said, 'I'll be your friend myself. Take the girl. I know you better than they do.'"[8] Despite Jervis Langdon's declaration of faith and Twain's own statements that he was not much afflicted with a mania for moneymaking, he did not believe he could earn a living by his pen alone. He also judged that lecturing was unsatisfactory. His letters to Olivia after their engagement became official on February 4, 1869, indicate a desire to end his traveling days, at least temporarily, and to settle into a permanent home where he could provide them both with the comfort and security she was enjoying at the Langdon house.

With these qualifications in mind, Twain set about negotiating for an editorial interest in several newspapers. His first choice was the *Cleveland Herald*. He hoped that Mary Fairbanks would be able to exert some influence on his behalf with her husband, Abel Fairbanks, one of the *Herald's* owners, thereby helping Twain to secure an interest in the paper and to establish himself and his future wife in Cleveland. During the intervening months of negotiation, the purchase amount fluctuated between one-eighth and one-quarter interest in the paper. But the *Herald's* owners were apparently slow to close the negotiations, and Twain began looking elsewhere. He approached the owners of the *Hartford Courant* about purchasing a one-third interest of that newspaper. The city of Hartford would have been an ideal place for Twain to settle. Jervis Langdon and his family had personal ties to the city. Also, Hartford served as the headquarters for the American Publishing Company, the subscription house that had produced several of Mark Twain's books and was in the process of preparing *The Innocents Abroad*. However, even with the added influence of Joseph Twichell on Twain's behalf, the owners, Joseph Hawley and Charles Dudley Warner, gave Twain's offer a cool reception. At that time, Twain was still reading proof for his travel narrative, and the *Courant's* co-owners "saw themselves negotiating with the latter-day Wild Humorist of the Pacific Slope."[9] Hawley and Warner

8. Kaplan, *Mr. Clemens and Mark Twain* (New York: Simon and Schuster, 1966), 91–92.

9. Steinbrink, *Getting to Be Mark Twain,* 32. Steinbrink provides the most thorough discussion of the negotiations with various newspapers, offering detailed supporting evidence from Twain's correspondence during this period (29–41).

would later regret their early rejection of Twain; after the enthusiastic reception of *The Innocents Abroad* six months later, followed by brisk sales, the Hartford editors tried to reopen negotiations with Twain, but by then he and Olivia had already settled upon Buffalo as their home. While awaiting the final outcome of these two transactions, Twain met Petroleum V. Nasby (David Ross Locke), who suggested that Twain join the *Toledo Blade*, but apparently the author never entertained any serious notions of settling there. When negotiations seemed stalemated at the *Herald* and the *Courant*, Twain made a half-hearted attempt to buy into the *Springfield Republican* in Massachusetts, but his attempt was rejected out of hand by the editor, Samuel Bowles.

In the end, it was Jervis Langdon who finally decided the issue, finding his future son-in-law an editorship at the *Buffalo Express* and advancing him $12,500, one half of the buy-in price of $25,000. The loan enabled Twain to purchase a one-third interest in the paper from Thomas Kennett. In early August 1869 the bottom had fallen out of negotiations with the *Herald;* within two weeks similar negotiations with the *Buffalo Express* were complete. Twain's partners there were George H. Selkirk, who handed most business matters, and Josephus Nelson Larned, the paper's political editor. As Steinbrink has suggested, Jervis Langdon profoundly influenced the course of Twain's early career, guiding him to what both considered a permanent position and his life's work as a newspaper editor in Buffalo. By the time that the Langdons had moved to Elmira in 1845, Jervis had begun to prosper in the lumber business. In Elmira that prosperity soared as he shifted his investments into coal, made his fortune, and participated prominently in abolitionist and other humanitarian causes.[10] He was, for example a "conductor" on the Underground Railroad, and Frederick Douglass, whom Twain would meet in Boston in early December 1869, was an honored guest in the Langdon home.

When Twain took up residence in Buffalo in early 1869, he encountered a vibrant commercial and industrial town, with a population of nearly 120,000. The city's growth began in earnest with the completion of the Erie

10. "Jervis Langdon," in *The Mark Twain Encyclopedia,* ed. LeMaster and Wilson, 440. I have also drawn upon Laura Skandera-Trombley's useful discussion of Langdon's abolitionist and related activities in *Mark Twain in the Company of Women* (Philadelphia: University of Pennsylvania Press, 1994).

Canal in 1825, an event that brought a tremendous economic boom to the community, attracting immigrants and boosting its population to nearly 10,000 at the time of its incorporation as a city in 1832.[11] The city became the logical gateway to America's frontier and initiated a rich commercial and manufacturing economy based on the transport and processing of raw materials. Trade with the expanding West grew rapidly during the Civil War. Buffalo's location led logically to its becoming a major railroad hub. In 1852, five small local lines were merged into the New York Central system. The growth of the city's population by the middle of the nineteenth century was spectacular, giving it all of the earmarks of a boomtown. Between 1845 and 1855, for example, the population more than doubled. While a fair number of these newcomers were native-born Americans migrating to the city from New England and rural New York, the greatest percentage were foreigners. In 1855 more than 60 percent of the nearly 75,000 people who lived in Buffalo were foreign-born. Almost half (31,000) were Germans, and a fifth (18,000) were Irish. Cramped together on the several streets of the city's East Side, and sandwiched in among a continually expanding German population, was a small but well-organized community of African Americans. By midcentury the more than 700 African Americans living in Buffalo had two churches and a separate, segregated school for their children. By the 1840s the black community had begun to attract national attention. The city's reputation as a critical junction on the Underground Railroad began to spread, and soon African Americans were coming to Buffalo. Yet, while the blacks lived in a strictly segregated community, they did interact with whites, particularly on the city's waterfront, where black and Irish day laborers worked together. More often, however, they met at strikes, where blacks were often used as strikebreakers. By the middle of the 1850s racial riots between the Irish and the blacks of the waterfront community had become common, and race relations in the city were further poisoned during

---

11. "Buffalo," in Encyclopaedia Britannica Online, http://www.britannica.com/eb/article-9017935 (accessed June 20, 1008). For detailed historical and related information concerning Buffalo, I have relied on Mark Goldman's *High Hopes: The Rise and Decline of Buffalo, New York* (Albany: State University of New York Press, 1983), 56–97, 124–52, and Richard O. Resisem's *Classic Buffalo: A Heritage of Distinguished Architecture* (Buffalo: Canisius College Press, 1999), 13–21.

the Civil War years by the imposition of a federal draft in the summer of
1862, in the aftermath of the Battle of Gettysburg.

By 1860 the population of Buffalo had grown to more than 81,000 people. The same year brought Buffalo's first streetcars. Wealth grew, and the
banking system developed to channel local capital into new industries. The
newly rich entrepreneurs worked to improve the aesthetic environment.
Impressive additions to the city such as Forest Lawn Cemetery (1849), the
Historical Society (1862), and Grosvenor Library (1870) all represented the
desire of Buffalo's leading citizens to create a culture appropriate to the city's
new economic prominence. The city government also enacted legislation
for an ambitious new park system, then lured the nationally known landscape architect Frederick Law Olmsted, who had previously designed New
York's Central Park, to create an ambitious pastoral refuge. He would be followed by a number of prominent architects, including Louis Sullivan, Stanford White, Edward Broadhead Green, and Frank Lloyd Wright, to name
only a few, who would leave their lasting mark on the city. After 1865, the
demands of the lumber industry and the iron ore flowing from Minnesota
promoted further rapid growth. Shipyards, iron and steel mills, meatpack-
ing plants, flour mills, and railroad car industries developed, and alongside
them the population grew unabated.

It was against this backdrop that Twain took up his new duties as editor.
The *Buffalo Express* occupied a four-story brick building at 14 East Swan
Street, just a few steps from a boardinghouse in which Twain lodged. Although his editorial duties were only vaguely defined, Twain actively assumed his post as managing editor on August 15, 1869. Evidently, he immediately threw himself into his new responsibilities. John Harrison Mills,
an artist on the editorial staff of the paper in 1869, later wrote: "I cannot remember that there was any delay in getting down to his work. I think within five minutes the new editor had assumed the easy look of one entirely at
home, pencil in hand and a clutch of paper before him, with an air of pre-
occupation, as of one intent on a task delayed."[12]

For all of Buffalo's vibrancy and culturally rich environment, along with
its attendant problems, Twain generally seemed little interested in local af-

12. Steinbrink, *Getting to Be Mark Twain,* 101. I have also relied for information on the excellent detailed biographical chronology provided by Louis Budd in *CTSS1,* 964–70.

fairs or social issues during his residency in the city, at least in terms of writing about them for the *Express* readers. He did write one sketch, "A Curious Dream: Containing a Moral" (April 30, 1870, and concluding in the May 7, 1870 issue), in which he exposed the dreadful neglect of local cemeteries. He also penned a negligible short, unsigned piece lambasting the city government's oversight of the irresponsible manner in which "Delaware Street is sprinkled about Virginia Street." To be sure, Twain never mined to any great extent the minute details of the various cities in which he lived or was acquainted, nor developed the urban environments in his writings as did, say, Henry James and William Dean Howells, much less Theodore Dreiser, Frank Norris, or Stephen Crane.

Although Clemens's first sketch signed as Mark Twain did not appear in the paper until August 21, 1869, he apparently began "retraining" reporters, making changes in the paper's appearance, and writing or collaborating in unsigned material, in particular contributing several items to a "People and Things" column. He also likely wrote four unsigned editorials prior to August 21, the day of his official debut with the paper. One of these deserves special attention, for it indicates the subtle influence that Jervis Langdon, even unwittingly, exerted. The editorial, "The Monopoly Speaks" (August 20, 1869), seems to have been written in order to please Jervis Langdon, Twain's future father-in-law and benefactor, as well as the owner of one of four coal companies that supplied virtually all of Buffalo's coal and had united to form the Anthracite Coal Association. Believing that this association amounted to a monopoly, which was driving prices higher, several Buffalo businessmen formed the cooperative Citizen's Mutual Coal Mining, Purchasing and Sale Company in an attempt to compete with the "monopoly." As Jeffrey Steinbrink observes, controversy engendered by the coal question warmed the editorial pages of the Buffalo papers, and Twain inserted himself squarely into the middle of the controversy by arguing that "up to the present we have heard only the people's side of the coal question, though there could be no doubt that the coal men had a side also." The *Express* up to this point had generally taken the side of the citizen's company against the monopolists. The *Express*'s turnabout was doubtless attributed to Twain's arrival, a circumstance not lost on rival newspapermen.[13]

---

13. Steinbrink, *Getting to Be Mark Twain,* 46–7.

In the *Express's* official announcement about Twain's arrival as editor, the paper stated: "As we speak now in advance of his occupation of the chair in which he will seat himself with us a few days hence, we can properly indulge these congratulations and confess pride that we feel in identifying the celebrity of the name and popularity of the writings of 'Mark Twain' with the *Express*." On August 21, 1869, Twain's "Salutatory" and his first signed sketch, "A Day at Niagara," appeared in the paper. Almost every Saturday one of his signed articles made its appearance. Determining conclusively that unsigned pieces were written wholly or partially by Twain is sometimes difficult, given his association with Josephus Larned, the paper's political editor. In a letter to Livy on August 21, 1869, only days after assuming his editorial duties, Twain described his daily routine:

> Larned & I sit upon opposite sides of the same table & it is exceedingly convenient—for if you will remember, you sometimes write till you reach the middle of a subject & then run hard aground—you know what you *want* to say, but for the life of you you can't say—your ideas & your words get thick & sluggish & you are vanquished. So, occasionally, after biting our nails & scratching our heads awhile, we just reach over & *swap manuscripts*—& then we scribble away without the least trouble, he finishing my article & I his. Some of our patchwork editorials of this kind are all the better for the new life they get by crossing the breed. (*L3,* 317)

Mark Twain had transformed himself from a vagabond travel writer and lecturer to a "settled" man with a solid financial interest, though even his new readers caught a glimpse of the old Twain in remarks he made in his "Salutatory" on August 21:

> I only wish to assure parties having a friendly interest in the prosperity of the journal, that I am not going to hurt the paper deliberately and intentionally at any time. I am not going to introduce any startling reforms, or in any way attempt to make trouble. I am simply going to do my plain, unpretending duty, and when I cannot get out of it; I shall work diligently and honestly and faithfully at all times and upon all occasions, when privation and want shall compel me to do it; in writing I shall always confine myself strictly to the truth, except when it is

attended with inconvenience; I shall witheringly rebuke all forms of crime and misconduct, except when committed by the party inhabiting my own vest; I shall not make use of slang or vulgarity upon any occasion or under any circumstances, and shall never use profanity except in discussing house-rent and taxes. Indeed, upon second thought, I will not even use it then, for it is unchristian, inelegant and degrading—though to speak truly I do not see how house-rent and taxes are going to be discussed worth a cent without it. I shall not often meddle with politics, because we have a political editor who is already excellent, and only needs to serve a term in the penitentiary in order to be perfect. I shall not write any poetry, unless I conceive a spite against the subscribers.[14]

Characteristically, Twain began his settled, permanent life in Buffalo by striking out on a lecture tour scheduled through James Redpath's Lyceum. Within two weeks of writing his first sketch for the *Express,* Twain had already agreed to a speaking tour that began on November 1, 1869. The tour started in Pittsburgh and took him through Pennsylvania, Rhode Island, Connecticut, Massachusetts, and New York before ending on January 20, 1870, near Elmira. Twain then had one week to recuperate from the rigors of the tour and prepare for his wedding to Olivia on February 2. For this season, Twain chose as his lecture "Our Fellow Savages in the Sandwich Islands," a departure from the previous year's lecture, "An American Vandal Abroad."

The lectures were well received, for the most part, as evidenced by a review in the *Boston Evening Transcript* on November 11, 1869, which was later reprinted in the *Express,* but Twain's letters to Olivia and others during this time indicate that he was travel weary and looking forward to returning to Elmira and eventually to Buffalo. The lecture tour and the brisk sales of *The Innocents Abroad* were sufficiently lucrative, however, that Twain was able to retire $15,000 of debt and still retain about $3,000 on hand. While on tour, Twain did manage to make frequent contributions to the *Express* by mail, including several "Around the World" sketches, which derived from his Western days in Nevada, California, and the Sandwich Islands and which he would later incorporate into his next book, *Roughing It.*

14. *Mark Twain at the "Buffalo Express,"* ed. McCullough and McIntire-Strasburg, 5.

Despite Twain's penchant for constant, even frenetic travel, he looked forward to his marriage to Olivia Langdon, after which he would be able to settle into a life of marital bliss and domestic harmony. To be sure, the prospects for supporting Livy in the manner to which she was accustomed were questionable, but Twain was optimistic about his future, both personal and professional. His marriage to Olivia on February 2, 1870, was a modest affair, taking place in the Langdon home in Elmira, with Thomas Beecher and Joseph Twichell performing the service. After spending their night with the family, Twain and his new bride, along with a small party of houseguests, took a private train to Buffalo, where Twain expected to move into a boardinghouse that had been arranged by a friend. Once arriving in town, the couple was delayed, while the rest of the party went to another location. The driver then took the newlyweds to 472 Delaware Avenue, one of the most prestigious streets in the city, where Twain was surprised by a wedding gift from Jervis Langdon, worth $40,000 (equivalent to perhaps $800,000 today): a house complete with a staff that included a maid, housekeeper, cook, coachman, and carriage. As Connie Ann Kirk suggests,

> The marriage and move into the new house had a profound effect on Twain. While he had been working on and off at a life of letters for several years by this time, he had no responsibilities to anyone but himself, and he had never held or kept a regular job with regular office hours. The lifestyle of an upper-middle-class literary man, which Jervis Langdon had set up for him, was something he would have to work to maintain and grow into to feel comfortable, and Clemens at that moment must have wondered if that was even possible for him to do. . . . He had spent years going from job to job and whim to whim wherever the winds may carry him. Gaining this level of responsibility and climb into social status in one fell swoop was a jolt, so in the early days he hid out from his duties at the Buffalo *Express* by having an extended honeymoon with Livy in the house. The young woman whose family once thought she might not marry because of her frail health enjoyed a healthy and satisfying romantic life with her new husband, and he with her.[15]

15. Kirk, *Mark Twain: A Biography* (Westport, Conn.: Greenwood Press), 55–59.

Now married and wishing to enjoy a life of marital contentment, and receiving substantial royalty checks from *The Innocents Abroad,* Twain began going to the *Express* offices only twice a week to fulfill his editorial duties. He also signed a contract in March with the New York–based *Galaxy* to supply a monthly humorous column, "Memoranda," for $2,000 a year, with the stipulation that he reserved all republication rights. While he continued to write for the *Express,* he felt that the *Galaxy* allowed him more freedom and national exposure. As Steinbrink astutely observes,

> Clemens's decision to write for the *Galaxy* did not so much foster as confirm his determination to keep his distance from the Buffalo *Express* and, at least indirectly, from Buffalo itself. In his estimation the magazine offered not only a wider scope for his talents than the newspaper but also a more literate and cosmopolitan readership, a national—or at least an eastern—audience far different from the one he associated with the narrow, parochial demands of the *Express.* The *Galaxy,* he told the Langdons, "gives me a chance to write what I please, not what I *must*" (April 1st, 1870). The celebrity he was gaining as the author of *The Innocents Abroad* no doubt contributed to his desire for greater freedom as well as for a wider, more literary forum than Buffalo could provide.[16]

However, while the future looked promising, both personally and professionally for Twain and Olivia, their happiness was short lived. In the summer of 1870 Jervis Langdon was diagnosed with cancer of the stomach. The Clemenses spent May in Elmira nursing Livy's father and canceled a trip to Europe that they had planned for that summer. Twain began to publish less and less in the *Express,* as he journeyed to Elmira for two weeks to help care for Langdon, often sitting at his bedside for four hours a night. The pieces that appeared during that time were inevitably those published in the *Galaxy.* But with Langdon appearing to be recovering in July, Twain made a trip to Washington, D.C., during which he met with President Grant and signed a contract with Elisha Bliss for a book that would later become

16. Steinbrink, *Getting to Be Mark Twain,* 101. I have also relied for biographical information on the excellent chronology provided by Louis Budd in *CTSS1,* 965–70.

*Roughing It.* Jervis Langdon's recovery, however, was brief. After suffering several setbacks, Olivia's father and Twain's friend and benefactor died on August 6, 1870.

Her father's illness and eventual death exacerbated Olivia's own frail health. She was pregnant with her first child, and Twain spent the months following Jervis Langdon's death nursing her and awaiting the birth of their son, Langdon, who was born one month prematurely on November 7, 1870. (Langdon would die of diphtheria on June 2, 1872.) Although these family matters consumed much of his time, Twain had further committed himself to finishing *Roughing It* by January, to continuing his monthly "Memoranda" column for the *Galaxy,* to fulfilling his Buffalo *Express* obligations, to completing a collection of sketches (finally published in 1875 as *Sketches, New and Old*), and to undertaking a book on the South African diamond mines based on data collected by John Henry Riley, a friend from his California days. For this latter project, Riley was to travel to South Africa, where a diamond frenzy similar to the Gold Rush days in Nevada was in progress. From there, he would send letters to Twain while he acquired a fortune in diamonds. Twain would write the book, and Riley would keep the diamonds. Unfortunately, by the time Riley was ready to supply Twain with material, Twain was fully engaged in the illnesses and deaths that marked his last days with the *Buffalo Express.* Twain put Riley off with excuses, and Riley contracted peritonitis from his trip and died in September 1872, before Twain could devote any time to the project.

Moreover, to add to the family woes, one of Olivia's close friends, Emma Nye, who had come to stay with them after Jervis Langdon's death, contracted typhoid fever and died at the family residence. With Livy falling dangerously ill with typhoid in February 1871, Twain decided to cease writing for the *Galaxy* in order to devote more time to the writing of books. Progress on *Roughing It* had come to a standstill, and Twain could barely keep up his commitments to the *Galaxy* and the *Express.* He also decided to put his house and interest in the *Express* up for sale, and, when Livy's health improved slightly, moved her to Elmira, where he attempted to complete his book. The house in Buffalo was advertised on the front page of the *Express* for six months and finally sold in December for $19,000, a thousand dollars less than Jervis Langdon had paid for it the previous year, not counting the carriage, coachman, staff, and furniture. Twain also lost money on his interest in the *Express* when he sold it in August 1871 to Colonel George F. Selkirk for $10,000 less than he had paid for it. The series of heartaches and tragedies that beset Twain and his family during this time seriously qualified the jubilation that he enjoyed with his marriage and residence in his Delaware Avenue home. In later years, he would describe this time as "the blackest, the gloomiest, the most wretched" of his life.[17] His immediate feelings toward Buffalo were succinctly stated in a letter he wrote to John Henry Riley on March 3, 1871, when he decided to move permanently away from the city:

> I have come at last to loathe Buffalo so bitterly (always hated it) that yesterday I advertised our dwelling house for sale, & the man that comes forward & pays us what it cost a year ago, ($25,000) can take it. Of course we won't sell the furniture, at *any* price, nor the horse, carriage or sleigh . . . We have doctors & watchers & nurses in the house *all* the time for 8 months, & I am disgusted. My wife came near dying, 2 weeks ago.
>
> I quit the Galaxy with the current number, & shall write no more for any periodical. Am offered great prices, but it's a no go. Shall simply write books. (*L4*, 337–38)[18]

As Twain closed the Buffalo chapter of his life and looked forward to his new life in Hartford, he probably had little awareness and virtually no perspective to assess the subtle, yet important, transformation that had occurred during this period. To be sure, many of his sketches in both the *Express* and the *Galaxy* are reminiscent of the burlesques, tall tales, and hoaxes that his audience had come to expect. But a more subtle moralism and social outrage can also be found that separates him from his image of "The Wild Humorist of the Pacific Slope." Steinbrink suggests that by aligning himself with the more prestigious New York magazine, the *Galaxy*, Twain was also aligning himself .

17. *Mark Twain in Eruption,* ed. Bernard DeVoto (New York: Harper and Brothers, 1940), 251.

18. Editors Victor Fischer and Michael Frank also note that "the furniture was worth '$10,000 or $12,000,' the horse, carriage, and sleigh between $3000 and $7000" (*L4*, 338n3).

more nearly with the eastern cultural establishment that supposedly provided him a discriminating, literate audience and that extended his credentials as a professional writer rather than a journalist. The Wild Humorist had become the Resident Humorist, a sign not so much that he had been tamed or traduced as that he himself was willing to exchange a measure of his touted "notoriety" for recognition as a writer of stature and substance. . . . The *Galaxy* and *Express* writing he did during the spring of 1870 shows Clemens becoming more clearly and coherently a moralist. Defining right behavior and impeaching bad had of course been a part of his satiric agenda from the beginning, but now, as he sought more and more deliberately to make his way as a professional writer, social criticism emerged unambiguously as a focus of his work.[19]

This social criticism and moral outrage can be seen in a number of places. For example, a recent court case that admitted temporary insanity as a defense strategy and resulted in acquittal provoked Twain to produce three sketches in 1870 assailing the insanity plea: "The New Crime," "Our Precious Lunatic," and "Unburlesquable Things." His ire can also be detected in his deepening racial conscience. He was particularly bitter about the unjust treatment of the Chinese in the West that he had witnessed as a reporter in San Francisco in 1865–1866 and assailed then. His most sustained attack on the problem, however, occurred while he lived in Buffalo. Imitating Oliver Goldsmith's famous series, "Letters from a Citizen of the World" (1760–1761), Twain wrote a short series comprising six letters in the *Galaxy* in October and November, 1870, under the title "Goldsmith's Friend Abroad Again." As Larry Berkove observes, "Using the fictitious Ah Song Hi, a naively idealistic Chinese Americaphile, as a narrator, Twain depicted him as deceived when he was recruited to become a coolie, when he was transported to San Francisco, and when he fell into the clutches of the law. The short series is shockingly realistic in its portrayal of the villainy of California's courts, the brutality of its jails, and the oppression of the underclass in them."[20] Likewise, his bitterly ironic "Disgraceful Persecution of a Boy," which appeared in the *Galaxy* in May 1870, assails the corrupt and brutal

19. Steinbrink, *Getting to Be Mark Twain,* 106–7.
20. "Goldsmith's Friend Abroad Again," in *The Mark Twain Encyclopedia,* ed. LeMaster and Wilson, 330.

police officers who victimize the local Chinese population. Shelley Fisher Fishkin points out:

> Twain focuses on a community that collects unlawful mining taxes from the Chinese not once but twice, whose courts convict the Chinese not just when guilty but always, whose police stand idly by when the Chinese are mugged by gangs—all occurrences he had witnessed in San Francisco. A young boy who has been taught by his elders that it was "a high and holy thing" to abuse the Chinese answers the call by stoning "a Chinaman" on his way to Sunday school. When the boy is arrested, the narrator decries the injustice of the fact that the boy "no sooner attempts to do his duty than he is punished for it."[21]

In a similar, bitterly ironic vein, Twain produced one of his most virulent attacks against miscarriages of justice in an unsigned editorial, under the title "Only a Nigger," in the *Buffalo Express* (August 26, 1869). This relatively little known piece clearly anticipates Twain's many angry responses to racial prejudices and merits reprinting in full:

> A dispatch from Memphis mentions that, of two negroes lately sentenced to death for murder in that vicinity, one named Woods has just confessed to having ravished a young lady during the war, for which deed another negro was hung at the time by an avenging mob, the evidence that doomed the guiltless wretch being a hat which Woods now relates that he stole from its owner and left behind, for the purpose of misleading. Ah, well! Too bad, to be sure! A little blunder in the administration of justice by Southern mob-law; but nothing to speak of. Only "a nigger" killed by mistake—that is all. Of course every high toned gentleman whose chivalric impulses were so unfortunately misled in this affair, by the cunning of the miscreant Woods, is as sorry about it as a high toned gentleman can be expected to be sorry about the unlucky fate of "a nigger." But mistakes will happen, even in the conduct of the best regulated and most high toned mobs, and surely there is no good reason why Southern gentlemen should worry themselves with the useless regrets, so long as only an innocent "nigger" is

---

21. "Racial Attitudes," in *The Mark Twain Encyclopedia,* ed. LeMaster and Wilson, 610.

hanged, or roasted or knouted to death, now and then. What if the
blunder of lynching the wrong man does happen once in four or five
cases! Is that any fair argument against the cultivation and indulgence
of those fine and chivalric passions and that noble Southern spirit
which will not brook the slow and cold formalities of regular law,
when outraged white womanhood appeals for vengeance? Perish the
thought so unworthy of a Southern soul! Leave it to the sentimental-
ism and humanitarianism of a cold-blooded Yankee civilization! What
are the lives of a few "niggers" in comparison with the preservation of
the impetuous instincts of a proud and fiery race? Keep ready the hal-
ter, therefore, oh chivalry of Memphis! Keep the lash knotted; keep
the brand and the faggots in waiting, for prompt work with the next
"nigger" who may be suspected of any damnable crime! Wreak a swift
vengeance upon him, for the satisfaction of the noble impulses that
animate knightly hearts, and then leave time and accident to discover, if they will, whether he was guilty or not.[22]

This piece is important for a number of reasons. That Twain did not sign
the piece was not, in itself, unusual, since he produced numerous unsigned
editorials while at the *Express,* some even dealing with controversial political issues, but the moral outrage contained in it anticipated racial subjects
that he would return to frequently. Twain may have recognized that the vit-
riolic nature of the piece, while deeply felt, might have created an undesir-
able controversy. Similarly, much later in his career he chose not to publish
his essay "The United States of Lyncherdom," in which he directed his outrage directly and without an ironic voice at his home state of Missouri concerning a subject about which he became obsessed. He also withheld from
publication some of his more controversial religious opinions found in
works like *Letters from the Earth* or the *Mysterious Stranger Manuscripts,* to
name only two, recognizing that the public was not ready for and would
not welcome such efforts.

In the end, despite Twain's assertion to John Henry Riley that he "loathed"
Buffalo, there is no denying that his time there played a crucial role in his
personal and artistic evolution. While he never completely abandoned his

22. Text reprinted from *Mark Twain at the "Buffalo Express,"* ed. McCullough and McIntire-
Strasburg, 22–23.

bohemian tendencies, and while he continued to travel often both in the United States and abroad, he discovered that he preferred the amenities and opportunities offered in urban environments. For one thing, even though he was always ambivalent about the benefits of wealth and power, he no longer wished to return to a life lived on the move with scant resources. With his move to Hartford and the completion of his second book, *Roughing It,* Mark Twain had, in some subtle and complex way, become urbanized.

# Mark Twain's Music Box

*Livy, Cosmopolitanism, and the Commodity Aesthetic*

KERRY DRISCOLL

**WHEN** Mark Twain first visited Hartford in 1868, he was dazzled by both the beauty of the city's natural environs and the gracious lifestyle of its prosperous inhabitants. He enthusiastically described his impressions of the city in San Francisco's *Alta California* newspaper, pronouncing it "the best built and handsomest town I have ever seen" and "a vision of refreshing green."[1] Indeed, "you do not know what beauty is," the writer smugly informed his western readers, "if you have not

I would like to offer special thanks to four individuals without whose assistance this essay would never have come to fruition. Patti Philippon, the Archivist at the Twain House and Museum in Hartford, and Bob Hirst, the General Editor of the Mark Twain Papers and Project at the University of California, Berkeley, were both instrumental in providing me with many of the primary documents I've used in constructing this narrative. Gerry Wright, the owner of Rita Ford Music Boxes, a Manhattan firm specializing in the restoration and sale of these antique devices, shared a wealth of technical information regarding the various types of music boxes manufactured during Twain's era and the diverse range of sounds that each produced. Julius Rubin, my dear friend and colleague at Saint Joseph College, through the many incisive questions he posed over coffee at Starbucks, helped me to shape and hone my argument about Twain's cosmopolitanism. All four were incredibly patient, generous, and kind in fielding my incessant questions.

1. Twain's descriptions of Hartford appeared as part of his "Letters from Washington" series, published in the *Alta California,* March 3 and September 8, 1868, respectively. The complete texts of these articles can be found online at www.twainquotes.com.

been here." Twain was particularly smitten with Hartford's broad avenues and stately dwellings, each situated in "about an acre of green grass, or flower beds or ornamental shrubbery, guarded on all sides by the trimmest hedges of arbor-vitae, and by files of huge forest trees that cast a shadow like a thunder-cloud." To the visitor's admiring gaze, the city seemed an oasis of genteel affluence; "Where are the poor of Hartford?" he mused, only to admit, "I confess I do not know. They are 'corralled,' doubtless—corralled in some unsanctified corner of this paradise whither my feet have not yet wandered." The urban Eden that Twain constructed in the pages of the *Alta*—a place where "morality and huckleberries flourished"—is a capitalist fantasy in which wealth and beauty are conflated, poverty is rendered invisible, and stylish comfort is the social norm: "Hartford has a population of 40,000 souls," he noted, "and the most of them ride in sleighs. That is a sign of prosperity, and a knowledge of how to live—isn't it?"

Twain's extravagant praise of Hartford attests, in part, to the vigor of the city's thriving economy. By the end of the 1860s, Connecticut's capital was a leading center of diversified industry—insurance, subscription book publishing, and firearms manufacturing—and widely heralded as "the richest city in the United States."[2] Yet his whimsical equation of sleigh riding with an optimal "knowledge of how to live" suggests that Hartford's allure transcended material wealth. The city in fact epitomized the "good life" to Twain, an ideal of elegance, status, and sophistication that he aspired to but could not then afford—ruefully acknowledging that "to live in this style one must have his bank account, of course." This vision of Hartford's "uniform grandeur," albeit cursory and ingenuous, nonetheless captivated the young writer and played a pivotal role in his decision to permanently relocate there three years later.

Twain arrived in the city in October 1871 at the age of thirty-six—ambitious, upwardly mobile, his literary star ascendant—with his pregnant wife and eleven-month-old infant in tow. The young family set up housekeeping in rented quarters at the Forest Street home of John and Isabella Beecher Hooker and began the gradual process of immersing themselves in the so-

2. Charles Hopkins Clark, "The Charter Oak City," *Scribner's Monthly* 16:5 (November 1876): 2; see also George Parsons Lathrop, "A Model State Capital," *Harper's New Monthly Magazine* 71:425 (October 1885): 715.

cial and intellectual life of the "sterling old Puritan community" (*L2,* 166) known as Nook Farm. This neighborhood, a one-hundred- acre wooded tract established in 1851 at the city's western edge by Hooker and his brother-in-law Francis Gillette, was regarded as Hartford's "choicest residential district."[3] Its professional, middle-class inhabitants were highly educated, well-traveled, and socially conscious; they also—rather ominously—collectively embraced a luxurious standard of living that often exceeded their means.

Sam and Livy concretized their commitment to this Gilded Age lifestyle in 1873 by purchasing a parcel of land on Farmington Avenue and hiring architect Edward Tuckerman Potter to design and build the stately nineteen-room mansion that would serve as the family's primary residence for the next seventeen years. Between 1874 and 1891, Twain amassed and subsequently lost a great fortune and became not only the most successful writer in America but also an international celebrity. The evolution of his status as a transnational figure may be gauged by many variables—the foreign sales of his books; the number of languages into which they were translated; his prominence in the world press. It is my contention, however, that the development of Twain's cosmopolitan identity can be read on a more intimate, domestic level by examining the lavish manner in which he and Livy decorated their Hartford home. For in the protracted process of selecting and acquiring these furnishings, the writer discovered that beauty, wealth, and style, while complexly interrelated, were by no means synonymous. The mysterious "knowledge of how to live" that he had observed in Hartford's sleigh-riding citizens back in 1868 also required the cultivation of discernment and good taste, ineffable qualities that could not be bought—regardless of the size of one's bank account—but derived only through careful imitation of models found both in books and in the abodes of more discriminating acquaintances.

The Clemenses' respectful deference to the aesthetic standards of their Nook Farm neighbors is illustrated by two anecdotes in Isabella Beecher Hooker's 1876 diary.[4] When Twain's lecture agent Frank Fuller and his wife visited Hartford on May 17, Sam and Livy took them to view the Hookers'

---

3. Kenneth Andrews, *Nook Farm: Mark Twain's Hartford Circle* (Cambridge: Harvard University Press, 1950), 4.

4. In the frontispiece of this unpublished document, housed at the Connecticut Historical Society in Hartford, Isabella wrote: "These notes are strictly private and to be read only by my

Mark Twain's Hartford home, circa 1885, as illustrated in *Harper's Monthly*. The accompanying text describes the writer's residence as "the most delightful of houses, [set] in the pleasantest part of the city, just where it ceases to be visible as city at all, and merges into rolling hill and dale." (Courtesy Mark Twain House and Museum, Hartford, Connecticut)

collection of European bric-a-brac. "They were thoroughly appreciative of these rooms," Isabella noted approvingly, "and seemed [particularly] carried away with the study, which is one memento of our travels."[5] Almost seven months later, on December 4, she reciprocated the social call, bringing one of her friends to tour the interior of the Clemenses' home. This visit, however—at least in Isabella's recollection—took an acrimonious turn

---

husband and children in case of my death." Below this inscription is a later notation in an unidentified hand: "Private diary of Isabella (Beecher) Hooker, wife of John Hooker of Hartford. Found in 1934 among waste in a barn in Hartford." Such are the sobering vicissitudes of time.

5. Hooker Diary, 5. Quoted with the permission of the Connecticut Historical Society, Hartford.

due to a pointed remark she made regarding one of the couple's recent purchases:

> [Nancy] enjoyed the house much but I had an unfortunate interview with Mr. C. . . . I joked with him about not caring for a pretty lampshade after he had found it so very cheap—& he was vexed & said something about things going around the neighborhood & explained that he had no taste or judgment himself & so when an established house said a thing was good & charged a good price for it he felt sure that it was worthy of Livy & that was all he cared for.[6]

This incident exposes an unpleasant dimension of Nook Farm's much extolled social intimacy: gossip. Despite the community's lofty, high-minded character, idle chatter of the most trifling sort permeated it; thus, the Clemenses' acquisition of a "cheap" albeit "pretty" lampshade bizarrely qualified as news. Moreover, Isabella's characterization of Twain's defensive behavior is quite revealing. Visibly discomfited at both the apparent scrutiny to which this insignificant object has been subjected as well as his neighbor's meddlesome stance as a self-appointed arbiter of household aesthetics, the writer blurts out an extraordinary confession—that he himself possesses "no taste or judgment"—and must therefore rely upon an extrinsic authority (in this case, a reputable merchant) in order to validate a thing's worth. Undeterred by this forthright admission of inadequacy, Mrs. Hooker continues her verbal sparring, blithely pointing out the risks of such naive, misplaced trust:

> I said oh that was handsomely said but really as a matter of fact I thought one often paid a high price for a homely article under such circumstances—which he didn't seem to like & again spoke of being talked about. When I said why it was all a joke as I heard it & retailed it—& one so given to joking as himself mustn't mind it etc.—but his eyes flashed & he looked really angry—though Livy coming in then & hearing only the last sentence about cheap things not being worth presenting, said most lovingly—'Why yes, dear I think they are—no matter how small the gift, the thoughtfulness & love make them valu-

6. Ibid., 193; quoted in Andrews, *Nook Farm*, 86.

able'—but as this helped my side he did not seem to relish it & I felt uncomfortable.[7]

The intensity of Twain's response—eyes flashing, temper flaring—suggests that much more is at stake in this conversation than a mere lampshade. Rather, the commodity functions as what Karl Marx terms a "social hieroglyphic,"[8] signifying status, class hierarchy, and an abstract ideal of beauty. In accusing the writer of "not caring for" this decorative object despite its attractive appearance, Hooker is impugning his lack of both taste and sophistication.

Just three years after this contentious encounter, however, a Scottish evangelist named Henry Drummond visited Clemens in his Hartford home. Recounting his meeting with the author in a letter to a friend, Drummond stated: "[Mark Twain] is funnier than any of his books, and to my surprise a most respected citizen, devoted to things esthetic, and a friend of the poor and struggling."[9] The "surprise" expressed in this statement is significant; expecting to find a tamed version of "the wild humorist of the Pacific Slope," Drummond instead encountered an urbane, sophisticated individual—a thoughtful, politically engaged citizen, a philanthropist, and, perhaps most remarkably, an aesthete—a far cry from the man who claimed to have "no taste" in December 1876. Notwithstanding the subjectivity that informs these radically disparate impressions, the writer's demeanor and domestic persona appear to have undergone a dramatic transformation during this period—but how? And more important, why?

## II

In large part, the answer to these questions lies in the sixteen-month sojourn Clemens and his family made to Europe between April 1878 and August 1879. This excursion was undertaken for several reasons—economic, creative, and cultural. By closing their Hartford house just three and a half

---

7. Hooker Diary, 194–95; quoted in Andrews, *Nook Farm,* 86–87.
8. Marx, *Capital,* trans. Samuel Moore and Edward Aveling (New York: Modern Library, 1936), 85.
9. Quoted in Albert Bigelow Paine, *Mark Twain: A Biography,* 2 vols. (New York: Chelsea House Publishers), 2:661.

years after moving into it, the Clemenses hoped to significantly reduce expenses related to entertaining, upkeep, and domestic staff. The months abroad also offered Twain both space and time—the first, a welcome reprieve from the stinging humiliation of the Whittier Birthday dinner debacle of the previous December; the second, an opportunity to write a new travel book and reassess a number of other stalled projects. In terms of the creation of the writer's cosmopolitan identity, however, the trip's raison d'être was cultural edification—a kind of midlife version of the "Grand Tour." During their extended stay abroad, the family members would not be idle tourists but students, engaged in an ambitious program of self-improvement orchestrated largely by Livy. The earnest, high-minded sense of purpose with which she embraced this agenda is reflected in a letter written to her mother in January 1879: "Munich is a fascinating, interesting city—we feel as if there is so very much here of interest to see, yet we are so busy with our studies that we seem to get little time for outside matters."[10] These "studies" involved learning to read and speak German (the family would also hire a French tutor in Paris); taking drawing lessons; attending the opera; and dutifully touring museums in each metropolis they visited. Livy undertook this last activity with particular diligence, spending four out of five mornings in one week at Florence's Pitti Palace and Uffizi Gallery; as she solemnly informed her mother, the appreciation of great art required both time and intense focus: "One ought to know no one when they are visiting picture galleries."[11]

Twain was, for the most part, a willing—if somewhat bemused—participant in this enterprise. Although he joked in a letter to Howells that "Mrs. Clemens even reads note-books in her hunger for culture" (*MTHL1*, 236), he also took great pride in her budding connoisseurship. In a Christmas note to Mrs. Langdon, he asked her to thank his sister-in-law Susan Crane for her generous holiday gift, explaining that Livy planned to use the money to buy him something special: "She has not made up her mind yet what she will select, *but no matter it will be well and wisely and tastefully selected*"

10. Olivia Langdon Clemens (OLC) to Olivia Lewis Langdon (OLL), January 1, 1879. Quoted with the permission of MTH&M.
11. OLC to OLL, October 21, 1978 (MTH&M).

(emphasis added).[12] Moreover, he privately shared Livy's desire for cultural enrichment, telling Joe Twichell in January 1879:

> My crude plans are crystallizing. As the thing stands now, I went to
> Europe for three purposes. The first you *know* and must keep secret,
> even from the Blisses; the second is to study Art; and the third is to ac-
> quire a critical knowledge of the German language. My MS shows that
> the two latter objects are already accomplished. It shows that I am now
> moving about as an Artist and Philologist, & unaware that there is any
> immodesty in assuming these titles. Having three definite objects has
> had the effect of seeming to enlarge my domain & give me the free-
> dom of a loose costume. It is three strings to my bow, too.[13]

Despite the obvious self-mockery of Twain's pretension in "moving about as
an Artist and Philologist," the overarching sincerity of his tone suggests that
he regarded these endeavors as fundamentally worthwhile—adding depth
and breadth to his worldview and simultaneously liberating him from the
narrowly confining role of humorist.

The ambitious course of studies Livy planned for her family also involved
a pragmatic corollary—shopping—lots of it. In cultivating an appreciation
of the Old Masters, she sought to develop a more discriminating sense of
personal taste, which would in turn inspire her confidence as a consumer.
Even though the Clemenses had lived in their Farmington Avenue home for
several years, the home's interior decor remained very much a work in
progress. Most of the furniture had come from their first residence in Buffalo, purchased as a wedding gift by Mr. and Mrs. Langdon. While Livy no
doubt had a hand in choosing the style and color of those original furnish-

12. Samuel Langhorne Clemens (SLC) to OLL, December 26, 1878 (UCCL 01617, MTPO,
2007). Quoted with the permission of the Mark Twain Papers, Bancroft Library, University of
California, Berkeley.
13. SLC to Joseph Hopkins Twichell, January 26, 1879 (UCCL 01577, MTPO, 2007). In a
letter to William Dean Howells written four days later, Clemens described the plan of *A Tramp
Abroad* similarly: "In my book I allow it to appear,—casually & without stress,—that I am
over here to make the tour of Europe *on foot* . . . but mount the first conveyance that offers,
making but slight explanation or excuse, & endeavoring to seem unconscious that this is not
legitimate pedestrianizing. My second object here is to become a German scholar; my third,
to study Art, & learn to paint" (*MTHL1*, 249).

ings, they overwhelmingly reflected the formal midcentury aesthetic favored by her parents' generation. The European excursion thus offered a
perfect opportunity for the Clemenses to decorate their Hartford house as
*they* saw fit—namely, in accordance with the prevailing international style
favored by the Hookers and other Nook Farm residents. The look Livy aspired to emulate—cultured, worldly, eclectic—is illustrated by the following description in *Harper's Monthly* of neighbor Charles Dudley Warner's
residence:

> The house is charming in all its appointments, and especially rich in
> bric-a-brac, much of it Oriental, collected by the owner during his
> several tours in Europe, the East, and Africa . . . over the sideboard
> [in the music room] hangs "The Martyrdom of Santa Barbara," by
> Vasquez, a contemporary, perhaps pupil of Velasquez. . . . The man-
> telpiece is unique. It is made of Saracenic tiles framed in California
> redwood. Most of the tiles are wall tiles from ancient houses in Da-
> mascus and Cairo, one from the Mosque of Omar, in Jerusalem, and
> some small ones at the side from the pavement of the courts in the Al-
> hambra.[14]

This cluttered, quintessentially Victorian interior is a pastiche of the exotic
and the antique; its rich profusion of bric-a-brac not only creates a distinctive ambience but also reifies Warner's identity as an aesthete and inveter-
ate traveler. These objects, assiduously "collected by the owner," represent
the culmination of a four-part process: consumption, possession, accumulation, and display.[15] In purchasing a diverse array of decorative objects
abroad, Livy hoped to infuse the public rooms on the first floor of their Hartford home with a similarly cosmopolitan flair.

   By all accounts, Mrs. Clemens was an eager, indefatigable consumer, repeatedly "tempted" (as she herself characterized it) and seduced by the
"singularly pretty" wares showcased in "such marvelous places" as Le Bon
Marche.[16] Her steadfast pursuit of this avocation is reflected in a Septem-

14. George Parsons Lathrop, "A Model State Capital," 726.
   15. Bill Brown, *A Sense of Things: The Object Matter of American Literature* (Chicago: University of Chicago Press, 2003), 48.
   16. The theme of temptation (along with its requisite corollary, guilt) recurs throughout

ber 1878 letter Twain wrote his mother-in-law from Geneva: "A day or two ago Livy & I drove to [Chamonix] in a two-horse carriage & remained a day—9 hours' drive thither & 9 hours back. It tired Livy out & she went to bed early last night—but she is out shopping again today."[17] Livy's passion for acquiring things typifies what Jean-Christophe Agnew calls a "commodity aesthetic"—"a way of seeing the world in general, and the self and society in particular, as so much raw space to be furnished with mobile, detachable, and transactionable goods." Such an aesthetic, Agnew contends, "celebrates those moments when the very boundaries between the self and the commodity world collapse in the act of purchase," and objects become "interchangeable" with the owner's identity, tacitly conveying information about his or her gender, social class, knowledge, and competence. A commodity aesthetic therefore regards consumption "not as a waste or use, but as deliberate and informed accumulation," out of which the self is "at once improvised and imprisoned, constructed and confined."[18]

Deliberate and informed accumulation was very much part of Livy's agenda for the trip. Before boarding the *Holsatia* in April 1878, she made a detailed list—complete with measurements—of various household furnishings she intended to purchase overseas. Her European diary, which more closely resembles an account book, contains page after page of notes such as "Pictures for hall, 2 ft. high & 1 ft. to 1½ ft. wide"; "glass transparency or something to hang in the northwest window of the bay in the drawing room 23¼ in by 40 in. inside the sash"; and "stands or fancy arrangements of any kind . . . 2ft. 6 in. long—as high as necessary. Not very

---

Livy's descriptions of shopping abroad, suggesting that—perhaps as a result of her early religious training—she had inherited a Calvinistic mistrust of the seductive power of material things. Anticipating her visit to Paris in the spring of 1879, for example, Livy wrote her mother from Munich: "Mrs. Smith from Heidelberg said when she was here that everything in Paris was beautiful and tempting beyond measure—so perhaps you better send me the measurements [for the guest room curtains], then in case I see anything that I feel sure about I can get it" (February 2, 1879, MTH&M). Similarly, after splurging on at least twenty pieces of furniture in Venice, she told her mother, "We are feeling very poverty-stricken just now [because] we have spent so much in Italy—I don't know as we have done right, but it is such a temptation when things seem so reasonable and you get such a good premium on your line of credit" (January 19, 1879, MTH&M).

17. SLC to OLL, September 1, 1878 (UCCL 01593, MTPO, 2007).

18. Agnew, "A House of Fiction: Domestic Interiors and the Commodity Aesthetic," in *Consuming Visions: Accumulation and Display of Goods in America, 1880–1920*, ed. Simon Bonner (New York: W. W. Norton, 1989), 135–36.

deep—because they are by the side of the door as you enter the room"
(MTP). She also actively enlisted her husband in this endeavor, as indicated by the following entry in his hand:

> Livy dear
> Dining Room
> From library door to window = 53 in.
>     "            to hall door = 55½ in.
>     "   sideboard to china closet door = 44 in.
>     "   sideboard to window = 39½ in. (MTP)

The specificity of these dimensions suggests that Livy's shopping was neither
capricious nor haphazard, indulging whatever passing fancy caught her
eye, but purposeful—even strategic. According to French theorist Jean Baudrillard, consumption is "an active form of relationship not only to objects
but also to society and to the world," wherein the materiality of things is su-
perseded by their "psychological and sociological reality": "Human beings
and objects are indeed bound together in a collusion in which the objects
take on a certain density, an emotional value—what might be called a 'presence.' What gives the houses of our childhood such depth and resonance in
memory is clearly this complex structure of interiority, and the objects within it serve for us as boundary markers of the symbolic configuration known
as home." Within the paradigm Baudrillard proposes, the object functions as
a *miroir parfait*—perfect mirror—"precisely because it sends back not real
images but desired ones," in terms both of the owner's identity and of how
he or she wishes to be perceived.[19] As such, the commodities Livy purchased
abroad were intended to construct an image of wealth, sophistication, and
refinement that would both enhance and advance her husband's reputation.

    In the same diary where Livy recorded her measurements of specific in-
terior spaces, she itemized the cost of each purchase she made in Europe;
these entries—in aggregate—document a shopping spree of truly epic proportions. Within a period of sixteen months, she spent nearly five thousand
dollars on household furnishings—a staggering sum, equivalent to ap-

---

19. Baudrillard, *The System of Objects,* trans. James Benedict (London and New York: Ver-
so Publishers, 1996), 217, 6, 14, 96.

proximately a hundred thousand dollars in today's currency.[20] The sheer volume of these goods filled some twenty-two freight packages (*Interviews*, 25), *excluding* the elaborately carved bedstead, library table, chest, chairs, and other miscellaneous furniture the family purchased in Venice and shipped home separately. The diary also reveals that Livy took little interest in haute couture or fine jewelry; her shopping focused not on personal adornment but on home decor. Many of her acquisitions related to entertaining—table linens, sterling silver, brass chargers, porcelain dishes, Venetian glass—while others were purely decorative in nature: pottery, rugs, mirrors, carved picture frames, and assorted bric-a-brac. She and Sam also bought reproductions of classical paintings they had seen and admired, such as Andrea Del Sarto's *Holy Family*, Rosso Fiorentino's *The Three Fates*, and a Rembrandt self-portrait (*N&J2*, 222); these artworks would grace the walls of their drawing room and library, visual reminders of the family's travels and cultured sensibility. In addition, they visited the studios of several American expatriate artists and purchased a few small pieces of original art—Elihu Vedder's *Young Medusa* and an unidentified watercolor by Gedney Bunce. Like bourgeois, law-abiding versions of the souvenir-hunting "American Vandal" whom Twain had satirized nearly a decade earlier in *The Innocents Abroad,* Mr. and Mrs. Clemens moved leisurely through Europe—armed not with chisels but with a sizable line of credit—amassing elegant objects for the ornamentation of their Hartford home.

Given that domestic economy was one of the primary reasons for undertaking the trip, expenditures of this magnitude seem counterintuitive, difficult to justify. Yet Sam and Livy rationalized them in two ways. First, furnishings of this sort cost less abroad than in the United States and were therefore "bargains." Twain's acceptance of this relativistic logic is reflected in a notebook entry from October 1878; under the heading "Bought to-day," he listed eight pieces of furniture, plus "1 carved Bellows" and "1 small picture," then added up the total cost, concluding with apparent satisfaction, "These things are amazingly cheap" (*N&J2*, 198). A second, more compelling, rationale was that, for the most part, they weren't spending their

20. For specific information on how this figure was derived, see "Five Ways to Compute the Relative Value of a U.S. Dollar Amount, 1790–2005" at www.measuringworth.com. My thanks to Dr. Shyamala Raman, professor of economics and international studies at Saint Joseph College, for directing me to this helpful Web site.

own money. Throughout their European stay, Livy's letters to her mother contain effusive expressions of gratitude for the periodic infusions of cash sent from Elmira: "Oh Mother you are too good to send us *so much money.* It is too much—you are so good to us," "so lavish with us in every way. We do appreciate it and thank you so much for it."[21] Although the exact amount of Mrs. Langdon's largesse is uncertain, a letter Livy wrote from Paris about a month before the family returned home suggests that her mother in fact subsidized the vast majority of the family's overseas purchases:

> I was reading over to Mr. Clemens yesterday the things that I had bought on this side with the money that you had given me. I said, *"When we get home Mother will see that about all the handsome things we have bought she has given us"*—Mr. Clemens said, "You better not tell Mother, she'll be wanting to take her money back"—I still have over three hundred dollars left, part of that is the Christmas money—I am going to get some stained glass with that when we get to London— Mr. Clemens suggested that I reserve it to pay the duties with, now wasn't that like a man? *I answered that if Mother would give me the things on this side, I would see to getting them home.* I feel as if I wanted you all to see the things at once and of course you can't until you come to Hartford. (emphasis added)[22]

As this passage attests, Livy's correspondence with her mother—chatty, confiding, at times unexpectedly girlish—sheds significant light on the interpersonal and cultural tensions underlying the excursion. Many of the let-

21. OLC to OLL, November 20, 1878, and April 28, 1879 (MTH&M). Prior to the family's departure for Europe, Mrs. Langdon gave her daughter a substantial cash gift, for which Livy thanked her profusely soon after arriving in Germany: "Mother the money that you gave me does make me feel so rich I feel on account of it some way taken care of by you. I feel so much freer because I have that money I shall write you everything that I buy with it—the only thing I have bought so far is some common gloves—they were very soft, nice kid, 3 buttons for 87 cents and 4 buttons for $1.00" (April 26, 1878, MTH&M). Livy was apparently true to her word, for almost every letter she wrote home contains detailed descriptions of her various purchases.

22. OLC to OLL, July 6, 1879 (MTH&M). Several months earlier, Mrs. Langdon had also generously offered Sam and Livy a thousand dollars to cover the expense of painting and wallpapering the interior of their Hartford home upon the family's return from Europe that fall. Although Livy graciously declined the money, stating, "Mother dear, I think you are the very best mother in the world how could you offer me that thousand dollars! [However] we have no need of it now," she insinuated that the gift would be welcome at a later date: "When we

ters, for example, have a poignant quality in that her spouse is frequently offstage, spending his days immersed in the composition of *A Tramp Abroad* at one of the many studios he rented for that purpose. Livy, in contrast, emerges as a woman of leisure—largely freed from the responsibilities of child care by the presence of nursemaid Rosina Hay—with a great deal of time on her hands. Shopping therefore was not merely an indulgence but a pleasant diversion with which to occupy her otherwise idle hours. Writing from Baden-Baden in August 1878, she described the quaint charm of browsing *en plein air*:

> Oh this is such a pretty town. The little shops are so very attractive, just think of shopping outdoors, how I do wish that I could give you some idea of these shops—the counters are right on the side walks so that you can do your errands without stopping inside the door—there is a dense shade from the trees & the shop keepers will sit out under these trees at little stands with their work, when they are warm, & when you indicate that you want to buy something and are not simply looking at the things then the shop keeper will leave the little table on the side walk and go inside the shop & wait on you—it all seems so leisurely & cool & pleasant—you are tempted to go there & walk up and down & look at things even if you don't want to buy.[23]

Given the manifold sensory delights of this experience—"so leisurely & cool & pleasant"—it is perhaps not surprising that Livy's European letters are filled with offers—to her mother, sister, sister-in-law, and friends—volunteering her services as a personal shopper: "Isn't there something that you want to send for?" she cajoled her brother Charlie in July 1878; "I like so much to do shopping over here and particularly if other people are to pay for the things that I get—then there is no drawback to the buying." Similarly, she told her mother that autumn, "I love dearly to have you send

---

get home we will talk it over and if it then seems best to decorate and you feel at that time that you have a thousand dollars that you desire to part with, I think a thousand dollars would do all to the house that we should care to have done—and I should be very glad to accept it—although I feel like a pig, mother, to contemplate accepting it at all" (April 28, 1879, MTH&M).

23. OLC to OLL, August 4, 1878 (MTH&M).

commissions for it is simply fun in these places where I have plenty of time—so send for anything that you may happen to want." As time passed, however, Livy's offers grew importune—"And Mother anything else that you or Sue or Ida or the children want and would like to trust Clara [Spaulding] and me to get, do send for it, for we are glad to have the errands to do"—suggesting that she felt bored, adrift, in need of some concrete task to lend structure and purpose to her days.[24]

Livy's letters to her mother also demonstrate that while she actively promoted the family's cultural edification, she nonetheless found it wearisome at times—more a duty, externally imposed by considerations of appearance and social class, than a genuine pleasure. In describing her thrill at the prospect of visiting Florence's Pitti Palace, for example, she giddily wrote, "Doesn't it seem wonderful I am seeing all these well-known places"; once inside the museum, however, she grew quickly fatigued and her attention flagged: "In the gallery . . . we did not feel real enthusiasm—I could not take in the pictures, so after staying a little while I came back to rest." Apparently, Livy found the *idea* of viewing great art more scintillating than the actual experience. Several days later, she reported: "We have had a rich week this past week enjoying the galleries—we spent four mornings . . . in them—two in the Pitti & two in the Uffizi & we should be glad if we had the time to spend four more. There are loads of pictures that are to us uninteresting but there are so many that are intensely interesting, attractive, pleasing, & many so strong."[25]

The banal generalizations Livy used to describe these masterworks of Italian Renaissance painting—"attractive," "pleasing," "so strong"—suggest a casual and, at best, superficial interest in art history. Similarly, after visiting Elihu Vedder's studio in Rome, she commented rather lamely, "he had such a large amount of pictures and such an infinite variety of subjects," but made no mention of either specific works or distinctive features of the artist's style; as at the Pitti Palace, her consciousness merely registered "loads" of undifferentiated canvases. Yet because Vedder was a living artist rather than an Old Master, she viewed his work through the lens of consumerism, perceiving it first and foremost as a commodity—expensive, highly desirable,

24. OLC to Charles Jervis Langdon, July 21, 1878; OLC to OLL, November 20, 1878, and February 2, 1879 (MTH&M).
25. OLC to OLL, October 21, 1878 (MTH&M).

but unfortunately out of reach—hence her telling remark: "I felt as if I could spend two thousand dollars there if I had it to spend."[26] In contrast to these anemic descriptions of art, Livy's prose positively sparkles when discussing her true passion—shopping. Writing to her mother from Venice in October 1878, she excitedly recounted—in language that is detailed, precise, and brimming with superlatives—the various pieces of furniture she had recently purchased:

> This week . . . I have done a good deal of shopping, how I should like to talk over all the things with you—When we get the things home you will see how many of them you have given us—We have bought several most beautiful pieces of wood carving & I am very anxious to see them in our house—There is now standing in the room a carved chest that I have bought for our hall . . . We have [also] ordered made a cabinet of drawers for the bay window in the library to stand where that little stand with books has always been. Then we found a most wonderful old carved bedstead that was a great beauty—that we got for our room—I do hope these things will all prove when we get them home what they seem to be—I am always afraid that there will be some rotten or bad place in them . . .
>
> Then this week we have been visiting old curiosity shops. They are wonderfully interesting—among lots of rubbish you find a great deal that you would like to own. I should even like the rubbish thrown in, but none of these things are cheap, there is such a demand for them that they ask high prices—& then you generally get a reproduction of the old & not the old itself—
>
> I found an old apron in one of these shops. It was very heavy silk tapestry with flowers woven on it—in asking the price of it I found that there was a little child's apron & two large sleeves that all belonged together—it will make plenty of stuff to cover a large chair & will I think be very pretty—I do hope you will enjoy what we buy when we get it home Mother dear.[27]

The obvious pleasure Livy derived from these objects—particularly the serendipitous junk shop discovery of three matching pieces of silk tapes-

26. OLC to OLL, November 10, 1878 (MTH&M).
27. OLC to OLL, October 13, 1878 (MTH&M).

try—corresponds directly with their anticipated use in her beloved Hartford home. Thus, in her mind's eye, the tapestry was instantly transformed
into a "very pretty" chair covering, while the custom-made cabinet was already ensconced in its designated nook beneath "the bay window in the library." These details suggest that, even while the Clemenses were abroad,
the family residence on Farmington Avenue indisputably remained the
emotional locus of Livy's being; in this respect, the tremendous energy she
invested in decorating it from afar proved therapeutic, an antidote to the
homesickness that plagued her throughout the excursion.

Indeed, shopping anchored and sustained Livy in several ways—af-
fording a safe, clearly delimited point of entry into European life on the
one hand, while simultaneously reaffirming her ties to Hartford on the other. "I am glad our home is in America," she enthusiastically announced to
her mother a few months after arriving in Germany; "I enjoy it as much as
possible here but *I should not like to think of living here always, of this being
any home*—I would rather live just where I do than any place that I know
of—and I can only hope that we shall always have money enough so that
we can continue to live there" (emphasis added).[28] Livy's letters also indicate that she found the moral laxity of European life troubling and offensive; when the family stopped in a small French town en route from
Switzerland to Italy in September 1878, for example, she observed disap-
provingly:

> Oh how different this town is on a Sunday from any American town—
> such quantities of idlers standing about—such an aimless look about
> everybody—the young women dressed in their Sunday clothes and
> standing in their shop doors—that seeming to be all of life to them—
> oh how I do dislike the French—and I am more and more thankful
> that I am an American—I believe the old puritan education brings bet-
> ter men and women than any of these looser methods—perhaps they
> were too severe but they certainly leaned toward the wiser course.[29]

Rather than acclimating to European life as the months passed, Livy found
her sense of cultural dislocation growing more profound; writing to her

28. OLC to OLL, June 9, 1878 (MTH&M).
29. OLC to OLL, September 15, 1878 (MTH&M).

mother from Paris in June 1879, she announced: "I have a great longing to get back to my settled ways—there seems no good bottom here—everything seems sandy and uncertain . . . how I should hate to bring the children up here—I am afraid it would take more strength of mind than I possess to draw the line where it ought to be drawn—I am glad we live in Hartford."[30]

Unlike Livy, Clemens was not especially enthusiastic about shopping; the curiosity shops she delighted in were his "pet detestation," filled with worthless junk sold at exorbitant prices. He grumbled in his notebook about visiting a number of such stores near Heidelberg, where he "examined 3 brass beer mugs (crippled) & 5 ancient & hideously ugly & elaborately figured & ornamented (noseless) Nuremberg earthenware ones. Price, brass, from 250 to 650 M each—the others from 550 to 1100 marks each. I wouldn't have such rubbish in the house. I do hate this antiquarian rot, sham, humbug; cannot keep my temper in such a place—& *never* voluntarily enter one" (*N&J2*, 256).

New commodities, particularly quaint folkloric objects produced by local craftsmen for the tourist trade, also elicited the writer's disdain. In *A Tramp Abroad,* he discusses how the experience of being surrounded by carved cuckoo clocks in Lucerne induced a brief frenzy of shopping: "The first day, I would have bought a hundred and fifty of these clocks if I had had the money,—and I did buy three,—but on the third day the disease had run its course, I had convalesced, and was in the market once more,—trying to sell. However, I had no luck; which was just as well, for the things will be pretty enough, no doubt, when I get them home" (*TA*, 262). Twain aptly characterizes consumerism here as a "disease," a fever of irrational enthusiasm and acquisitiveness to which he succumbed, then quickly recovered. In the clear-eyed sobriety of the incident's aftermath, he sought to divest himself of these inane timepieces; failing that, he rationalized the expenditure by declaring that they would look "pretty enough" back in Hartford. Clemens's ambivalence toward material possessions, both old and new, suggests that he had not internalized the "commodity aesthetic" as fully as his wife had; nonetheless, his frame of reference in evaluating their merit was identical to hers—a culturally loaded concept of "home." As he informed Howells from Heidelberg in June 1878, his goal was to always

---

30. OLC to OLL, June 1879 (MTH&M).

have sufficient income "to live in Hartford on a generous scale" (*MTHL1*, 237).

Despite his aversion to shopping, the writer was by no means immune to the seductive power of things. On December 2, 1878, for example, he thanked his mother-in-law for her "sumptuous birthday present" of a brass pitcher (which she paid for, but Livy selected and bought in Munich), declaring: "A covered Krug of beaten brass (& gilded in addition,) is not a common spectacle in any country; & we all enjoy the grace & splendor of this thing as much as we do its utility & its rarity."[31] Twain's description of the pitcher offers an important insight into his mind-set as a consumer: he admires not only the physical beauty of the object's luster and well-proportioned shape but also its status as a "rarity"—explicitly noting that such a thing is "not a common spectacle *in any country*" (emphasis added). Perhaps even more tellingly, his use of the term *spectacle*—with its denotation of public, quasi-theatrical display, intended to impress—suggests that Twain shared Livy's vision of home as a cosmopolitan showplace and willingly assisted in its creation. Indeed, the twin criteria of "rarity" and "splendor" guided many of Mr. and Mrs. Clemens's purchases abroad—though not with uniformly positive results. While in Venice, they made several visits to the workshop of cabinetmaker Valentino Besarel, where they ordered at least eight pieces of ornately carved, ebonized furniture. Soon thereafter, however, they apparently experienced serious misgivings about the proportions of the relief figures on the base of a large table intended for their Hartford library. Questioning the validity of their taste, beset with anxiety that the finished product would be ostentatious and hopelessly vulgar, the couple eventually grew so discomfited that Twain dispatched a letter to the cabinetmaker from Rome requesting a modification in the table's design. Although this document no longer exists, the nature of their concerns can be readily deduced from Besarel's response, written in gracious, if somewhat fractured, English:

> In promptly answer your very highly esteemed favor of the 25th instant, I am very sorry indeed to could not agree your wish as the table you kindly ordered me is not only begun but very advanced in the

31. SLC to OLL, December 2, 1878 (UCCL 01611, MTPO, 2007).

work.—I am glad however to assure you that I have had in evidence to do the lions not so massive and heavy as you have remarked on the other one and I don't doubt that by receiving of my sending you shall remain entirely satisfied.[32]

This letter offers an instructive glimpse of Sam and Livy as parvenus—hesitant, self-conscious consumers for whom the act of purchase was not the unqualified "celebration" Jean-Christophe Agnew describes in his discussion of the commodity aesthetic but rather a source of stress. Their fear that the table's carving would be too "massive and heavy," when interpreted within the framework of Agnew's notion of the interchangeability of the commodity and the self, is symptomatic of a deeper, more unnerving concern—that the objects they collected overseas might betray the inadequacy of their aesthetic standards and thereby subvert the image of cultured refinement they so diligently sought to create.

But of all the commodities the couple purchased in Europe, the lavish gifts they exchanged to commemorate one another's birthdays in November 1878 best illustrate the convergence of Livy's dual agendas of cultural edification and consumerism. Nearly three months before the actual occasion, each partner carefully selected an expensive personal item for the other—Sam bought Livy an intricate necklace crafted by the renowned Roman goldsmith Augusto Castellani ($165.00; N&J2, 238); she, in turn, bought him a Swiss watch ($180.00).[33] In addition, they purchased objets d'art for one another, intended for strategic display in their Hartford home. Twain's gift to Livy was a watercolor of an unidentified young girl by the Italian impressionist Daniele Ranzoni, which he discovered in a gallery window while strolling in Milan and purchased on impulse:

> In the arcade stumbled on a water color in a window which was without form—just random dull-colored splotches—like a palette which hadn't been cleaned. Stepped back 15 feet was so carried away with rapture over the beauty of the picture & the sweetness of the face that I said to myself, "I know by my perfect joy in this thing that it is the

32. Valentino Besarel to SLC, October 27, 1878 (MTP).
33. OLC, European Diary, 1879–1879 (MTP).

very worst piece of art that has ever defiled the world. But to my vulgar & ignorant eye it is divine. I wish it were within the possibilities of my purse. But of course it isn't. I will go out of the reach of its fascinations. Ah, if I could only get it for a thousand francs I would snatch it & fly—& economise in clothes. Then the pew-rent occurred to me—I could stand 2000." I went in & asked the price: 250 francs! My soul stood still for gladness. I said "I will give you 200." After some talk he said, "Take it for 200." So I took it. (*N&J2*, 188)

This painting, which later occupied an honored place on the carved Scottish mantel in the library, was affectionately dubbed "Emmeline" by the family and became an integral component of Twain's evening storytelling ritual with his daughters. As he recalled in his *Autobiography*, "Every now and then the children required me to construct a romance—always impromptu—not a moment's preparation permitted—and into that romance I had to get all that bric-a-brac [on the mantel]. I had to start always with [the framed oil painting of] the cat and finish with Emmeline" (*MTA*, 204). At the moment of the watercolor's purchase, however, the question of aesthetic merit predominated; the writer's perception of the work's beauty was immediately undercut by a fundamental mistrust of his ignorant, untrained eye.

Livy's corresponding gift to her husband was an elegant music box made of "handsome walnut root" by the Swiss firm of Samuel Troll, Fils. In an era preceding the advent of recorded sound, this device, which—according to the sales invoice prepared for U.S. Customs—played "10 airs with Orchestra & Flute Basso accomp[animent]," was both a novelty and a technological wonder.[34] This quintessential luxury item—nobody's necessity—also had the distinction of being the single most expensive commodity the family purchased abroad. It cost $400—ten times the price of the Ranzoni watercolor, and more than twice the annual salary of their German nursemaid Rosina Hay[35]—the equivalent of approximately $8,000 in today's currency. Yet the instrument's astronomical price tag ultimately proved to be far less than the immense toll it levied on the writer's psyche. The convoluted saga of the music box—from Twain's maddening inability to select the songs

34. Custom invoice from Samuel Troll, Fils, to SLC, April 24, 1879 (MTP).
35. In an unpublished note Twain made for his autobiography circa 1877 (MTP), he listed the annual salaries of six members of his household staff as follows:

Assorted bric-a-brac, much of which was acquired abroad in 1878–
1879, set atop the carved Scottish mantel in Twain's Hartford Library.
The Italian watercolor of "Emmeline," purchased in Milan as a birthday
gift for Livy in 1878, is visible at the far left. (*Harper's Monthly*, 1885,
courtesy Mark Twain House and Museum)

The customs invoice for the Swiss music box Clemens purchased in Geneva in September 1878. (Courtesy Mark Twain Papers and Project, University of California, Berkeley)

it would play to the logistical challenges of its safe transport across the Atlantic, followed by his "grievous disappointment"[36] in the flawed device that finally arrived in Hartford—is fraught with symbolism, a metonym of the many difficulties the writer faced in aspiring to become cosmopolitan.

## III

According to an unpublished essay entitled "The Music Box," originally intended for inclusion in chapter 47 of A Tramp Abroad,[37] everything about this object signified exclusivity and cachet in the writer's imagination. Purchased from what he termed the "best music box establishment" in Geneva, it was no average model displayed on the showroom floor. Rather, the large "trunk-like box" that Twain chose was kept in a back room, "the holy of holies of the establishment" (MTP), and available only upon special order. In its splendor and rarity, the music box was the antithesis of a crudely carved, mass-produced souvenir like the cuckoo clock; moreover, it epitomized European high culture—sophisticated, elite, transnational—in contrast to the provincial folk tradition represented by the timepiece.

The device's allure was further enhanced by the fact that the playlist of the model Twain selected was customized according to individual preference; its range of melodies—usually featuring arias and overtures from celebrated European operas—thus reflected the owner's unique sensibility. As such, Livy's gift symbolically affirmed her husband's genteel taste; however, a problem soon arose that neither of them anticipated. What should have been a relatively simple process of choosing the music box's ten airs instead

---

| German housemaid | $155 per year |
| Irish housemaid | $150 |
| Irish laundress | $150 |
| Black cook | $240 |
| Black butler | $360 |
| Irish coachman | $600 +gas, hot and cold water and dwelling next to stable |

As thse figures illustrate, only coachman Patrick McAleer earned more than the cost of the Geneva music box.

36. SLC to George Baker, October 27, 1879 (UCCL 02408, MTPO, 2007).

37. Twain's intention is explicitly indicated by a notation at the top-left-hand corner of the first page of this manuscript: "Put this into the Geneva chapter—say at the end of it" (MTP).

vexed and eluded Clemens for close to six months, prompting him to desperately solicit advice from more musically inclined friends both at home and abroad. The nagging unease elicited by his indecision—though comical on the surface—was in fact overdetermined, bred of insecurity and self-conscious cultural anxiety. The music box became a fetish for Twain, invested with the irresistible "magic" of status and refinement. As its later conspicuous placement in the front hall of the family's Hartford home suggests, this object was intended to impress; a playlist of "common," second-rate music would therefore undermine the very purpose of its acquisition and had to be scrupulously avoided.

Unfortunately, the present location of Twain's Swiss music box is unknown; hence, its exact roster of songs remains a mystery.[38] The writer's notebook from October 1878, however, contains two lists of proposed melodies—one in his hand, the other unidentified—indicating the type of music under consideration (N&J2, 212–13). Twain's list of eighteen titles, an eclectic array of classical music, traditional ballads, and popular contemporary songs, illuminates the nature of his dilemma. Many of the selections seem forced, de rigueur, an obligatory genuflection at the altar of highbrow European culture rather than a genuine expression of personal taste. He includes, for example, two of the best-known melodies in nineteenth-century opera, the "Miserere" aria from Verdi's Il Trovatore and the overture to Rossini's William Tell; in addition, he names two Wagner compositions—"The Wedding March" from Lohengrin and "The Lorelei" from Das Rheingold—then fumbles with the third, vaguely identifying it only as "Tannhauser (where the heroine is taken into the lower regions)" (N&J2, 212). Twain's ambivalence about these choices is indicated by the interpolation, "Ich weiss nicht" (I don't know), which he jotted between two Wagner

38. The customs invoice prepared by Samuel Troll, Fils, dated April 24, 1879, specifies that Twain's music box included "Special Tunes" (MTP). Based on Twain's November 1878 note to Sue Warner and Clara Clemens's reminiscence of the music box in MFMT, five of the ten songs on its playlist can be positively identified: three Wagner arias ("The Wedding March" from Lohengrin; "The Pilgrim's Chorus" from Tannhauser; and "The Lorelei" from Das Rheingold), Verdi's "Miserere" from Il Trovatore, and "The Russian National Anthem." The other five tunes remain unknown. According to Gerry Wright, the owner of Manhattan's Rita Ford Music Boxes, the Wagner and Verdi titles were standard fare in this era; "The Russian National Anthem," on the other hand, while not unique, nonetheless represents a quirkier, more individualized selection. In light of the mainstream nature of these five choices, Twain's protracted indecision over the music box's playlist seems all the more peculiar.

titles and then promptly canceled out. Moreover, the writer's relative unfamiliarity with classical composers is demonstrated by his misspelling of Felix Mendelssohn's surname not once but twice ("Mendellson" and "Mendelsson") in the last notation of the series, followed by the abbreviated, somewhat misleading title, "Hymn." In all likelihood, this note refers to Mendelssohn's Symphony Number 2, known in its entirety as "Lobgesang" or "Hymn of Praise," which was composed in 1840 to commemorate the four hundredth anniversary of the invention of printing. While the occasion of the symphony's creation would doubtlessly have intrigued the former printer's devil from Hannibal, the generic shorthand of his title, indicating the piece as a whole rather than a specific movement within it, offers virtually no clue as to the actual melody under consideration.

The remaining titles on Twain's proposed list are much more revealing, culled from an English folk tradition of vernacular ballads, such as Thomas Moore's "Last Rose of Summer," Robert Burns's "Bonnie Boon" and "Auld Lang Syne," and Lady Dufferin's "Lament of the Irish Immigrant." Several popular American songs also appear—the anonymous antebellum "Way Down in Tennessee" ("The poor old slave has gone to rest / We know that he is free. / His bones, they lie, disturb them nay. / Way down in Tennessee"), Thomas Bayley's 1830 "Long, Long Ago" ("Let me forget that so long you have rov'd / Let me believe that you love as you lov'd, / Long, long ago, long ago"), and a tune he called "Day after Day"—an apparent misnomer that may allude to the plaintive refrain of Septimus Winner's 1871 "Drifting from Home" ("Drifting from home o'er the wide sea / Day after day drifting further from thee"). These romantic songs of loss and unrequited love, which the writer characterized as "freighted with infinite pathos," represent the democratic inverse of the grand operatic tradition. Their appeal, as he told Livy in an 1868 letter, was profoundly personal: "Tunes are good remembrancers. Almost everyone I am familiar with, summons instantly a face when I hear it. It is so with the Marseillaise, with Bonny Doon, and a score of others" (MFMT, 23).

Three additional titles on Twain's list express his unique musical preferences rather than the impersonal standards of high culture: the overture from François-Adrien Boieldieu's now forgotten 1800 comic opera, The Caliph of Baghdad; the patriotic 1833 "Russian National Hymn"; and Miloslaw Könnemann's 1853 composition "Der Fremersberg," which was based on a medieval German legend set in the Black Forest.[39] As the writer reports in *A Tramp Abroad,* he heard "Der Fremersberg" performed outdoors in Baden-Baden during the summer of 1878 and found the "beautiful air [that] ran through the music without ceasing" (*TA*, 235) deeply pleasurable. In this respect, Könnemann's composition seems a perfect choice for inclusion on the playlist of Twain's music box—an evocative souvenir of the richly storied German landscape he had visited—capable, like Proust's madeleines, of transporting him back·through space and time—but no. He instead dismisses "Der Fremersberg" as "the very lowest of low-grade music," on the basis of two peculiar, albeit telling, criteria—its popular appeal and its thrilling emotional power:

> I suppose the Fremersberg is very low-grade music; I know, indeed, that it *must* be low-grade music, because it so delighted me, warmed me, moved me, stirred me, uplifted me, enraptured me, that I was full of cry all the time, and mad with enthusiasm. My soul had never had such a scouring out since I was born . . . it seemed to me that nothing but the very lowest of low-grade music *could* be so divinely beautiful. The great crowd which the Fremersberg had called out was another evidence that it was low-grade music; for only the few are educated up to a point where high-grade music gives pleasure. I have never heard enough classic music to be able to enjoy it. I dislike the opera because I want to love it and can't.
>
> I suppose there are two kinds of music,—one kind which one feels, just as an oyster might, and another sort which requires a higher faculty, a faculty which must be assisted and developed by teaching. Yet if base music gives certain of us wings, why should we want any other? But we do. We want it because the higher and better like it. But we want it without giving it the necessary time and trouble; so we climb into that upper tier, that dress circle by a lie: we *pretend* we like it. I know several of that sort of people,—and I propose to be one of them myself when I get home with my fine European education. (*TA*, 237)

39. The factual information regarding these various titles—their dates of composition and so on—was derived from Oxford University Press's vast electronic archive, Grove Music Online, which includes the full texts of *The New Grove Dictionary of Music and Musicians,* ed. Stanley Sadie and John Tyrrell, 2d ed., 29 vols. (London, 2001); *The New Grove Dictionary of Opera,* ed. Stanley Sadie, 4 vols. (London, 1992); and *The New Grove Dictionary of Jazz,* ed. Barry Kernfeld, 2d ed., 3 vols. (London, 2002).

Twain frames his assessment of "Der Fremersberg" within a series of po-
larized dichotomies—"base" versus "high-grade" music, "the great crowd"
versus the elite "upper tier," the "mad" enthusiasm of sensory delight versus the "higher faculty" of cool intellectual discernment—that reveal why
selecting the music box's melodies proved so daunting and onerous a task.
Good taste, in the writer's estimation, was inextricably linked with education and social class; on that basis, he deemed his innate aesthetic sense—
whether in relation to painting, architecture, music, or any other art form—
suspect, unreliable, even treacherous. Like his rapturous response to the
"Emmeline" watercolor in Milan, Twain's admiration of Könnemann's "di-
vinely beautiful" composition conversely signals its inferiority rather than
its worth; his appreciation of such "low-grade music" thus threatens to expose him as a consummate boor, an unthinking "oyster" who knows only
how to feel. Small wonder, then, that "Der Fremersberg" was stricken from
the list of titles under consideration. The music box—as a touchstone of
cultural refinement intended to demonstrate the worthiness of Twain's inclusion in the coveted "dress circle" of the cosmopolitan upper class—could
play only "high-grade" music that he "pretended to like" rather than the
popular melodies that genuinely moved him.

In this regard, the list anonymously inscribed on the flyleaf of Twain's
1878 notebook offers an intriguing counterpoint to the writer's own selections. As Robert Hirst, the general editor of the Mark Twain Project, has
perceptively noted, the handwriting bears a close resemblance to that in
two letters concerning the music box that Clemens received in April 1879
from either Samuel Troll himself or a representative of his firm; in all likelihood, the entries were made in Troll's Geneva showroom soon after the
box's purchase on September 9. The strict numeric sequencing of this second list indicates that it was constructed as a unified set of ten melodies,
perhaps in anticipation of the instrument's domestic use as a soothing backdrop during dinner parties or other social events. Three songs originally
identified by Twain recur—Wagner's "Wedding March," the Overture from
*William Tell,* and the "Russian National Hymn." Felix Mendelssohn is also
invoked, though with a different selection—his Opus 63 ("I Would that
my Love") now standing in for the elusive "Hymn." The differences between the two lists, however, are far more revealing than the similarities.
Only one Américan title appears—Reverend Samuel Francis Smith's patri-

otic 1831 anthem "America," more familiarly known as "My Country 'Tis of Thee." The remaining six selections—all European in origin—commingle the sacred (an unidentified "Chorale" arranged by Martin Luther) and secular, and comprise a wide variety of musical forms. The titles range from grand opera (the introduction to Verdi's *Rigoletto*) to more popular, middlebrow entertainment (Vincent Wallace's *Maritana* and Charles Lecocq's comic operetta, *La Fille de Madame Angot*) and also include two contemporary waltzes—Charles Godfrey's "The Flower Girl" and Lecocq's "Tournez, Tournez."

This Eurocentric list of nineteenth-century "lite" favorites apparently did not satisfy Clemens either, causing him to seek advice further afield. In frustration and bewilderment, he turned to a long-familiar benchmark of culture and good taste—the community of Nook Farm. In a letter written to Joe Twichell on November 20, 1878, Twain enclosed a note to his neighbor Susan (Mrs. Charles Dudley) Warner, a gifted musician whom his daughter Clara would later recall as "the best amateur pianist in town" (*MFMT*, 188), earnestly pleading for her assistance:

> I ordered a perfect love of a music box in Geneva, & for 2 months have been trying to select the 10 tunes for it.—Won't you help me? Its best hold is not loud, or staccato or rapid music, but just the reverse—a soft, *flowing* strain—its strong suit is the plaintive. I have selected 4: The Lorelei, the Miserere from Trovatore, the Wedding March from Lohengrin, & the Russian National Anthem—& at that point I *stuck*. You are just the person who can suggest some tunes to get the wanting 6 out of. This box is great on rich chords—pours them out like the great god Pan—or any other man. She's not one of the thumping or banging or tinkling sort, with castanets & birds & drums & such-like foolishness—no, her melody is low-voiced, & flows in blended waves of sound. Her forte is to express pathos, not hilarity or hurrah. Come, will you help me? I shall wait to hear from you. (Yale manuscript quoted in *N&J2*, 212)

It is unclear whether or not Susan Warner responded to Clemens's request; if she did, her recommendations have not survived. In any event, Twain's indecision regarding the music box's playlist persisted for another two months. It was not until February 23, 1879, that he announced, with obvious relief, in a letter to his mother-in-law:

> I've got the airs for my music box selected at last, thanks to goodness—been five months at it. If I ever get the thing home I'll give you some musical chords which you will say are the softest and sweetest you ever heard. The sounds are more suggestive of the violin or a combination of violins (softly played) than anything else. I had never seen a box of the sort before. It is to play 10 tunes and cost $400. It is small in size—comparatively speaking—but has virtues of large dimensions.[40]

Twain's description of the music box in these two letters indicates his progressive idealization of its sublime sound. The "rich," "low-voiced" strains he commended to Susan Warner in November resonate within his memory and three months later become the "softest and sweetest" musical chords "ever heard." This inflated rhetoric, reflecting both his pride of ownership and his eager anticipation of the delight his possession will elicit in future listeners at home, suggests that he regarded the music box as not only a showpiece but also a talisman, possessing mysterious "virtues of large dimensions." The writer's exaggerated recollection of the instrument's sound was no doubt reinforced by Troll's letter of April 12, 1879, which stated: "I am happy to say your Box is completed & *to my satisfaction;* a telling but mellow tone, & all the airs have been arranged in accordance with your Inst'ns; I am certain you will be as pleased as myself" (MTP). A second letter from Troll, written on April 24, details the care with which the music box was packed for transatlantic shipping: with its mechanical movements padded and protected by corks, it was placed in a specially constructed tin-lined case that was soldered shut before being sent to the Cunard Line's office in Liverpool. Troll concludes: "Let me once more repeat that the Inst'mt is fully up to my expectations, & I have no doubt you will be well satisfied with the way in which I have carried out your order" (MTP).

Given the degree of Twain's imaginative investment in this commodity,

---

40. SLC to OLL, February 23, 1879 (UCCL 01635, MTPO, 2007).

the crushing disappointment he experienced upon its arrival in Hartford was perhaps inevitable. As he explains in the deleted "Music Box" passage of *A Tramp Abroad,* he was hardly "well satisfied" with the device Troll sent him: "When I at last opened the blessed thing in America, the first turn of the crank brought forth an agonizing jingle and squawk and clatter of bells, gongs, drums, and castanets, with never a solitary strain of flute or fiddle! It was like ordering a serenade of angels, and getting a shivaree in place of it" (MTP). To Twain's ear, the shrill cacophony of this instrument bore no resemblance to the "richly blended chords of flutes and violins playing in concert" that had captivated him a year earlier in Geneva; indeed, the disparity between the two was so glaring he could only conclude: "She is not the box I ordered" (MTP).[41] While the possibility of an egregious shipping error cannot be completely discounted, such a mix-up seems unlikely in that the music box was custom-made, and—as the manufacturer repeatedly proclaimed—completed in strict accordance with the writer's specifications. Rather, I believe his peremptory rejection of the device was psychological in origin—an expression of acute buyer's remorse.

Within a week of returning to Hartford in October 1879, Twain's chagrin over the music box prompted him to compose a long, irate letter to George Baker, the salesman from whom he had purchased it. Significantly, this document survives only in draft form, as an enclosure in an unsent note to Mr. L. T. Adams, the American consul in Geneva:

> Dear Sir:
> Being under the impression that I am personally acquainted with you, I am going to venture to write you a rather private sort of note. The enclosed letter is the rough draft of one which I have just

41. According to music box expert Gerry Wright, no nineteenth-century device reproduced the sound of violins. The closest approximation to Twain's recollection of the "soft, long-drawn strains and richly blended chords" of the instrument he *thought* he ordered would have been an "expressive" music box, which featured the delicate sounds of a mandolin and piccolo flute. Samuel Troll's April 1879 customs invoice, however, explicitly identifies Twain's music box as an "Orchestra" model with "Flute Basso accompaniment"—exactly the kind he claimed he did not want—"freighted with a nerve-wrenching accumulation of aggravating devices such as little bells, & gongs, & drums, & castanets, & wing-flopping, beak-stretching singing-birds" (MTP). In Wright's estimation, the "Flute-Basso" designation complicates matters further, since it can refer to either a dainty flute organ sound (which might conceivably be described as violins) or a more robust reed organ sound, reminiscent of a church organ.

mailed to Mr. Geo. Baker, Manager for M. Troll, fils, 6 Rue Bonivard, Geneva. It explains itself.[42]

The very fact that the writer contemplated—though ultimately decided against—the need for diplomatic intervention in resolving this problem bespeaks his impression of its magnitude and gravity. Moreover, despite his claim to the contrary, the letter to Baker hardly "explains itself"—its skewed rendition of events must be interpreted with care. The series of forthright and, at times, frankly accusatory questions that Twain poses throughout the document, for example, portray him as a frustrated consumer seeking immediate redress of a wrong that has been unjustly foisted upon him:

> Don't you remember? The box I ordered was to be like the one you played on in the back room—the room through which you pass to go to the workshop where the music-master was writing some sheet music. You played on only one box in that room (there were boxes of various prices, but *it* was the only 2000 *f* box in the house) & the next day you played it again, for Mrs. Clemens & the young lady. That box had no *drum* in it; it had no *bells* or *gongs; it* produced *no tinkling music-box sounds.* It produced no sounds whatever but richly blended *continuous* chords, like a number of violins playing softly together, with the *vox humana* threading its way through them.[43]
>
> As I have said, there were no tinklings, no bells, no drums. But the instrument you have sent me *has,* alas! I have talked so much about my wonderful box that was coming, that descriptions of it have wandered about among the newspapers from here to California—but alas! Well, the descriptions were all right enough, & I could have shown the people a box that would justify all those praises, if no mistake had been made in constructing it. What shall we do? Will you build me the right instrument, with nothing in it but violins & vox humana? . . . And what shall I do with this present box?—ship it back to you?[44]

42. SLC to L. T. Adams, October 29, 1878 (UCCL 01704, MTPO, 2007).

43. The term *vox humana* refers to a pipe-organ stop that produces tones resembling the human voice. According to Gerry Wright, this terminology is not at all applicable to the range of sound made by music boxes; he was therefore mystified by Twain's use of the phrase in this context.

44. SLC to George Baker, October 27, 1879 (UCCL 02408, MTPO, 2007).

The writer is so resolute in his conviction that Baker made a terrible mistake that he never questions the accuracy of his own memory—and therefore overlooks the inherent paradox of one of his key assertions—that if the instrument he ordered was in fact "the only 2000 ƒ box in the house," how could it possibly have been confused with another model? Even more significant, Twain deliberately exaggerates the public humiliation he has suffered as the result of this alleged error, claiming that descriptions of his music box have been widely circulated in "newspapers from here to California." He thus characterizes himself as doubly victimized—first, by the shipment of the wrong instrument and, second, by the ensuing damage to his reputation. He also stubbornly refuses to admit any embellishment in his representation of the music box's sound, insisting, "Well, the descriptions were all right enough, & I could have shown the people a box that would justify all those praises, if no mistake had been made in constructing it." The patent absurdity of this statement captures the essence of the whole music box fiasco; after bragging so shamelessly about this wondrous commodity—the chief trophy of his extended European stay—he was painfully embarrassed by the pathetic reality of its "tinkling" sound.

The problem of the music box, as Twain informed Baker, was compounded by the fact that it had been damaged in transit: "The ships and railways managed to break the strong bolt that fastened the row of bells at the right hand end short off, & also two of the teeth of the short bass comb at the left-hand end." These mechanical issues, he acknowledged, were "easily repaired" by a local Swiss craftsman, who "removed the corks & cards & put the box through its paces, & it discoursed excellent music." But this restoration did little to obviate the writer's dissatisfaction, since he remained convinced that the instrument—even in proper working order—"wasn't the kind I wanted—I wanted violins and vox humana exclusively—as originally agreed upon." On this basis, he repudiated the device, deeming it inadequate and unworthy: "What shall I do with this present box?" he asked Baker in exasperation; "Ship it back to you?" Having invested so much time, money, and psychic energy in the procurement of this symbolic commodity, however, Twain was understandably reluctant to incur any further expense in returning it to Geneva. His dilemma—which exacerbated an already intense case of buyer's remorse—is particularly evident in two passages stricken from the draft, both pertaining to the payment of additional freight charges and import duties. After proposing the music box's return, he bluntly inquired, "And must I pay the freight & duties again, the error not being mine but yours?—or will you pay them?"; similarly, he added in closing, "If this box goes back to you, I suppose there would be *no* duties on the one which came in its place. Our Consul of Geneva, Mr. L.T. Adams, will know about that."[45] This allusion to Adams may have been what motivated Clemens to compose the note to the American official in the first place, informing him—as a matter of courtesy—that he had invoked his name and authority in the matter.

Twain concluded his letter to Baker with the statement, "Hoping for an early reply," which the penultimate paragraph of the deleted "Music Box" chapter indicates he did receive, although the whereabouts of the actual response—from either Baker or Troll himself—is unknown:

> She is not the box I ordered. Mr. Troll says she is; but as I was present and he was not, perhaps I ought to know better than he. He frankly offers to take her back if I will ship her to Geneva, and says he will give me the other kind of box. That is creditable, and is all he could be expected to do; but as my life and limbs are valuable to me I am not going to try to pack that thing in these times when accident policies are so high. (MTP)

"The Music Box" manuscript itself is undated; however, evidence suggests that it was composed during the first three weeks of November 1879—after Twain sent the letter to Baker on October 27 but before informing Howells on November 23, "My book is really finished at last" (*MTHL1,* 281). Since it took at least a week for mail to cross the Atlantic, this timeline demonstrates that Clemens's complaint was taken seriously and given a prompt, professional response, although clearly not the one he anticipated. Troll's insistence that he had shipped the correct music box stymied the writer, sending him into a tailspin of confusion, as evinced by a letter written on December 5, 1879, to his friend and former agent Frank Fuller in New York:

45. Ibid.

> See if the musical box people haven't got an expert who can run up
> here right away & tell me what is the matter with a $500-box which
> I ordered in Geneva, & what sort of box it is, & how much it is dam-
> aged & what it will cost to repair it. The man will need to be a person
> who has actually made or repaired boxes, I judge, for this thing is so
> mysterious a machine that it will easily baffle an amateur. The matter
> is important, because I am about to put a chapter in my book which
> must not go in if the Geneva people have not done me a dishonesty.[46]

Some six weeks after writing to Baker, Twain's assurance had dissolved into
utter bewilderment; he therefore solicited an impartial authority to deter-
mine both the type of music box he owned and the degree of damage it had
sustained, as well as an accurate estimate of the cost involved in its repair—
all, as the last line of the letter states, to preclude the possibility of being
sued for libel by the Swiss manufacturer.

It is uncertain whether Fuller ever sent an expert to Hartford as request-
ed; the next exchange of letters between the two men suggests otherwise.
On December 19, Clemens seems to have begged off, explaining that his attention had been preempted by other, more urgent matters: "I'm leaving the
music box business alone till I get out of this awful press of work. Then I'm
going to get you or the other man to fix it."[47] In addition, no invoices or receipts exist in the Mark Twain Papers documenting the instrument's repair;
however, two entries in the writer's 1880 notebook, reminding himself to
"Send Music box man" (*N&J2*, 371–72), imply that the "fix"—whatever it
may have been—was neither simple nor easy, but entailed an ongoing series of fine adjustments.

Despite the overwhelming aggravation caused by the music box, Twain
ultimately chose to omit any mention of it in *A Tramp Abroad*. While the legal concerns mentioned in his letter to Fuller no doubt figured prominently in this decision, several other factors were also involved. The instrument
was, after all, a birthday gift from his beloved spouse; to excoriate it in print
would have been a callous—and perhaps unforgivable—affront. But, more
important, I suspect that the writer recognized and was embarrassed by the
unfavorable light that this painful, protracted comedy of errors shed on his

46. SLC to Frank Fuller, December 5, 1879 (UCCL 01733, MTPO, 2007).
47. SLC to Frank Fuller, December 19, 1879 (UCCL 01742, MTPO, 2007).

character, particularly the foolishness of his overreaching desire for status and refinement. In this regard, the suppressed "Music Box" essay—an ironic cautionary tale about the pitfalls of consumerism in which the writer found himself inadvertently ensnared—is a richly instructive text. Throughout the manuscript, Twain uses comic hyperbole to satirize not only the gratuitous extravagance of his purchase but also the conformist mentality underlying it: "Everybody orders a watch, in Geneva, and a music box. Neither of these things was a necessity to me, but I ordered both, because I did not like to seem eccentric." With the bitter clarity of hindsight, he rues the cost—literal as well as figurative—of yielding to this mindless material impulse: "With duties, freights, and so on, [the music box] had cost me six hundred and fifty dollars—a pure waste, for I could have got a guillotine for half the money" (MTP). The harshness of Twain's denunciation—declaring the expenditure "a pure waste"—is a sweeping indictment of both his frivolous spending habits and the foibles of his social aspirations. Moreover, the provocative analogy he draws between the music box and a guillotine reveals how dramatically his perception of the device had shifted within the space of a month. The delicate object that he sought to protect from further damage in late October by locking it "in a vacant bedroom [so] nobody can get at it to handle it"[48] is here characterized as a "machine capable of producing almost instant death"—in other words, a fearsome weapon against which both the residents of his household and the entire neighborhood must be defended. Indeed, the device's destructive power is so immense that he abandons the anachronistic figure of the guillotine at the end of the essay in favor of a more lethal, technologically advanced machine—the Gatling gun. Whereas a guillotine executes its victims individually and in silence, a machine gun—like the music box—is both indiscriminate and deafeningly loud, capable of mass slaughter.

It is therefore befitting that Twain used the language of insurance—specifically, an extended metaphor of liability—to describe the quandary of owning such a hazardous device:

> I did not know what to do with it. It did not seem safe to have it about
> the house where innocent and unsuspecting persons might meddle

---

48. SLC to George Baker, October 27, 1879 (UCCL 02408, MTPO, 2007).

> with it and *I be held for damages* on the inquest; neither would it be
> right to ask any storage-house to take charge of it without explaining
> *its dangerous nature;* I could not keep a policeman to watch it, for *I could
> not afford to pay for that policeman in case he came to grief;* I would not
> trust it in the cellar, for there was a good deal of machinery about it
> which nobody understood, and there was no sure thing that it would
> not go off of its own accord, and of course *I could not collect any insur-
> ance on the damage it would do the house, for a fire-risk does not cover de-
> struction wrought by a music box;* I thought of burying it, but the sexton
> did not like to handle it. There was really no way out of the scrape.
> (MTP; emphasis added)

The danger posed by the music box is of course not to "life and limbs" as the
writer claims but—no less fatally—to his genteel self-image. Recognizing the
potential "damage it would do the house," he determines that the instrument
can neither be kept on the premises (even in the basement) nor safely stored
in a warehouse; even burial in consecrated ground is out of the question.
Twain's much-vaunted possession thus becomes an onerous, inescapable bur-
den, an uninsurable "risk." In desperation, he attempts to dispose of the music box by giving it to a neighbor who "put some wires to it, and started in to
use it for a burglar alarm"; however, this strategy backfires as well:

> The first time it went off, (it was doing the Anvil Chorus,) this man,
> instead of rising up and killing the burglars, went quaking to them and
> offered them all his wealth to kill the music box. But they fled.
> She is on my hands yet. I am willing to trade her for an elephant,
> and give boot. Or, I will agree to fight her with an elephant, the victor
> to yield up his champion to the vanquished. (MTP)

*Kill* the music box? Arrange for it to *fight* an elephant? Twain's playful
(though admittedly peculiar) diction not only personifies the device but also
invests it with an uncanny, almost wraithlike power; given the inherent
"deviltries in its composition," the instrument imperils all "innocent and un-
suspecting persons" who encounter it.

But the most intriguing aspect of the "Music Box" manuscript is the convoluted manner in which Twain finally acknowledges his own culpability
in the fiasco. Although he continues to insist that Troll shipped him the

wrong box, the writer also admits—for the first time—that the error was not an act of duplicity or carelessness but a misunderstanding grounded in his inability to select the ten melodies the instrument would play:

> It was my own fault that I never got [the box I ordered]. I thought I had ten favorite tunes, but easily found I had only four. It took me eight months to furnish the other six. Meantime I suppose that that young man had forgotten what kind of a box I had ordered. . . . The moral of this little tale is, when you order a music box in Geneva, furnish your tunes at once, then no mistake will be made, and you will get what you order. But if you delay as I did, Mr. Troll's young man's memory may become uncertain and cause a disappointment to be inflicted upon you. No intentional wrong will be done you, for it is an honorable and trustworthy house, but no matter, if you delay too much you may have the bitterness of seeing that the charming instrument you have been waiting for is not that enchanting instrument at all, but a Gatling gun in disguise. (MTP)

As this passage implies, Twain's procrastination is symptomatic of a larger underlying problem—the poverty of his musical background: "I thought I had ten favorite tunes," he confesses, "but easily found I had only four." His exaggeration of the time line, claiming that the tortured process of decision making extended over a period of eight months rather than five, further underscores this impression of inadequacy. Yet the prescriptive moral tagline he offers in the essay's conclusion ultimately skirts this uncomfortable issue, instead identifying the symptom—paralyzing indecision—as the root cause of the music box ordeal: "Furnish your tunes at once," he advises other well-heeled American tourists contemplating a similar purchase abroad; "then no mistake will be made, and you will get what you order." The model of swift, decisive action Twain advocates is of course tacitly grounded in self-assurance—the very quality he lacked in selecting his playlist. Thus, in warning other consumers not to follow his example, he intimates that they should ignore the pressures of social convention he succumbed to and confidently choose music they personally like—only then will the outcome prove satisfactory. One cannot help but speculate that the writer's music box would have featured "Way Down in Tennessee" rather than Wagner's "Wedding March" had he been able to heed this pragmatic advice.

The manuscript of "The Music Box" contains few corrections or revisions; however, two of Twain's most significant changes occur in the paragraph quoted above. Initially, he emphasized the adverse effect that his procrastination had on George Baker's behavior: "If you delay as I did, Mr. Troll's young man's memory may become uncertain and *cause him to inflict* a disappointment upon you." In revising this sentence, he shifted from active to passive voice, substituting the impersonal construction, "and *cause a disappointment to be inflicted* upon you." While the outcome—disillusionment—remains the same in both versions, the revision delicately sidesteps any explicit ascription of agency or blame. Similarly, in the essay's closing line—"If you delay too much you may have the bitterness of seeing that charming instrument you have so long been waiting for suddenly transformed into not that enchanting instrument at all, but a Gatling gun in disguise"—Twain struck out the verb phrase "suddenly transformed into," replacing it with the colorless predicate "is" (MTP). In terms of semantics, this slight change of diction may appear unremarkable, but it is nonetheless revealing. While "suddenly transformed into" suggests a dynamic process of outward, objective change whereby one thing becomes another (due to a manufacturing or shipping error, for example), Twain's revision connotes a subjective perceptual shift. The metamorphosis he describes thus occurs not in the music box itself but rather in the way he sees it—as the commodity's charm and enchantment vanish, so too does its status as a fetish.

While "The Music Box" may capture the poetic truth of Twain's complex relationship with this object, his characterization of its sound as both a "shivaree" and a "Gatling gun in disguise" is challenged by the fond recollections of two other members of the Clemens household. According to longtime servant Katy Leary, the device was an integral component of the family's nightly dining ritual:

> Mrs. Clemens always put on a lovely dress for dinner, even when we was alone, and they always had music during dinner. They had a music box in the hall, and George would set that going at dinner every day. Played nine pieces, that music box did; and he always set it going every night. They brought it from Geneva, and it was wonderful. It was foreign. It used to play all by itself—it wasn't like a Victrola, you know.

It just went with a crank. George would wind it up and they'd have pretty music all during the dinner. Oh, it was lovely! And the children was just delighted with it.[49]

Daughter Clara also remembered the instrument with incredulous wonder:

One of the early miracles in my life was a huge music box Father bought in New York when I was about five years old. Could such a thing really be true? A great brown case of polished wood that resembled a coffin, and out of it floated the most enthralling melodies and harmonies! My sisters and I were fascinated by these first tones that we had ever heard from the great world of music. The "Pilgrim's Chorus" from *Tannhauser* and the *Lohengrin* "Wedding March" were our favorites. Well do I remember Father's delight over the joyful amazement expressed by us all. (*MFMT,* 31)

These accounts complement and corroborate one another in several ways—both, for example, represent the music box as an apparent "miracle," a technological novelty capable of playing "all by itself." They also concur that its lovely ethereal sound was a source of abiding fascination and pleasure for the Clemens children. In Katy's estimation, however, much of the object's allure lay in its exotic, Old World origin, as implied by the missing conjunction linking the discrete statements, "They brought it from Geneva, and it was wonderful [because] It was foreign." Clara, who mistakenly identifies the music box as American, perceives its foreignness differently. She endows it with mysterious, vaguely supernatural qualities, claiming that the case "resembled a coffin" out of which "floated" disembodied strains of "the most enthralling melodies and harmonies." In her recollection, the instrument functioned primarily as a teaching tool—an imaginative portal of entry into the "great world" of European music—demonstrating that Livy's plan for the girls' cultural edification extended well beyond the duration of their overseas excursion. But the most surprising detail in Clara's reminiscence, particularly when juxtaposed with the

49. Mary Lawton, *A Lifetime with Mark Twain: The Memories of Katy Leary, for Thirty Years His Faithful and Devoted Servant* (New York: Haskell House Publishers, 1972), 8.

anger and shame Twain expressed throughout "The Music Box," is her allusion to *his* delight—not in the device itself, but in observing the "joyful amazement" it elicited in his children.

Several questions inevitably arise in attempting to reconcile these wildly conflicting accounts of the music box. What did it actually sound like? Did Twain eventually overcome his ambivalence toward this commodity and come to enjoy it as Clara alleged? In the course of my research, I have been unable to locate any other contemporary descriptions of the music box, in either the letters or the memoirs of the many visitors who stayed in the family's Hartford home. Howells does not mention it in *My Mark Twain,* nor does Lillian Aldrich in *Crowding Memories,* although both narratives contain detailed information about the house and its convivial ambience. Is it possible that the device was never played for guests but reserved exclusively for the family's entertainment? And might this accommodation represent the way in which Clemens finally made peace with his flawed, frivolous expenditure?

Indeed, Twain's disinfatuation with the goods he and Livy acquired overseas was by no means limited to the music box. As he glumly informed his friend Hjalmar Boyesen soon after returning to Hartford: "We arrived safely ourselves, but our things are all broken. Our unpacking room looks like a furniture hospital." Livy's perspective, on the other hand, was far more sanguine: "The house here looks wonderfully pretty already although it is not settled yet," she told her mother on November 16; "The new things look so pretty."[50] This gradual process of settling-in would continue for two more years—culminating in the hiring of Louis Comfort Tiffany's design firm, Associated Artists, to paint and stencil the walls throughout the home's first floor in 1881. Only then did Livy's grand vision of a cosmopolitan home achieve fruition.

IV

According to strangers and intimate friends alike, the results were most impressive. An anonymous reporter from the *Chicago Daily Tribune* who visited the house in early 1884 lauded the "very fine style" in which the au-

---

50. SLC to Hjalmar H. Boyesen, November 6, 1879 (UCCL 01707, MTPO, 2007); OLC to OLL, November 16, 1879 (MTH&M).

thor and his family lived. The home's flamboyant exterior, he noted, "is quite as funny as its proprietor"; like a classic Twain tale, it "rambles" off in three directions at once, bristling with fanciful "peaks and chimney pots, and seems to be made up of an aggregate of extensions." Its quirky architectural style, the writer declared, is "a crystallized expression of an encounter between Mark Twain and Queen Anne with the humorist in good feather and the monarch signing small." Inside, however, this eccentricity vanished, replaced by a resplendent atmosphere of luxury and wealth. "Within it is simply a palace," the reporter gushed. "The parlor is a dream of pale-blue satin, stained glass, rich curtains, carved furniture, and articles of vertu. A buck negro attends the door and ushers the guests through a great central ante-room luxuriously appointed into the parlor, drawing-room, dining-room, and other apartments which open out of it."[51] The reporter's exaggerated language—characterizing the drawing room as "a dream of pale-blue satin," for example—imparts a fairy-tale quality to Twain's life and domicile; however, the most significant detail in the *Tribune* article is the phrase "articles of vertu," used in reference to the parlor bric-a-bric. An orthographic variant of the French *virtu*, "vertu" is an archaism for connoisseurship—a knowledge and love of, or excellent taste in, fine art. These unspecified "articles of vertu"—the decorative commodities Livy purchased overseas—thus become the tangible hallmarks of Twain's worldly sophistication.

Later that year, Thomas K. Beecher, the minister who had married the couple in 1870, visited his sisters Harriet and Isabella at Nook Farm and stopped in to see the Clemenses. In a note written upon his return to Elmira, he complimented Livy on the gracious, congenial character of their abode: "You must know . . . that yours is one of the few *restful* homes in which intelligence, culture, luxury, and company combine to the compounding of a pleasure which every visitor longs to taste again."[52] Beecher's observation is perceptive: the heady fusion of material opulence, lively conversation, and warm camaraderie was precisely what made a visit to

---

51. "The Metropolis: Mark Twain's House," *Chicago Daily Tribune,* April 6, 1884, p. 17. Interestingly, the reporter took pains to inform his readers that Twain's splendid mansion owed its existence not to his success as a writer but to Livy's family assets: "Although many persons, even in Hartford, suppose that to literature is due the palatial home, the fact is that Mrs. Clemens is the source of the bulk of the wealth from which all this sprang."

52. Quoted in Andrews, *Nook Farm,* 94.

Twain's home so unforgettable. Throughout the 1880s, the Farmington Avenue mansion functioned as an elaborate stage set, where the Clemens girls literally performed plays and a larger social drama was simultaneously enacted. A steady procession of literary luminaries and other notables—Matthew Arnold, Henry Morton Stanley, and Edward Bellamy, among others—came to call and be sumptuously entertained. The lavish hospitality Mr. and Mrs. Clemens routinely bestowed upon their guests is illustrated by Louisiana writer Grace King's description of a dinner given in her honor on June 19, 1887:

> The table was beautiful—round with an exquisite cut glass bowl in the centre filled with daisies, ferns, and grasses—a bunch of white roses was at each one's plate. . . . The candelabra were of twisted silver, with yellow candles and shades. Olives, salted almonds, and bonbons in curious dishes were on the table and decanters of quaint shape and color held the wine. The soup was "Claire"—the clairest you ever saw, delicious flavor—sherry. Then fresh salmon, white wine sauce—Apollonaris water—sweet breads in cream, served I vow, in what looked like porcelain pots—with covers (little flat round ones, exquisitely painted in blue). Claret, broiled chicken, green peas and new potatoes (they are very rare here), [and] tomato salad. I really cannot write a description of this—the salad dish is an immense deep plate of Hungarian ware. On the lettuce leaves were placed the tomatoes, sliced but still in shape—over it all was poured the mayonnaise—and such instruments for serving—gold and silver—and carving. The dessert was a most magnificent dish—Charlotte Russe and wine jelly with candied cherries in it, with whipped cream. . . . The butler in full evening dress served from the side table, and I assure you each plate was simply a chef d'oeuvre of artistic porcelain. Their cook must be a French one. Never in New Orleans have I seen such beautiful dishes, or such exquisite flavoring.[53]

The Clemenses' 1878–1879 European excursion is evoked by many details of this feast, from the cosmopolitan touches on the menu (consommé, im-

---

53. Grace King to Nina Ansley King, June 19, 1887 (manuscript 1282), Grace King Papers, Louisiana State University. Quoted with the permission of the Special Collections Department, Hill Memorial Library, Louisiana State University, Baton Rouge, La.

ported German mineral water, a trendy French dessert invented to honor Czar Alexander I) to the beautiful hand-painted dishes of "Hungarian ware" and "artistic porcelain" used in serving the food. These exotic commodities, epitomizing Baudrillard's concept of le miroir parfait, dazzle King—precisely as they were intended to—with the "exquisite" elegance and civility of her hosts.

When the Clemenses were forced to close the house in 1891 due to mounting financial pressures, they returned once again to Europe—not for cultural edification but rather for economic frugality. After traveling through France, Germany, and Switzerland, they settled for nine months (September 1892–June 1893) at the seventeenth-century Villa Viviani outside Florence. Describing the soaring ceilings and cool stone floors of the villa's sparsely furnished twenty-eight rooms in his *Autobiography,* Twain meditated on the fundamental difference between European and American interiors:

> There is a trick about an American house that is like the deep-lying untranslatable idioms of a foreign language—a trick uncatchable by the stranger, a trick incommunicable and indescribable; and that elusive trick, that intangible something, whatever it is, is just the something that gives the home look and the home feeling to an American house and makes it the most satisfying refuge yet invented by men— and women, mainly women. The American house is opulent in soft and varied colors that please and rest the eye, and in surfaces that are smooth and pleasant to the touch, in forms that are shapely and graceful, in objects without number which compel interest and cover nakedness; and the night has even a higher charm than the day, there, for the artificial lights do really give light instead of merely trying and failing; and under their veiled and tinted glow all the snug coziness and comfort and charm of the place is at best and loveliest.[54]

Although he never specifically mentions his Hartford residence in this passage, it is clearly the implied benchmark against which the villa is being measured. From the vantage point of his involuntary exile, Clemens rues all he has left behind on Farmington Avenue—the colors, textures, and forms

54. *The Autobiography of Mark Twain,* ed. Charles Neider (New York: Harper and Row, 1959), 226–27.

that make an American home "the most satisfying refuge yet invented." In
particular, he laments the loss of "objects without number"—bric-a-bric, in
other words—not for their practical utility, but for their intrinsic aesthetic
value in "compelling" visual interest and "cover[ing] nakedness." Ironically, it is only in the absence of these commodities that Twain can finally recognize their true worth; he appreciates them not as individual signifiers of
wealth and status but collectively, for their role in creating an ambience of
"snug coziness" and security.

Three years after his stay at Villa Viviani, in March 1895, Twain returned
alone to Nook Farm prior to embarking on his worldwide lecture tour. He
stopped briefly at home, not realizing it would be the last time he would
enter the premises, and poignantly described the experience in a letter to
Livy, who was then living with the girls in Paris:

> When I arrived in town I did not want to go near the house, & I
> didn't want to go anywhere or see anybody. I said to myself, "If I may
> be spared it I will never live in Hartford again."
>
> But as soon as I entered this front door I was seized with a furious
> desire to have us all in this house again & right away, & never to go
> outside the grounds any more forever—certainly never again to Eu-
> rope.
>
> How ugly, tasteless, repulsive, are all the domestic interiors I have
> ever seen in Europe compared with the perfect taste of this ground
> floor, with its delicious dream of harmonious color, & its all-pervading
> spirit of peace & serenity & deep contentment. You did it all, & it
> speaks of you & praises you eloquently and unceasingly. It is the loveli-
> est home that ever was. I had no faintest idea of what it was like. I sup-
> posed I had, for I have seen it in its wraps & disguises several times in
> the past three years; but it was a mistake; I had wholly forgotten its
> olden aspect. And so, when I stepped in at the front door & was sud-
> denly confronted by all its richness & beauty minus wraps & con-
> cealments, it almost took my breath away. Katy had every rug & pic-
> ture & ornament & chair exactly where they had always belonged, the
> place was bewitchingly bright & splendid & homelike & natural, &
> it seemed as if I had burst awake out of a hellish dream, & had never
> been away, & that you would come drifting down out of those dainty
> upper regions with the little children tagging after you. (*LLMT*, 312)

This text addresses many of same themes Twain discussed in his description of the Villa Viviani, such as the superiority of American homes to those of Europe and the creative use of color in producing a tranquil atmosphere; however, its tone is intimate, specific, and unabashedly personal whereas the excerpt from his *Autobiography* is generic and abstract. Dramatizing the moment when he steps across the threshold into the front hall, the writer is spellbound by the abundant "richness and beauty" of his environs. As he gazes at the evocative tableau of familiar objects, "every rug & picture & ornament & chair" unveiled for his special viewing by the family's loyal servant Katy Leary, he is transported backward through time to a blissful era when his daughters were young. The "hellish dream" of his present reality—the disaster of bankruptcy and painful separation from his loved ones—thus yields briefly to a potent fantasy of reunion. In his imagination, the house represents a sanctuary from all earthly care; once reassembled under its gabled roof, the family need "never go outside the grounds any more forever." This imagery uncannily echoes Twain's depiction of Hartford as Eden nearly thirty years earlier in the *Alta California*, though his vision has contracted and turned inward over time: paradise is no longer conceived as a lush oasis of trees and flowers but is instead an inviolable domestic fortress where "peace & serenity & deep contentment" reign supreme. In a sense, these two documents serve as bookends of the writer's years in Hartford, symbolically marking the trajectory of his material aspirations, achievement, and irrevocable loss.

Even more suggestively, Twain personifies the household furnishings in his 1895 letter, telling Livy that the objects throughout the first floor—many of which had been collected abroad in 1878–1879—"speak . . . eloquently and unceasingly" of her aesthetic discernment. Arranged "exactly where they had always belonged," these commodities (among which the Swiss music box is conspicuously absent) become a panegyric to his absent spouse. "You did it all," he fervently declares, pronouncing their former residence "the loveliest home that ever was." In seeking to emulate the eclectic international aesthetic of their Nook Farm neighbors, Livy succeeded—at least in the eyes of her devoted husband—in outstripping both her models and the European originals that inspired them, creating an interior in "perfect taste." The writer's appreciation of these furnishings, moreover, underscores a profound metamorphosis in his own sensibility—in the nearly two decades that had elapsed between his telling Isabella Beecher Hooker he possessed "no taste or judgment" and this elegiac declaration of "perfection," Mark Twain had become a cosmopolitan.

# "Not an Alien but at Home"

## Mark Twain and London

PETER MESSENT

> When he came to my name . . . there was such a storm of applause as you
> never heard. . . . I did not know I was a lion. . . . I am by long odds the
> most widely known & popular American author among the English. . . .
> How have I been received? Just the same as if I were a Prodigal Son
> getting back home again.
>
> —Samuel Clemens to Olivia L. Clemens and to Mary Mason Fairbanks

> I have received since I have been here, in this one week, hundreds of
> letters from all conditions of people in England . . . and there is in them
> compliment, praise, and, above all and better than all, there is in them a
> note of affection. (Loud cheers.) . . . All these letters make me feel that
> here in England—as in America—when I stand under the English flag,
> I am not a stranger, I am not an alien, but at home.
>
> —Mark Twain speaking to the Pilgrim's Club

 FROM the start of his professional career to its end, Mark Twain
and his British (and especially his London) audience were
deeply appreciative of one another. When Twain first traveled to London in September 1872, he found that he was already well
known through the success of *The Innocents Abroad* (1869),[1] and he was im-

---

1. See, for instance, *L5*, 179.

mediately feted by London society. Soon after his arrival, on September 11, he wrote to his wife, Olivia: "confound this town, time slips relentlessly away & I accomplish next to nothing. Too much company—too much dining—too much sociability." He then added, in brackets, "But I would rather live in England than America—which is treason" (*L5*, 154–55).

Indeed, in certain ways, his early celebrity in England out-matched that in his native country. As Howard G. Baetzhold notes: "To be sure, Mark Twain was accepted more as a personality than as a literary giant, but the 'literary gods of New England' had accorded him no such enthusiasm as did the English lord mayors, lord chief justices, industrial magnates and literary men."[2] Twain's early letters from the capital are full of references to the various dinners he attended and the clubs to which he was invited. (In 1899, the Savage Club—composed of authors, journalists, and artists—would make him only its fourth honorary member, after Fridtjof Nansen, Henry M. Stanley, and the Prince of Wales.) And during the three visits he made between late summer 1872 and January 1874, he would meet a good number of celebrities and men of social substance from various walks of life and develop many close friendships among them.

Twain's main visits to London span four main periods, the first being the three linked occasions mentioned above. He made the initial trip alone, reaching the city on September 2, 1872 (following his August 31 arrival in Liverpool), and leaving on November 10 or 11 (he departed from Liverpool on the twelfth). His plan was to gather material for a book on England (provisionally titled *Upon the Oddities and Eccentricities of the English*) and, probably, to check out the possibilities of lecturing there. Although he did some work on the book, that project would gradually collapse. One of the main reasons seems to have been Twain's worry that, after his English friends had taken him into "their inner sanctuary," to then describe in a book conversations that had taken place, and the domestic manners and customs that he had seen, would be a betrayal of trust.[3] But there may have been other reasons too. In 1879, he was asked by an interviewer, "Why have you never written a book on England?" He replied:

2. Baetzhold, *Mark Twain and John Bull: The British Connection* (Bloomington: Indiana University Press, 1970), 10. Baetzhold's work provides more detail on the people Twain met and the events he attended.
3. See *L5*, 205 and esp. 540.

I have spent a good deal of time in England (your question is not a new one to me) and I made a world of notes, but it was no use. I couldn't get any fun out of England. It is too grave a country. And its gravity soaks into the stranger and makes him as serious as everybody else. When I was there I couldn't seem to think of anything but deep problems of government, taxes, free trade, finance—and every night I went to bed drunk with statistics. I could have written a million books, but my publisher would have hired the common hangman to burn them. One is bound to respect England . . . but she is not a good text for hilarious literature.[4]

Twain returned to London, this time with his wife, her friend Clara Spaulding, and his young daughter Susy, landing in Liverpool on May 27, 1873, and reaching the capital the next day. He came to expedite the British publication of *The Gilded Age* (1873) but also to lecture. Traveling from mid-July to early September (to York, Edinburgh, Dublin, Chester, and Condover Hall, the home of the amateur naturalist Reginald Cholmondeley), and with a visit to France in the first week of October, the family left London sometime on or after October 19, sailing from Liverpool on the twenty-first. With further lectures arranged, Twain stayed less than a week in America before turning around, disembarking at Liverpool on November 18, 1873 (and reaching London by the nineteenth). On this trip—lasting until his January 13, 1874, departure from Liverpool—he was accompanied by poet and travel and memoir writer Charles Warren Stoddard, who acted as his secretary and companion. Stoddard was homosexual: thus Twain's supposed reference to him as "such a nice girl" (*L5*, 456).

The lectures Twain delivered on these last two trips ("Our Fellow Savages of the Sandwich Islands" and "Roughing It on the Silver Frontier") were highly successful. There is valuable evidence of Twain's performance, and of the appeal of his comic delivery to a new and different London audience, in the newspaper reports of the time. The *Times* of October 14, 1873, reports on the previous night's lecture (Twain's first in London) and gives a full description of Twain's distinctive way of providing his own introduction:

4. Robert Regan, "'English Notes': A Book Mark Twain Abandoned," *Studies in American Humor* o.s. 2:3 (1976): 168 (from an interview in the *New York World*, May 11, 1879).

Last evening "Mark Twain" (Mr. S. L. Clemens), the well-known American humourist, delivered a lecture on "Our Fellow Savages of the Sandwich Islands" at the Hanover-square Rooms. . . . The lecturer, on making his appearance on the platform, was warmly greeted. He stated that . . . he should ask their permission to introduce to them "Mr. Mark Twain," a gentleman whose varied learning, historical accuracy, veneration for the truth, and devotion to science were only equalled by his personal comeliness, his grandeur of character, and native sweetness of disposition. It was of himself that he gave that vague and modest description; and, finding that it was the custom in this country to introduce a lecturer, and not wishing, though he disliked it, to break through that custom, he had chosen to make the introduction himself, with the object of getting in all the facts. In view of the liberality of England, who had sent to America all the lecturers that she could spare, he had felt it nothing but right and fair that the United States, in however imperfect a way, should reciprocate the compliment and he had, therefore, voluntarily thrown himself into the breach. He was present that evening under those circumstances, not in his own insignificant individual capacity, but as a representative and exponent of the gratitude of America, and so firmly was he impressed with the importance of his diplomatic mission that to make amends for past neglect he should insist on sending to Great Britain in future fourteen Yankee lecturers for every one who left these shores.

The report then gives a brief précis of the rest of his lecture.[5] The two-way traffic in lecturing that Twain humorously comments on here suggests the cross-cultural fertilization of information, ideas, politics, and humor that was very much a part of the transatlantic world of Twain's day, and to which he himself would so greatly contribute.

In a report on the "Roughing It" lecture—Twain having been to America and back meanwhile—the *Times* on December 12 paid more attention to his comic delivery. This story provides a carefully drawn account of Twain's lecturing style from the perspective of a non-American observer—and suggests the ease of the cultural crossing his comedy made. It also indicates something of the way in which Twain tailored his material for his

5. Since this was a newspaper report, there can be no guarantee of the accuracy of the transcription.

London audience. Having given a very short description of the lecture's content, the writer continued:

> While we thus briefly indicate the matter of Mr. Mark Twain's discourse, we give no notion of the exquisite humour of his manner, or of the quiet irony with which he makes a narrative that might be exceedingly dismal a cause of perpetual mirth. A smile never appears on his lips and he makes the most startling remarks as if he were uttering the merest common-place. At times, indeed, he describes in glowing terms the beauties of Lake Tahoe, but his great forte, like that of Artemus Ward, is his sustained irony, and this reaches its perfection when, at the end of his description of horrors, he grimly expresses a hope that he has not said anything which might tend to depopulate England, through a vast emigration to Nevada.

I will concentrate on the first English trips because of their impact on Twain. But he would return to London off and on throughout his career, passing three other significant periods there as well as short stays such as the July 20–August 18, 1879, visit following his *Tramp Abroad* trip.[6] Though this visit is scarcely mentioned in his published book, Twain's growing disaffection with the British at this point is hinted in his comments on London manners and the discourteous treatment accorded any "lady" walking the streets alone, even "by men who carry the look and wear the dress of gentlemen" (*TA*, 545). (Baetzhold fully traces the ups and downs of Twain's relationship with England in his book. Twain was an Anglophile at the start and end of his career, but his admiration for the country dipped in the late 1870s and 1880s, and "during the first few months of 1890, the breach between Clemens and England gaped its widest.")[7]

The next significant time Twain spent in London was much later: from between September 11 and 13, 1896, until July 17 or 18, 1897. By early October 1896 the family was established at 23 Tedworth Square in Chelsea (having moved from Guildford, its temporary home following Twain's round-the-world lecture tour). In early July of the following year, when the

---

6. Here, and at other points in the essay, I rely on information from the Mark Twain Papers at Berkeley provided by Victor Fischer. My thanks to him for his invaluable help.

7. Baetzhold, *Mark Twain and John Bull*, 162.

lease ran out, the family left Tedworth Square for the Hans Crescent Hotel, just off Sloane Street. This whole period was a quiet time of mourning following the shattering news of Susy Clemens's death on August 18, 1896 (an October letter to Poultney Bigelow reads, "We keep in hiding because we are four broken hearts, and I do not go out and my wife and daughters never see anybody").[8]

Twain and his family were next based in London from May 31, 1899, to October 6, 1900, at the end of this same extended period of European expatriation—though with time also spent at Sanna in Sweden from early July to September 27, 1899, when Jean took treatment for her epilepsy. By late June 1900 (and until early October) they were living in Dollis Hill House, the main residence of a picturesque estate in northwest London. This was Twain's favorite British residence. "He had," he said, "never seen any place that was so satisfactorily situated, with its noble trees and stretch of country, and everything that went to make life delightful, and all within a biscuit's throw of the metropolis of the world."[9]

The author's final, and highly emotional, trip to London came in his late years, from June 18 to July 13, 1907. He had come to collect—alongside Kipling—an honorary degree from Oxford University on June 26 (part of a three-day stay in that town). Twain was the subject of absolute welcome, even adoration, by the British crowds. And when he received his degree, the previous applause changed to a "roar": as Kipling remembered later, "even those dignified old Oxford dons stood up and yelled."[10] Twain's own pleasure in this trip is clearly evident in a letter to Jean written on June 30:

> Jean dear, I have had a lovely time every day of the fortnight since we arrived. . . . I prodigiously enjoyed every hour of my three days in Oxford. When we moved, gowned & mortar-boarded, in a single-file procession to the Sheldonian between solemn walls of the common people, their hearty welcome deeply touched me all the way, & brought back to mind the welcome of the stevedores when I went ashore at

---

8. Copy in MTP (Library of Poultney Bigelow, Malden-on-Hudson).
9. See "Gladstone Park," http://www.brent-heritage.co.uk/dollis_hill_house.htm (accessed June 26, 2008).
10. See Baetzhold, *Mark Twain and John Bull*, 246.

Tilbury dock. I enjoyed the noisy welcome of the undergrads when the degrees were conferred—& I was privately very vain of the common remark that it was the largest one of the day—for I was born vain, & can't seem to get over it.

I enjoyed all the fine old time-worn ceremonies, & the march back to All Souls, & the garden-party & the luncheon (ancient official name of it "gaudy,") & also the other gaudies of the succeeding nights & days—except the having to make speeches.[11]

This event was shortly followed by Twain's moving last farewell to England at the Lord Mayor's Banquet in Liverpool on July 10. In an extended and richly figurative passage at the end of his speech, he told of the meeting at sea between a small "coasting sloop in the dried apple and kitchen furniture trade," with its "frivolous little self-important captain . . . always hailing every vessel that came into sight, just to hear himself talk," and a "majestic Indiaman . . . with course on course of canvas towering into the sky . . . her freightage of precious spices lading the breeze with gracious and mysterious odors of the Orient." Hailed by the sloop's captain, the Indiaman identifies itself as "The *Begum of Bengal,* a hundred and twenty-three days out from Canton—homeward bound!" When the sloop's captain is asked for his own details, his vanity is "all crushed out of him" and he "humbly . . . squeaked back: 'Only the *Mary Ann*—fourteen hours out from Boston, bound for Kittery Point with—with nothing to speak of!'" Twain then applied this elaborate metaphor to his present position:

And what is my own case? During perhaps one hour in the twenty-four . . . I stop and reflect. Then I am humble, then I am properly meek, and for that little time I am "only the *Mary Ann,*" fourteen hours out, and cargoed with vegetables and tinware; but all the other twenty-three my vain self-satisfaction rides high and I am the stately Indiaman, plowing the great seas under a cloud of sail, and laden with a rich freightage of the kindest words that were ever spoken to a wandering alien, I think; my twenty-six crowded and fortunate days seem multiplied by five, and I am the *Begum of Bengal,* a hundred and twenty-three days out from Canton—homeward bound! (*Speaking,* 582–83)

11. Copy in MTP (Mark Twain Museum, Hannibal).

The paradoxical note right at the end, with one who is a "wandering alien" nonetheless "coming home," perfectly captures Twain's own (repeated) sense of being someone whose dislocated and transnational status—a "citizen of the world" and, to an extent, rootless according to that very definition[12] always warred with his deeply felt sense of American identity and nationality. (The move between wandering alienation and "home" is further complicated by his representation of England also as his home, as in my epigraphs.)

## II

I now return to Twain's first visits to London to focus on his early reactions to the city itself, "the metropolis of the world." It is clear that Twain—probably with his proposed book in mind—did explore the city and must have been aware of its status as a standard-bearer of modernization, with its associated benefits and discontents. Xavier Baron describes some of the city's many contradictions during the last decades of Queen Victoria's reign: "Paradoxically as London emerged as the premier world capital in the nineteenth century, celebrated by residents and visitors as an international centre of culture, elegance and sophisticated taste, it was also condemned by other natives and visitors as a concentration of the looming problems of the age of industrialization and empire: pollution, dehumanization and corruption."[13] Twain appears to have been peculiarly silent about the more negative side of this picture.

This is not the case when we turn to other writers. Twain's various stays in London span four and a half decades at a time of constant growth and change, so any blanket generalizations about the city must be treated with caution. Nonetheless, a constant theme of both native and foreign commentators, running through the whole period, concerns the social problems characterizing the London of the time, particularly the massive gaps existing between the different social classes. Fyodor Dostoevsky, writing in 1863—a decade before Twain's first visit—focused on the working classes

12. The phrase is from Dennis Welland, *Mark Twain in England* (London: Chatto and Windus, 1978), 164.

13. Baron, "The Character and Spirit of Late Victorian and Early Modern London: Conflict and Stability," in *London 1066–1914: Literary Sources and Documents,* ed. Xavier Baron, vol. 3, *Late Victorian and Early Modern London, 1870–1914* (Mountfield, East Sussex: Helm, 1997), 14.

and what he had learned of the degenerate and depressed nature of their existence:

> I have been told . . . that on Saturday nights half a million working men and women and their children spread like an ocean all over town, . . . guzzle and drink like beasts to make up for a whole week. . . . Great jets of gas burn in meat and food shops brightly lighting up the streets. It is as if a grand reception were being held for those white negroes. . . . Everyone is drunk, but drunk joylessly, gloomily and heavily. . . . Anyone who has ever visited London must have been at least once in the Haymarket at night. It is a district in certain streets of which prostitutes swarm by night in their thousands.[14]

Twenty years later, in 1883, it was again the lower-class "outcasts" of London who haunted Andrew Mearns as he conducted his religious fieldwork among the poor. Repeating Dostoevsky's white-slavery motif, he wrote: "Few who will read these pages have any conception of what these pestilential human rookeries are, where tens of thousands are crowded together amidst horrors which call to mind what we have heard of the middle passage of the slave ship." (The generic term *rookeries* comes from "The Rookery," an area of tightly packed lodging houses renowned for its iniquity, in the St. Giles part of London. The district was an oppressive and dangerous honeycomb of narrow alleys, cul-de-sacs, and small courts.) Mearns went on to describe the "100 gin-palaces" in the area surrounding his Orange Street chapel in Leicester Square, the "motley, miserable crowd" within these "glittering saloons," and the "fetid courts" (of housing) just behind them. The "low parts of London" he described as "the sink into which the filthy and abominable from all parts of the country seem to flow. Entire courts are filled with thieves, prostitutes and liberated convicts."[15]

Another two decades on—in 1905, just prior to Twain's visit for the Oxford degree ceremony—Ford Madox Ford wrote *The Soul of London*. For Ford, London was the very epitome of "the Modern." Its status as a "world

14. Dostoevsky, *Winter Notes on Summer Impressions* (1863), in *The Oxford Book of London,* ed. Paul Bailey (Oxford: Oxford University Press, 1995), 174–75.

15. Andrew Mearns, *The Bitter Cry of Outcast London* (1883), in *Late Victorian and Early Modern London,* ed. Baron, 282, 285.

town" was, however, a product not of its "vastness" but of "its assimilative powers, because it destroys all race characteristics, insensibly and, as it were, anaesthetically." He noted, too, how the city separated into its individual districts: for instance, the "Bloomsbury of dismal, decorous, unhappy, glamorous squares," and the Camden Town "of grimy boxlike houses, yellow gas and perpetual ring of tram-horse hoofs." Describing the different historical strata of the London street map, and the city's changing shapes and "enormously increased size," he suggested how such factors "militate against our nowadays having an impression, a remembered bird's-eye-view of London as a whole." (This contrasts with Michel de Certeau's more recent work on city space and especially his description of "seeing the whole" of New York from the 110th floor of the—then standing—World Trade Center. For Ford, nineteenth-century London precisely resisted the panoptic gaze and the sense of authority and control associated with it.) But Ford drew particular attention to the fissure in class and social experience between the leisured and the unemployed, groups who nonetheless inhabited adjacent city spaces: "go down Piccadilly to Hyde Park Corner on a pleasant summer day. On the right of you you have all those clubs with all those lounging and luxuriating men. On the left there is a stretch of green park, hidden and rendered hideous by recumbent forms. They lie like corpses . . . a great multitude of broken men and women."[16]

All writers, however, have their different agendas, and—in the case at hand—chose to represent urban experience in various ways. The first chapter of Henry James's 1905 *English Hours* describes the London of 1888. It does refer to the city's "uglinesses, the 'rookeries,' the brutalities"—but only deliberately to omit them from the larger impressionist picture of the welcoming city: "I think the romance of a winter afternoon in London arises partly from the fact that, when it is not altogether smothered, the general lamplight takes [the] hue of hospitality. Such is the colour of the interior glow of the clubs in Pall Mall, which I positively like best when the fog loiters upon their monumental staircases."[17] What is remarkable, though,

16. Ford, *The Soul of London: A Survey of the Modern City* (1905), in *Late Victorian and Early Modern London,* ed. Baron, 124, 125, 144–45; de Certeau, *The Practices of Everyday Life,* trans. Steven Randall (Berkeley: University of California Press, 1988), 91–92.
17. James, *English Hours* (1905), in *Late Victorian and Early Modern London,* ed. Baron, 442–43.

about Twain's depiction of London, both in his private letters and in the published writings about the city, is just how invisible are its large-scale social problems, and how little attention he pays to the strains and stresses of rapid growth and modernization in the metropolis.

Nonetheless, Twain does seem to have made a real effort to get to know his London environment during the early visits. London was considerably larger than New York, the city from which he had just come: "by the mid nineteenth century London was not merely the biggest city in the world, it was the biggest city the world had ever known." London's population in 1871 was 3,254,266, while it was only during the 1870s that New York's passed one million.[18] Twain was duly impressed by both London's size and its sights. His September 22, 1872, comic speech to the Savage Club mocks aspects of British class exclusivity and makes pointed remarks at the expense of London's public memorials—especially the just completed Albert Memorial. But the underlying sense here is of a newcomer to a much bigger city than he has previously known genuinely delighting in the new experiences and possibilities it offers:

> Everything in this monster city interests me. . . . I cannot express to you what entire enjoyment I find in this first visit to this prodigious metropolis of yours. Its wonders seem to me limitless. I go about as in a dream of enchantment. . . . Hour after hour I stand—I stand spellbound, as it were—and gaze upon the statuary in Leicester Square. I visit the mortuary effigies of Henry VIII, and Judge Jeffreys, and the preserved gorilla, and try to make up my mind which of my ancestors I admire the most. I go to that matchless Hyde Park and drive all *around* it, and then I start to enter it at the Marble Arch—and—am induced to "change my mind." . . . I drive round and round Hyde Park, and the more I see of the edges of it the more grateful I am that the margin is extensive. . . . [Twain then speaks of the monuments the country has built] in honor of two or three colossal demigods who have stalked across the world's stage, destroying tyrants and delivering nations, and whose prodigies will still live in memories of men ages after their monuments shall have crumbled to dust—I refer to the Wellington and Nelson columns and—the Albert Memorial. (*Speaking,* 70–71)

18. See "The Nineteenth-Century City," http://www.st-andrews.ac.uk/~city19c/viccity/pop.html (accessed June 26, 2008).

(In Leicester Square, a dilapidated royal statue had its head, limbs, and other parts, missing. Only the private carriages of the wealthy and fashionable were allowed in Hyde Park, not public cabs. The imposing Albert Memorial and the disparity between the magnificence of the monument and the relative insignificance of the man it immortalized also prompted Twain to write a longer satiric piece.)[19]

What then did Twain see, and what sightseeing trips did he make, during these early London visits? He certainly did most of the things that would have been on the tourist round of the time (the guidebook he used is still extant). He visited the Crystal Palace (originally built for the Great Exhibition of 1851), the Tower of London, St. Paul's Cathedral, the British Museum, the Zoological Gardens in Regent's Park, the Old Bailey, the Albert Hall (where he attended a production of Handel's *Messiah*), Newgate Prison (where public hangings had been halted only recently, in 1868), Westminster Abbey, the Doré Gallery in New Bond Street, and the Royal Academy (for an exhibition of Edwin Henry Landseer's paintings).[20] Trips outside London included stag hunting at Wargrave, near Henley; an expedition to Stratford-on-Avon with his wife (Olivia was told their destination was "Epworth" to preserve the surprise nature of the visit);[21] and outings to Salisbury and to Brighton to visit the aquarium and the Royal Pavilion.[22] He also planned a "prowl through rural England 'unbeknowns' to anybody" with Joaquin Miller, the American poet, notorious in London for his flamboyant western clothes (*L5*, 411, 413).

But there is evidence that Twain did not confine himself to conventional tourist sights and saw at least something of London street life—rather than just the insides of clubs, the mansions where formal dinners were held, and well-to-do private homes. Indeed it would be difficult to imagine any newcomer to London *not* exploring something of the huge variety of the city life then on display (some of it of the less respectable kind). Thus Twain wrote to his wife during the first of his London visits: "I have been bumming around in a vagrant sort of way, today, through the Seven Dials & such

19. See Twain's English Journals, as eventually published in *L5*, 592–95.
20. See *L5*, 155, 173–74, 179–81, 599–610, 614; *L6*, 11–12.
21. See Welland, *Mark Twain in England*, 55–56.
22. See *L5*, 205, 334–35, 158, 381. For the short piece on the Brighton Aquarium and Royal Pavilion in Twain's English Journals, see 588–91.

places. Nothing remarkable, except a street of *second-hand shoes*—every cellar full, & more displayed on the sidewalk. Scrawny people & dirty &
ragged ones rather abundant, but *they're* no sight" (*L5*, 199).

Charles Dickens had written about Seven Dials thirty-plus years earlier
(in the 1836 *Sketches by Boz*), and no doubt much had changed in the meantime, but one cannot help feeling that Twain's artistic eye and imagination
just failed to respond to the human variety and dense urban experience to
be found in such areas, in the way that Dickens's undoubtedly does:

> The stranger who finds himself in "The Dials" for the first time, and
> stands . . . at the entrance of seven obscure passages, uncertain which
> to take, will see enough around him to keep his curiosity and atten
> tion awake for no inconsiderable time. From the irregular square into
> which he has plunged, the streets and courts dart in all directions, un
> til they are lost in the unwholesome vapour which hangs over the
> house-tops, and renders the dirty perspective uncertain and confined;
> and lounging at every corner, as if they came there to take a few gasps
> of such fresh air as has found its way so far, but is too much exhaust
> ed already, to be enabled to force itself into the narrow alleys around,
> are groups of people, whose appearance and dwellings would fill any
> mind but a regular Londoner's with astonishment.[23]

(Though I have not been able to consult this book, Maude Stanley's 1878
account of her work as a district visitor in the early 1870s, *Work around the
Seven Dials,* would no doubt provide a useful update on Dickens. Seven Dials is now an up-market shopping and commercial area on the fringe of the
West End theater district, at the intersection of Monmouth, Earlham, and
Mercer streets and Shorts Gardens.)

The only other references I have found to Twain's experiences of London
street life are, first, in a description by Stoddard, his travel companion, of
their activities following a late-morning breakfast: "a lazy stroll through the
London parks, or an hour in some picture-gallery, or a saunter among the
byways of the city in search of the picturesque."[24] Then, on November 20,

---

23. Dickens, *Sketches by Boz* (New York: Charles Scribner's, 1898), 82.
24. Quoted in *L5*, 476. The references to art galleries thus far undermine Twain's self-
representation (in the travel books) as something of a cultural barbarian.

1873, in a letter to Olivia, Twain describes the view from the window of his—favorite—Langham Hotel (fronting both Portland and Langham Place, and opened just eight years earlier):

> As far up Portland Place as I can see, the glittering Horse-Guards are filing in stately procession; out here on Langham Place . . . that same beadle is behind a pillar "laying" for a tramp who has half a mind to venture inside the iron railings; that same one-legged crossing-sweeper is coming around the circle of the railings, & is humping himself too, to help a lady into a Hansom; that very same Punch & Judy man has arrived with a tap or two of his drum, a toot or two of his pipes & a wild, shrill remark from Punch himself. . . . These sights are things that you & Clara always liked. (L5, 478)

But no more of this type of material, or any record of Twain's other impressions of the "byways of the city" and the life inhabiting them, seems to exist. When he did write about London during this period he described the tourist sights (Westminster Abbey at night in "A Memorable Midnight Experience"), state occasions (the visit of the Shah of Persia), and other odd incidents, anecdotes, and character sketches ("Rogers").[25]

London changed greatly during the time spanned by Twain's various visits: in its physical geography and infrastructure, and in its social conditions. But, whatever impression it made on Twain, the modern city scarcely found its way into his published work. London (and one of its then "slum" areas, "Offal Court") did feature, in earlier historical form, in *The Prince and the Pauper* (1881). And in "The £1,000,000 Bank-Note" (1893) he did draw attention to the city's extremes of wealth and poverty as he got his narrative started. That he failed by and large to give much attention to the city is not necessarily surprising, however, when we consider that, despite his extensive knowledge of New York, and the years that he lived there, that large and fast-growing city also fails to feature significantly in his better-known writing.[26] There may be a clue to Twain's

25. Twain's London writings are scattered, though see Appendix C, "Mark Twain's English Journals," in L5, 583–629. Some material is in the early pamphlet *Mark Twain's Sketches: Number One* (1874), and some (including the rarely published letters reporting the Shah's visit) is in the posthumously published *Europe and Elsewhere* (1923) and *Letters from the Earth* (1942).

26. Though, during his 1867 residency, he did write a series of letters about New York for the San Francisco *Alta California*.

failure to engage with the urban scene around him in his comment on the populace of the Seven Dials that *"they're* no sight." He followed this remark, in the same letter to Olivia, by adding: "The truth is, there *are* no sights for me—I have seen them *all* before, in other places. . . . Consequently I do just as little sightseeing as possible, but try to see as many *people* as I can" (*L5*, 199).

Twain does describe aspects of European city life in *The Innocents Abroad* (1869), but it is usually by way of a particular comic / satiric scene or anecdote, or a focus on one distinctive place or experience, rather than in any attempt at sustained urban description. The American city Washington, D.C., features strongly in his two Colonel Sellers novels—with descriptions of boardinghouse life and of labor meetings in the 1892 *The American Claimant*. But, as a rule, Twain does not seem to have had any great urge to describe the full impact of the city environment on those who moved through it, as Howells and (later) Dreiser would do. His best fiction is set in the past, not the present-day and urban world, and though modernization is a constant theme in his work, it is usually represented indirectly, as, for example, through the impact of Hank Morgan's "improvements" on Arthurian England in *A Connecticut Yankee* (1889). It may be that the type of approach we associate with literary realism and naturalism in which the conditions of urban life have an increasingly deterministic influence on character just did not suit his artistic outlook.

Twain wrote that it was "people" rather than "sights" that stimulated him, but the urban masses and the conditions of their lives seem, for him, to have come under the latter rather than the former category. He appears to have had little interest in describing such a social class, or their immediate environment, either in his fiction or in his nonfiction. He did occasionally concentrate on a specifically urban topic ("The German Chicago"—on Berlin—in 1892), but it was not his particular forte. Martin Priestman describes Sherlock Holmes's late-Victorian London as a "sprawling anonymous city perceived as virtually unknowable."[27] Such modernistic anonymity and unknowability is a long way from Twain's normal writerly territory. "*People*" on the other hand, or at least people of a certain type, very much were of interest to him, and—in his own London life—it was his private social in-

27. Quoted in Lee Horsley, *Twentieth-Century Crime Fiction* (Oxford: Oxford University Press, 2005), 29.

teractions, in his mind very definitely unsuitable for literary representation, that made the city such an exciting and stimulating place.

There may, however, be another way of looking at all this. Twain, on his first visit to New York as a seventeen-year-old in 1853, lived in a boardinghouse, worked as a journeyman printer, and found it hard to maintain his separate identity in the context of the urban crowd ("this mass of human vermin") that pressed him on every side: "when I get in [the crowd], I am borne, and rubbed, and crowded along, and need scarcely trouble myself about using my own legs; and when I get out, it seems like I had been pulled to pieces and very badly put together again" (*L1*, 10). When he returned to the city after his long stay in Virginia and California, it was as a journalist and humorist-on-the-make and as part of bohemian society.

It is possible, then, that with the rise in social and professional status that came with his marriage and successful early career, Twain was deliberately turning his literary back on the hustle and bustle of lower-class urban life and the poverty and degradation at its margins (a type of social "otherness" that may well have threatened him by its closeness in his own younger years). Instead, it may be that his writing on London, and his own social self-representation in that urban world, was deliberately constructed as *cosmopolitan*—as he remade himself as an urbane and well-traveled citizen of the world who had little concern for the city's streets and the brute conditions to be found there.

### III

Twain's introduction to the cosmopolitan London environment, and the time he spent there, undoubtedly had a far-reaching effect on his work, fostering the status he would come to have as a genuinely *transnational* writer. Twain's travel, and his exposure to international events and opinions, would mean that he would finally be never quite fully "at home" (to recall that "Begum of Bengal" speech) either in America or elsewhere in the larger world. And—from an early point in his career—such experience meant that he found himself able to comment on the affairs of both his own country and others from a relatively detached and comparative perspective. He was unusual in this respect.

Twain was, to foreign audiences, the very epitome of the American. A picture in the June 29 *Illustrated London News* of his "interview with the King [Edward VII] at the Windsor Garden party" during the 1907 trip is headed "The King and the King of American Humour." Previously, the *Times* reported, on May 23, 1899, "The American Newspapers have been calling Mr. Clemens 'the Ambassador at large of the U.S.A.'" But this quasi-ambassadorial role was primarily cultural (Twain as a distinctively "American" presence) and did not mean that he represented his country in terms of its political actions. Rather, he came more and more to question narrowly nationalistic perspectives and to see his native country from a broader and international perspective.

By the 1860s, traffic between England and America was already substantial. Thus we find advertisements for American products in the British magazines—the *Illustrated London News* of October 19, 1872, contains one for "Colt's new breech-loading, large-bore, Deringer pistol [which] can be carried in the waistcoat pocket. Shoots accurately and with great force." American entertainments, too, were routinely staged in London. The same magazine, on May 27, 1873, advertised a concert at St. James's Hall by "The Jubilee Singers (from Fisk University, USA)." (The Jubilee singers were one of Twain's favorite musical groups. Indeed, he wrote an enthusiastic publicity letter for this very European tour.)[28] And Twain's October 13, 1873, lecture, in which he mentions the number of British lecturers who have visited America, suggests something of the two-way nature of this cultural and commercial exchange. But when he arrived in London for those first early visits, Twain must have found his horizons considerably widened just by living in such a vast city, and—particularly—one at the hub of an international empire. At the start of Joseph Conrad's *Heart of Darkness,* serialized in 1899, the narrator Marlow describes London as "the biggest, and the greatest, town on earth."[29] This was just as true earlier when Twain first arrived there.

Upon arriving in London, Twain found a political and social system that was very different from anything in his previous experience. Necessarily, the

28. See Shelley Fisher Fishkin, *Was Huck Black? Mark Twain and African American Voices* (New York: Oxford University Press, 1993), 150n12.

29. Conrad, *Heart of Darkness,* in *Youth: A Narrative and Two Other Stories* (Edinburgh: John Grant, 1925), 45.

newspapers and journals focused on the European and wider international scene (particularly as it affected the interests of the British Empire) to a much greater extent than was the case back in the United States. This— I would suggest—had two main effects. First, there was an immediate check on any tendency that Twain might have had to take his country's values and politics as an accepted norm. The review in the *Times* of Twain's *Collected Works* on December 27, 1900, praised the author as "always immaculately honest" and for his hatred of "literary Chauvinism." We might extend this to say that his experience of other countries and cultures, and particularly the time spent in London, made him wary of all types of narrow nationalism and the celebratory rhetoric associated with it.

Twain was initially struck by the beauty of the English countryside and by the deep-rooted sense of tradition he found in the culture. "God knows," he wrote to Mary Fairbanks on July 6, 1873, "I wish we had some of England's reverence for the old & great" (*L5*, 403).[30] His time in Washington (from late 1867 to the early spring of 1868), journalistic background, and keen interest in public affairs had already made him fully aware of the flaws of the American political world. But the obvious comparison with the more hierarchical and less democratic—but nonetheless attractive—British system could only have heightened that sense of dissatisfaction. In a speech prepared for an Independence Day dinner for Americans in London in 1873 (but that went undelivered when the presiding U.S. minister cut the speeches short), he praises the American democratic tradition: "we have a form of government which gives each man a fair chance and no favor. With us no individual is born with a right to look down on his neighbor and hold him in contempt." Yet his sharp satire on the wrong turns the American political, economic, and legal system had recently taken more than outweighs that praise:

> This is an age of progress, and ours is a progressive land. A great and glorious land, too—a land which has developed a Washington, a Franklin, a William M. Tweed . . . a Jay Gould, . . . a recent Congress which has never had its equal—(in some respects). . . . We have a

30. See too Twain's November 1872 letter to Susan Crane (*L5*, 213).

criminal jury system which is superior to any in the world; and its in-
efficiency is only marred by the difficulty of finding twelve men every
day who don't know anything and can't read. . . . I think I can say, and
say with pride, that we have some legislatures that bring higher prices
than any in the world. (*Speaking,* 75–76)[31]

Twain and Charles Dudley Warner had already written *The Gilded Age*
(1873) by this point, so such criticisms were well rehearsed. But it is significant that the composition of that book took place directly following the
first English visit.

Twain found himself much impressed by the efficiency of the British political system. As Baetzhold suggests: "To compare officials like the 'great
state Judges' of England, whom he described to Olivia, with the Higginses
and Dilworthys of his own country" (Higgins and Dilworthy were shady
political operators in *The Gilded Age,* a roman à clef, much of it based on
actual events and people) "must indeed have given Clemens pause. In England—whose form of government he had been taught to consider corrupt,
tyrannical, and oppressive toward the masses—it seemed that the 'best'
people, rather than almost the worse, occupied the position of authority."[32]
The comparative mode of thought, which Twain's London experiences undoubtedly encouraged, would have its effect throughout his career. For he
would continue to judge English society and politics in the light of America, and vice versa, in the coming years, swinging this way and that in terms
of the strengths and faults he would foreground. *A Connecticut Yankee* and
*The American Claimant* are particularly crucial texts in this regard (Baetzhold covers this whole subject in detail).

But Twain's London experiences also helped to prompt a second and
wider effect on his work and thinking. For his developing views on social
structures and political events were not focused through the lens of a
British-American comparison alone. The initial periods in London, and
those that followed—especially when put alongside Twain's other world

31. "Boss" Tweed of New York was a notoriously corrupt politician of the time; Jay Gould,
the financier associated with large-scale stock market manipulations.
32. Baetzhold, *Mark Twain and John Bull,* 13. See also Baetzhold's other comments on the
effects of Twain's "approval of the British system" and, especially, on his writing of "The Curious Republic of Gondour" (24–27).

travels—necessarily encouraged a much broader international perspective. London was the center of Empire, and its newspapers had a strong international dimension. Given the social world in which he moved, it is hard to see how Twain could have remained unaffected by this environment, especially given his own strong and lifelong interest in all aspects of contemporary political affairs.

The *Illustrated London News* during the period of Twain's first two (1872 and 1873) visits to London featured a number of key newsworthy topics and events, both at home and abroad. These included the diamond diggings in South Africa, the Tichborne claimant trial, the Stanley and Livingstone story (ongoing, following their November 1871 meeting in Africa and Stanley's return to London), the Modoc Indian War in the United States (Twain and his wife would nickname their young daughter Susy "Modoc"), the opening and burning down of the Alexandra Palace, the financial crisis in the United States, and—perhaps most conspicuously—the London visit of the Shah of Persia. The Tichborne case would intrigue Twain throughout his life, and he would write about it in *Following the Equator* (1897) and at greater length in the longer English edition of this book, *More Tramps Abroad*. But it was the Shah's visit that most spurred Twain's professional activity at the time, in a series of letters written for the *New York Herald*. These letters contain little in the way of inspiration. Twain's comic play on the misunderstanding that, when the *Herald's* representative tells him to "go over to Belgium and help bring the Shah to England," he is being asked to take personal responsibility for the Shah's trip, does not take him far. And, generally, he is overattentive to the "imposing processional pageantry" of the visit. He does, however, show his awareness of political inequities in Persia (the persecution of the Parsees) toward the end of the series of letters, commenting on this in the context of the state hospitality being offered: "if the mountains of money spent by civilized Europe in entertaining the Shah shall win him to adopt some of the mild and merciful ways that prevail in Christian realms it will have been money well and wisely laid out."[33] We see Twain here beginning to look beyond the America-London axis toward the larger political world.

Undoubtedly the later periods spent in London also affected Twain's out-

---

33. "O'Shah," in *Europe and Elsewhere* (New York: Harper's, 1923), 31, 64, 81.

look greatly. Debates about the course of British Empire—and especially about South African affairs—clearly fascinated him. He was in London in 1879 during the Zulu Wars. He was there again in 1897 (the sequestration in Tedworth Square) when the newspapers were full of material about the political inquiry following the Jameson raid: a failed attempt at the turn of 1895–1896, prompted by Cecil Rhodes, to undermine Boer rule in the Transvaal in favor of British political and commercial interests. Twain's own recent time in South Africa (he was there four months after the raid), and his own visits to Jameson's men in the Pretoria prison, gave him a deep interest in South African colonial affairs, one that spilled over into *Following the Equator* and—much more so—into *More Tramps Abroad*.[34]

I am suggesting that, even when we do not know much about Twain's day-to-day activities during his later English visits, it is almost certain that he was reading the newspapers carefully and closely monitoring overseas affairs (and no doubt discussing them with the British friends he did meet). There is evidence of his wide-ranging and cosmopolitan attitude in his response to the Chinese Boxer rebellion, which was in the news during his residency in 1900 at Dollis Hill House. The *Times* covered this series of events in detail, when the antimissionary and antiforeign Chinese "Boxers" became engaged in full-scale conflict with an international eight-nation army—including a group of U.S. marines—following a series of murderous attacks on Chinese Christians and foreign missionaries ("Boxers" was the name given by western correspondents to the violent and powerful Chinese secret society involved). Twain obviously followed the situation closely. Around July 9 he wrote a letter to C. F. Moberly Bell (manager at the *Times*), which, however, remained unsent.[35] Twain's cosmopolitanism here is signaled in his ability to stand apart from the general press condemnation of the Boxers and to offer—from a relativistic and comparative perspective—criticism of missionary activity (something he felt strongly about) and of the possible dangers of foreign interference. These are extracts from the much longer letter:

34. On the differences between the two versions of the text, see Dennis Welland, "Mark Twain's Last Travel Book," *Bulletin of the New York Public Library* 69 (January 1965): 31–48.
35. It was not unusual for Twain to vent his feelings in letters that remained unsent.

Sir: . . . I do not know why we respect missionaries. Perhaps it is because they have not intruded here from Turkey or China or Polynesia to break our hearts by sapping away our children's faith & winning them to the worship of alien gods. We have lacked the opportunity to find out how a parent feels to see his child deriding & blaspheming the religion of its ancestors. We have lacked the opportunity of hearing a foreign missionary who has been forced upon us against our will lauding his own saints & gods & saying harsh things about ours. If, some time or other, we shall have these experiences, it will probably go hard with the missionary. . . .

Wherever the missionary goes he not only proclaims that his religion is the best one, but that it is a true one while his hearer's religion is a false one; that the pagan's gods are inventions of his imagination. . . . The missionary has no wish to be an insulter, but how is he to help it? All his propositions are insults, word them as he may. . . .

And have [the Chinese] not reason for [their hatred of the missionary]. When a white man there kills a Chinaman is he dealt with more severely than he would be in Europe? No. When a missionary is killed by a Chinaman, are the Chinese blind to the difference in results? When an English missionary was lately killed there in a village, a British official visited the place & arranged the punishments himself . . . : a couple of beheadings . . . ; a heavy fine; and the village had to put up a monument & also build a Christian chapel to remember the missionary by. If we added fines & monuments & memorial churches to murder-penalties at home—but we don't, & we do not add them in China except when it is a missionary that is killed. And then they are insults, & they rankle in the Chinese breast, & bring us no advantage, moral, political, or commercial. . . .

[T]he missionary has always been a danger, & had made trouble more than once. . . . He has surpassed all his former mischiefs this time. He has loaded vast China onto the Concert of Christian Birds of Prey; & they were glad, smelling carrion; but they have lit & are astonished, finding the carcase alive.

Twain then talks of the likelihood of disagreement among this international "Concert" and the possibility even of "European War" as a result, concluding: "The time is grave. The future is blacker than has been any future which any person now living has tried to peer into" (MTP).

I quote at relative length here to suggest how Twain's residency in London gave him immediate access to extensive coverage of breaking international news. His various stays in the city, together with his international travel and experience, had also strongly fostered his deep interest in world affairs. His transnational positioning—crossing between countries, and retaining a certain objectivity and independence as a result—allowed him to hold political views that cut against hegemonic national interests (in this case both British and American). In his later years Twain would increasingly voice anti-missionary and anti-imperialist sentiments, and though he was wrong in the immediate case of 1900 China, he was absolutely right in foreseeing where international competition in a colonialist context would eventually end.

But even when he wrote about such matters, there was a part of Twain that retained his commitment to, and affection for, the two countries, America and England, that were closest to his heart. After a midcareer wobble, he was in his final years once more a firm Anglophile—undoubtedly, in good part, as a result of his various London experiences, his close friends in that city, and the view of British government he first gained there. All this led him, in the last analysis, to support Britain and its foreign policies, despite his general dislike of colonialist practices. That dislike was modified (following the world lecture tour) by his genuine admiration for British rule in India and by the "new conviction" he gained "of the importance of Anglo-American solidarity."[36] (This did not mean that he was always in full sympathy with the actions of either party in that pairing. See, for instance, his barbed comments on Britain and the United States being "kin in sin" as a result of their policies in South Africa and the Philippines, made during a speech introducing Winston Churchill in New York in December 1900 [*Speaking*, 368–69].) That solidarity was signaled, in a more personal sense, in the seating plan for the Pilgrims Club luncheon of June 25, 1907, on Twain's last London trip, with "upon its cover a portrait of Mark Twain surmounted by the Stars and Stripes and the Union Jack side by side." Twain's

---

36. Baetzhold, *Mark Twain and John Bull*, 207.

relationship to England (and to London in particular) is summed up in that one twinned image. Augustine Birrell (chief secretary for Ireland) toasted Twain at that dinner, praising him as "the true consolidator of nations . . . [whose] delightful humour . . . dissipates and destroys national prejudices."[37] One suspects that Twain deeply appreciated that remark.

37. *Times* of London, June 26, 1907, p. 3.

# Mark Twain in Vienna

*A Diplomat without Pay*

JANICE MCINTIRE-STRASBURG

THROUGHOUT his lifetime as a public figure, Mark Twain was asked to comment on public affairs—an opportunity he seldom refused. As early as 1869, when he took over editorship of the *Buffalo Express*, he began writing on issues of local and national importance in his weekly sketches. In "The Monopoly Speaks" he supported the coal magnates—including his soon-to-be father-in-law, Jervis Langdon, and commented on the then current debate over changing the national capital to St. Louis. Another favorite topic was congressional graft and scandal ("The Facts in the Case of George Fisher, Deceased," "War and Wittles"), and, though less frequently, he also commented on transnational affairs ("The European War!!!" and "Ye Cuban Patriot").[1] He spoke out against the treatment of Chinamen on the Pacific Coast and supported the Burlingame Treaty and anti-expansionism. Most often, these early sketches exploited his nom de plume's clown pose, taking advantage of hyperbolic humor, facetiousness, and downright silliness. He endorsed Grant's presidential bid as well, although his early forays into the political arena were marked by both caution and inconsistency. As Louis

1. *Mark Twain at the "Buffalo Express,"* ed. Joseph B. McCullough and Janice McIntire-Strasburg (DeKalb: Northern Illinois University Press, 1999).

Budd observes, "Twain himself was not worrying much about the overall picture. He had been earning most of his living as a topical columnist who served up the news with a humorous sauce and met his deadlines without agonizing over consistency."[2]

His actual political stance was a confusing mishmash of Whig ideals from his childhood and a Republican acceptance of laissez-faire business—no doubt influenced by Jervis Langdon, his new status as one-third owner of the *Buffalo Express,* and a weather-eye toward increasing his book sales. His public positions vacillated between defense of the common man as the underdog (some ethnic minorities included, while notably the Irish and Native Americans were not) and endorsement of big business monopolies. During the early part of his career, these included the coal and railroad monopolies and later came to include Henry Huttleston Rogers at Standard Oil as well as Andrew Carnegie. Throughout the 1870s and 1880s, at the peak of his career as a publishing author, Twain "manages to amuse without offending—to appear as a seemly sage, full of opinions but generally holding forth well within the bounds of respectability."[3] His support for causes never flagged; however, such support never jeopardized his book sales or the image of "Mark Twain" that he wished to promote: that of a serious American author. His increasing financial success and the concomitant rise in social status caused him to exercise increasing care in airing his opinions publicly. This inoffensive stance allowed him to form alliances with the rich and powerful social elite—to become a member of the in-group to which he aspired.

This "acceptance anxiety" that permeated the first half of his public life—stemming from his attempt to balance his perceived social position with influences from a childhood solidly anchored in the middle class—can be directly compared to the twin images of his persona: "Mark Twain," the Washoe humorist to whom news items and political commentary were subservient to humor and reader entertainment; and Samuel Clemens, the successful writer and businessman ambitious to be accepted as a serious writer and member of high society. While this analogy is clearly an oversimplifi-

2. Budd, *Mark Twain, Social Philosopher* (Columbia: University of Missouri Press, 2001), 38.
3. Leland Krauth, *Proper Mark Twain* (Athens: University of Georgia Press, 1999), 321.

cation of the Twain/Clemens persona and a wealth of discussions concerning it, I invoke it here only as an analogy to the problems he encountered in his attempt to shift his reputation from "mere humorist" to serious writer and successful businessman. He respected and admired the captains of industry and inventors, longed for acceptance into their ranks, and constantly schemed to join the millionaire class through his own investments and inventions.

As a consequence of these two competing forces in his life—humanitarianism and capitalism—Twain's political writing before the 1890s is a combination of humorous naïveté and rhetorical sophistication that depends for its stance on contemporaneous influences in the author's life. As the black slave comments to a youthful Twain in "Corn Pone Opinions" (1901)—"a man is not independent, and cannot afford views which might interfere with his bread and butter" (*CTSS2*, 507). He became, in essence, the "bounded Twain" of Leland Krauth's 1999 study, *Proper Mark Twain*. We can see a radical shift in Twain's personal life during the 1880s and beyond—a shift that also marked the beginnings of a sea change in the nature of his published and unpublished political essays and public speeches.

Between the publication of *A Connecticut Yankee in King Arthur's Court* in 1889 and Mark Twain's triumphant appearance in Vienna in 1897, the author had bankrupted himself trying to keep Charles Webster Publishing Company afloat and financing the Paige typesetter; become an exile from America in his efforts to economize on his personal spending; completed an around-the-world speaking tour to pay off his debts; and lost his oldest daughter, Susy, to spinal meningitis. In addition, he suffered the loss of his brother Orion in December 1897, shortly after his arrival in Vienna. Livy was already suffering from heart trouble, Jean had been diagnosed with epilepsy, and his own health was not the best. He was a sixty-year-old man who had been traveling and lecturing for a year, strapped for cash and worrying about financial support for his family should anything happen to him: "Since my daughter's death my interest has centered itself upon the books: they will be the only support of my family in case of my death; yes and their only support while I remain alive, for I am done with the platform. For a year or more, at any rate" (*MTHHR*, 243) His personal problems were exacerbated by his status as a public figure. His is perhaps the most public personal bankruptcy in American history. The newspapers published items concerning the amount of his debt and publicized his around-the-world tour, touting the fact that he intended to pay his creditors to the penny. The *New York Herald* even set up a fund to which readers could contribute to help the author pay off his debt—a plan his wife refused outright. When Clara took a fall from a carriage, the newspapers reported it, and Livy arrived in New York in 1896 to read about her daughter Susy's death in the local papers.

Amid all these personal problems, Twain completed *Following the Equator* for subscription publication in ten months. Everett Emerson describes it as "Twain's most elegant" travel book, made so by careful revision to act in concert with the image of himself that Twain wished to project.[4] The image is that of a man whose presence among the wealthy and influential is unquestioned. The tone is unostentatious and even decorous as he records his cosmopolitan life in Paris, his invited visits to mayors, governors, princes, and generals—even meetings with God and Satan.[5] He describes encounters with indigenous people in Australasia and India as well, although the text makes it clear that these people, no matter how sympathetic Twain is toward their plight, are his inferiors. Unlike *The Innocents Abroad,* in which "the narrator struggled to create status for himself by contentiously disputing the conduct of his fellow travelers, the reliability of conventional guidebooks, and the accuracy of traditional histories," in *Following the Equator,* "Twain has no need to establish his authority; it is a given, the product of his literary achievement and of his skill and fame as a lecturer."[6]

The completion of *Following the Equator,* Henry Huttleston Rogers's successful negotiation of a uniform edition of Twain's work through Harper and Brothers, the agreement with Frank Bliss to publish the travel book through subscription, and Rogers's successful investment of the funds Twain deposited with him while lecturing offered the author financial security for the first time in ten years; as a result, Twain felt less pressure to publish for purely monetary reasons. His letters to Rogers during negotiations demonstrate the heavy

---

4. Emerson, *The Authentic Mark Twain: A Literary Biography of Samuel L. Clemens* (Philadelphia: University of Philadelphia Press, 1984), 205.

5. Krauth, *Proper Mark Twain,* 223.

6. Ibid., 225.

toll that financial worries exerted on his creative life. He states in his February 26, 1897, letter that he has "grown so nervous about the contracts that such sleep as I get doesn't do much good, and so my work drags badly and lacks life" (MTHHR, 265). By November 11, he was writing exasperatedly:

> I throw up the sponge. I pull down the flag. I cannot bear the weight any longer. It totally unfits me for work. I have lost three entire months now. In that time I have begun twenty magazine articles and books— and flung every one of them aside in turn. The debts interfered every time and took the spirit out of the work . . . a man can't possibly write the stuff required of me unless he have an unharassed mind. My stuff is worth more in the market today than it ever was before—and yet in 3 months I have not succeeded in turning out fifty acceptable pages. (MTHHR, 303)

Twain's financial solvency, achieved in January 1899, marks the end of "writing for the creditors" (MTHHR, 303). He wrote William Dean Howells on December 30, 1898, that "the dread of leaving the children in difficult circumstances has died down" and that he can "sleep as well as anyone" (Letters, 669). His newfound financial security allowed him the luxury of choosing his writing projects according to his own tastes. It also gave him the freedom to interest and involve himself in the events taking place in Austria and elsewhere. Following the Equator and subsequent projects differ from Innocents and other early works in that they represent a more studied—and often more sophisticated—cosmopolitan view of the world. During the world tour and after, Twain examined the cultures he interrogated less as an imperialist and more as a moral idealist. Such a stance would have been impossible for him previously. He wrote to please himself and as a method of assuaging his grief. Writing to Joseph Twichell on January 19, 1897, he stated: "I am trying to add to the "assets" which you estimate so generously. No, I am not. I am working, but it is for the sake of the work—the 'surcease of sorrow' that is found there. I work all the days, and trouble vanishes away when I use that magic. This book [Following the Equator] will not stand between me and it now—but that is no matter, I have many unwritten books to fly to for my preservation" (Letters, 641). In fact, Twain had already made a good start on those "many unwritten books." Carl Dolmetsch observes that in Vienna he wrote "more and in a greater variety of forms" than "during all but a few comparable stretches in his career," including plays (and translations of German drama), short fiction, essays, and longer projects.[7] In this sense, his presence in Vienna and his improving financial situation appear to have inspired an increase in his creative imagination. Twain observed to Rogers from Lucerne in August that he was "writing a novel, and getting along well with it"—most likely "Chronicles of Young Satan" (*Letters*, 641). Most of his novel projects, however, would remain uncompleted and unpublished within his lifetime.

When Samuel Clemens detrained in Vienna in September 1897, he arrived as "Mark Twain"—international celebrity. Arguably the most-traveled man of his century, he had visited or lived in nearly every region of America; traveled to and written about the Sandwich Islands, Europe, the Holy Land, Australasia, Africa, and India; and was one of the most highly acclaimed American authors and lecturers of his time.[8] Andrew Lang had recently proclaimed *Adventures of Huckleberry Finn* the great American novel.[9] Twain had completed a highly successful lecture tour, a new travel book, and achieved (or was soon to achieve through Rogers's efforts) financial solvency. Viennese newspapers trumpeted his impending arrival three days in advance. Reporters clamored for interviews, which Twain gave from his hotel room, as an attack of gout kept him bedridden for much of the first month. One enterprising reporter even invented a humorous interview with "Our Famous Guest" when he could not gain access to the great man. During his stay there, the Hotel Metropole—Twain's home away from home from the fall of 1897 to the summer of 1898—"became a sort of clearinghouse of the Viennese art and literary life, much more like an embassy than the home of a mere literary man" (*MTHHR*, 657).[10] He could not go any-

7. Dolmetsch, *"Our Famous Guest": Mark Twain in Vienna* (Athens: University of Georgia Press, 1992), 11.

8. William Dean Howells retained the number-one spot on J. K. Bank's list, published in *Literature*, of the top-ten living writers, a fact Twain mentioned in a letter to Howells on April 2, 1899. The poll was taken from February to April. On March 17, the list read: Howells, Twain, Fiske, Aldrich, Henry Jones, Stockton, Harte, S. Weir Mitchell, Warner, and Cable. *SMTHL*, 330.

9. William R. Macnaughton, *Mark Twain's Last Years As a Writer* (Columbia: University of Missouri Press, 1979), 24.

10. Ironically, the Hotel Metropole, as Dolmetsch notes, later became the headquarters of the Nazi SS in World War II.

where in Vienna without being the center of attention. In his initial interviews, he told reporters that he had come to Vienna so that Clara could
study piano with Theodor Leschetizky and to find new material to write
about, even though letters to Howells, Twichell, and Rogers indicate that he
had already begun several more sustained projects and magazine articles.
After years of writing for pay and worrying about his financial situation,
"Mark Twain," it seems—and a bit to his own surprise—had arrived.

## MARK TWAIN: OUR MAN IN VIENNA

A study of Twain's later sociopolitical writing must begin with *Following
the Equator,* his last travel book, completed contemporaneously with his arrival in Vienna. Though Louis Budd critiques the text as neither happy nor
good, he observes that the book "deserves to be read if only because it shows
that [Twain's] values had firmed up in an unexpected way." Twain's stances
on human-rights issues fluctuate much less and depend less upon the eth-
nicity of the culture involved. On this last trip, having seen more of the
world and its cultures than almost any other author of his time, Twain seems
to have settled in his mind the "fact" of a universal brotherhood of mankind.
Though not unmitigated by pessimism—and in some cases, elitism—in his
notebook entries from the time, Twain clearly states a belief that "the hearts
of men are about alike all over the world, no matter what their skin-
complexions may be."[11] His later pessimistic thoughts recorded in essays
such as "What Is Man?" aside, such a statement can be read as Twain's support for a moral imperative of human equality as demonstrated early on in
*Adventures of Huckleberry Finn;* indeed, there is no question that Twain's canon
supports such a reading. However, in light of his also well-documented pessimism, the statement cuts both ways, as one of Pudd'nhead Wilson's New
Calendar maxims suggests: "The universal brotherhood of man is our most
precious possession—what there is of it" (*FE,* 256).

As an example of the first proposition, the aborigines of Australasia gain
the respect and sympathy denied to the indigenous people of his own country when Twain records his visit there. He immortalizes the Big River Tribe
of Tasmania, honoring their bravery and military acumen (sixteen men with

11. Budd, *Mark Twain Social Philosopher,* 168, 169.

only spears and clubs for defense, nine women, and one child against forty thousand British colonists), and satirizes their treatment after surrender: "These were indeed wonderful people, the natives. They should not have been wasted. They should have been crossed with the Whites. It would have improved the Whites, and done the Natives no harm" (*FE*, 265). Yet these natives *were* "wasted" according to Twain: placed in small settlements on neighboring islands, dressed in British clothing, forbidden tobacco, and instructed in Christianity, until "one by one their hearts broke and they died" (*FE*, 265). As one of Twain's earliest unambiguous anti-imperialist statements, and one in which he neither modified the account to placate British sentiments nor toned down his criticism of Christian missionaries, these passages stand out as a clear personal stance:

> Whites always mean well when they take a human fish out of the ocean and try to make them dry and warm and happy and comfortable in a chicken coop; but the kind-hearted white man can always be depended on to prove himself inadequate when he deals with savages. He cannot turn the situation around and imagine how he would like to have a well-meaning savage transfer him from his house and his church and his clothes and his books and his choice food to a hideous wilderness of sand and rocks and snow, and ice and sleet and storm and blistering sun, with no shelter, no bed, no covering for his and his family's naked bodies and nothing to eat but snakes and grubs and offal. This would be hell to him; and if he had any wisdom he would know that his own civilization is a hell to the savages. (*FE*, 267)

Twain advocates an anomaly in the nineteenth-century age of progress: a cultural pluralism that allows indigenous people to continue their lifeways unhindered (and "unimproved") by European sociocultural mores. While he stops short of recognizing their rights as original inhabitants from whom the land was stolen—a process present in every European colonization in the "new world"—he champions, at least, a laissez-faire attitude toward their cultural autonomy, using the Tasmanians as a clear example of the disastrous effects of forced cultural assimilation.

Yet the author clearly retains the vestiges of a nineteenth-century European cultural elitism when critiquing his visit to India. He exhibits considerably less sympathy for that country's natives. On the one hand, he finds

much to praise in Hindu religious practices. His description of Mina Ba-
hadur Rana overflows with the man's personal accomplishments, intellect,
and devotion. He finished the sketch with his own paean to reverence "that
is difficult"—that is, reverence for the "political or religious attitude of a
man whose beliefs are not yours" (*FE*, 514). Twain uses the story and its
moral to generalize concerning a less admirable quality of the "brotherhood
of man"—the inability of any civilization to recognize and honor reverence
for religious tenets and holy places other than its own. In this instance, he
is defending the Taj Mahal against British and American tourists' picnick-
ing on the ground of a shrine. However, the majority of Twain's descriptions
of India and Indians compare their civilization unfavorably with that of the
British colonists, lauding the British for bringing law, order, and progress to
a backward civilization. He describes the shops as "unbelievably small and
impossibly packed with merchantable rubbish, and with nine-tenths-naked
natives squatting at their work of hammering, pounding, brazing, solder-
ing, sewing, designing, cooking, measuring out grain, grinding it, repairing
idols—and then the swarm of ragged and noisy humanity under the horses' feet and everywhere the pervading reek, fume and smell!" (*FE*, 408). Although he finishes the description by stating that it was all "wonderful and
delightful," the style and tone are reminiscent of the more culturally critical Twain in *The Innocents Abroad* describing his travels through the Holy
Land, and clearly demonstrate his belief in his own superiority. It appears
from his text that the aborigines of Australasia fall into the "noble savage"
category; Indian peasants, on the other hand, are the "bloodthirsty" type.

He relates with horror the murder of a twelve-year-old girl for her jewelry, the trial for which coincided with his stay in Bombay. Although he admits that such a murder could happen anywhere, his dramatic description
of the case makes it obvious that he believes that the value placed on human life in his own cultural mores is radically different from that in the
mores of the Indian natives. Relating the incident to earlier stories of
Thuggee—murderous bands of criminals roaming India and preying on
travelers—Twain appears most appalled by the "cold, business-like quality" of the incident: "this Indian murderer does his deed in the full light of
day, cares nothing for the society of witnesses, is in no way incommoded by
the presence of the corpse, takes his own time about disposing of it, and the
whole party are so indifferent, so phlegmatic, that they take their regular

sleep as if nothing was happening and no halters hanging over them" (*FE,* 392). The preponderance of such sketches, including the history of Thuggee and his more lightly humorous sketches describing his Indian servants, show Twain's political sentiments regarding India, at least, to be more enthusiastic about British rule, which he saw as bringing needed reforms in law and order, progressive inventions that advanced the culture to late-nineteenth-century standards (including train travel across the country-side), and sociomoral responsibility.

It is tempting to view Twain's inconsistency within *Following the Equator* as an extension of the vacillation Budd and other scholars document in Twain's earlier writing. Krauth quotes a later passage in *Following the Equator* where the author states that soon all savage lands will come under European control, and that such change will bring "peace and order and the reign of law" (*FE,* 626). However, he also asserts that Twain's opinions on colonial rule are lodged in a more sophisticated moral imagination—one that can separate out the ameliorating effects of technological advances and the "humane end to factional strife and oppression," all the while recognizing the deleterious effects of colonial rule on indigenous cultures.[12] This last travel book shows a Twain less likely to accept the all-or-nothing proposition of imperialism and more likely to question the human consequences of it—a decidedly more sophisticated view of his world. As a political commentator, he has begun to notice shades of gray and recognize that besides bringing advancements to "primitive" peoples, colonialism has the potential to erase entire cultures.

Twain brought this slightly more pluralistic worldview with him to Vienna and applied it to the political events he observed there. His stay coincided with several historical watersheds in Viennese politics, and the reporter in him could not resist joining the fray. He wrote Twichell on October 23, 1897, that if he "had time to run around and talk, I would do it; for there is much politics agoing, and it would be interesting if a body could get the hang of it. It is Christian and Jew by the horns—the advantage with the superior man, as usual—the superior man being the Jew every time in all countries" (*Letters,* 647). The reference is to the events of October 1897, when Twain was present at a marathon filibuster session in the Reichsrath—

12. Krauth, *Proper Mark Twain,* 228.

the upper house of the German Parliament—and the subsequent ouster of "troublemakers" from the meeting hall. When the gallery was cleared, the author's fame found him a place with the London *Times* correspondent in the first gallery.[13] Twain thus missed "none of the show" and published his report of it, "Stirring Times in Austria," in 1898. The essay draws upon Twain's reportorial skills from his early days, served up with his trademark irony.

His legendary predisposition to dislike and disparage the French had already caused him to defend Dreyfus as a man framed purely on account of his being a Jew. Although Twain's own understanding of Jews was often marred by the stereotypical conventional wisdom of his time, he was totally unprepared for the vilification of Jews he encountered while a visitor in Austria.[14] Cynthia Ozick refers to the Vienna of 1897 as "notoriously, stingingly, passionately anti-Semitic,"[15] a characterization apparently unknown to Twain when he arrived. He found out soon enough. Innocently unaware of the separation of Jewish from non-Jewish newspapers and magazines within Vienna, Twain gave interviews without any thought to individual papers' politics. As a result, the first few interviews came out in Jewish newspapers. Christian venues viewed this as an affront, and disparaging political cartoons labeled him "Das Juden Mark Twain" for days afterward. Stung by this public criticism, Twain was more judicious in his choices of publication and his public commentary thereafter; however, he did not discontinue expressing his opinions. He published both "Stirring Times" and "Concerning the Jews" in *Harper's*, keeping his opinions safely in New York.

William Macnaughton calls "Stirring Times" a fine essay by any standard. He observes that this piece unites "the subject itself, the writer's perspective on the subject, and his sense of the audience for whom the piece is writ-

13. Twain offered further comment on his bird's-eye view of the Reichsrath in an interview for the *New York World* on December 13, 1897: "A scene I witnessed in America once was what approached it most nearly. It was when one gentleman had gone off on another man's horse—by mistake—and was caught and brought back. Well, there was an assembly then something like this Reichsrath that began by hanging the accused, and then sat in judgment over him afterward. I daresay a good deal of language then used was like what I heard tonight, but which, to my regret, I did not always catch correctly" (*Interviews*, 331).
14. Dan Vogel discusses references to Jews throughout the Twain canon in *Mark Twain's Jews* (Jersey City, N.Y.: KTAV Publishing House, 2006).
15. Ozick, "Mark Twain and the Jews," *Commentary* 99:5 (May 1995): 56–57.

ten."[16] In it, Twain offers the reader a masterful description of Austrian fac-
tionalism, newspaper censorship, and the government's skill in deflecting
Austrians' attention to other matters—primarily the insidious infiltration of
Jews into the superstructures of Austrian business and government. His report of the Reichsrath meeting is humorously ironic, depicting the members as incorrigible children clamoring for attention in any way possible:
they "pose for the gallery"; tear sections from the desks and pound them on
anything available, creating a deafening noise over which the speakers cannot be heard; and outshout and outvulgarize each other in name calling. He
details the duplicitous passage of the Lex Falkehayn and its effect on leg-
islative debate: "it was plain that nothing legitimately to be called a vote"
had taken place and that the subsequent ouster of the dissidents was an
event that "history will be talking of five centuries hence . . . a free parliament profaned by an invasion of brute force" (*CTSS2*, 237, 242). He notes
that these events signaled a crash of the Bandini government, a popular outbreak here and there, and three of four days of rioting in Prague, of which
Germans and Jews were the object. Unaccountably—at least for Twain—
"in all cases, the Jews had to roast, no matter what side he was on" (*CTSS2*,
243). Here Twain recognizes that the Jews, who at the time had no representation in either the German or the Opposition parties and were, therefore, nonparticipants, received the brunt of the punishment in the riots that
followed.

Unlike the political vacillation Twain's earlier writing demonstrates, his
support for Austrian Jews was rock solid, even though it proved to be an
unpopular stance at the time. While the artistic community in Vienna of
which Twain had become an accepted member contained a large contingent
of the Jewish population, he was also feted by elite political movers and
shakers whose antipathy for Jews was well known. A younger Twain, still
advancing his career as a writer, might have been more judicious in his support for an unpopular minority. Indeed, his standard toss-away line of the
early years, "No Irish need apply," demonstrates this to be the case. However, here he clearly threw his support to an unpopular cause—an approach
he continued to take when he returned home to castigate America's annex-
ation of the Philippines. That he declined comment for the Austrian papers

16. Macnaughton, *Last Years,* 65–66.

and published his account in the United States merely shows his increasing sophistication as an astute political observer; an awareness of his own precarious position within the country as a guest who had already been chastised for his unwitting support of Jews. His observations on this occasion and others prompted him to publish "Concerning the Jews" the following year, also in *Harper's*.

In this essay, Twain uses a rhetorical device that had served him well in his early *Express* sketches and elsewhere: the occasion is a response to a letter received from a reader of "Stirring Times." Although it is quite likely that Twain did receive letters concerning this essay, whether or not the actual letter he quotes from was ever received is irrelevant. What the quoted passage offers him is an opportunity to quickly and easily set the thesis for his commentary. He is then free to glide effortlessly into the discussion he wishes to have without addressing thorny questions of theology. The question his "reader" asks concerns the deliberation of the Ausgleich, in which Jews had no party or representation of any kind and thus were absolute nonparticipants.[17] Yet the majority of the violence in its aftermath fell upon them. He asks, "Will a Jew ever be permitted to live, honestly, decently, and peaceably like the rest of mankind?" (*CTSS2*, 354). On its face, the question has far wider implications than the particular case in point for the "brotherhood of man" that fascinated Twain all of his life in one way or another. It is an extension of the conundrums of slavery, reconstruction, and religious intolerance for which Twain had been trying to find an answer in *Adventures of Huckleberry Finn, Pudd'nhead Wilson,* and *A Connecticut Yankee in King Arthur's Court* and which permeate later, ultimately unpublished projects.

Unfortunately, Twain finds no real answers in "Concerning the Jews." Readers will find unconditional support and admiration for an oppressed and unappreciated minority, albeit support that is garnered through white western European stereotypes common at the time and still present today. It is a masterpiece of classical rhetorical argumentation, borrowing from biblical and historical sources for its support. Through this logic, Twain de-

17. The Ausgleich was the compact formed in 1867 that united Austria and Hungary. By the terms of its formation, it was to be revisited every ten years as the needs of the involved countries changed. The change suggested in this (1897) legislation—and what caused all the trouble—was that the legal language be the local vernacular rather than German. Austrians viewed the proposal as a loss of their control over the region.

termines that fanaticism—that is, in the sense of religious persecution—has little or nothing to do with the treatment of Jews from the earliest recorded history to the present. Across a series of historical examples, he demonstrates that the need for all cultures to suppress Jews stems from the inability of other cultures to compete with them in an open market in the areas of intellect and business acumen. His suggestion for Jews who wish to improve their situation is to organize into blocks to gain political strength. In short, his suggestion mirrors his belief in American democracy and its political efficaciousness. Rather than "scattering their votes" the Jews ought to consolidate their power as other groups had. Hindsight from the vantage point of the twenty-first century makes Twain's advice appear naive, to say the least. His declaration that religious persecution "has already come to an end" and that "among the high civilizations he [the Jew] seems to be very comfortably situated indeed, and to have more than his proprotionate share of the prosperities going" shows a lack of cultural insight and a misjudgment of the actual position of Jews in Austria at the time (CTSS2, 368). The argument is fundamentally flawed due to Twain's lack of experience and knowledge of Jews and their problems. As was often the case in Twain's earlier forays into the political arena, he has impulsively thrown his support to this cause without a complete understanding of the situation. As Dan Vogel suggests in *Mark Twain's Jews*, his heart is in the right place, though his understanding is lacking.

## THE VIENNA YEARS:
## MARK TWAIN'S CREATIVE LIFE

Although he published several short essays and gave some interviews during his Vienna days, Twain published little fiction during that time; his letters to Rogers, Howells, and Twichell all mention writing furiously on several projects, but his only published fiction of note was "Which Was the Dream?" and "The Man That Corrupted Hadleyburg." It may be that the social whirl of Vienna was not conducive to sustained creative effort. Twain was certainly caught up in receptions, concerts, parties, and other social functions.[18] He was also still dealing with the aftermath of grief that he and

18. For a complete description of Twain's social life in Vienna, there is no better source than Dolmetsch's *"Our Famous Guest."*

his family experienced at the one-year anniversary of Susy's death. It is clear from his notebooks and letters that he was dividing his time between the manuscript for the "Early Days" section of his autobiography, "Chronicles of Young Satan," "Schoolhouse Hill," "Hellfire Hotchkiss," "The Great Dark," and "Tom Sawyer's Conspiracy."[19] His creative efforts toward novel-length material were divided roughly between a fascination with reality and dream states; a desire to return to the material of Hannibal by bringing Huck, Tom, and Jim back for another adventure; and tales whose denouements rely on temptation and the moral corruption of man.

Most of the dream stories contain thinly veiled elements of autobiography in which the characters' lives are shattered by events and/or realizations that are beyond their control. They also indicate a fascination with the precarious nature of human consciousness, as noted by John S. Tuckey in *Mark Twain and Little Satan*. On the surface, in writing "Which Was the Dream?" Mark Twain was working his way out of bankruptcy and coming to grips with his grief over the loss of Susy. Major General X leads the picture-perfect life of a war hero whose successful business dealings bring him the same kind of wealth and recognition that Twain's novels had brought him in the 1870s and 1880s. It draws from *Tom Sawyer* both for the protagonist's first name and for his meeting with his future wife, Alison; and the General's daughters engage in many of the same activities and pastimes as Clemens's own daughters—playacting and listening to stories written by a doting father. The characters live in "a world of enchantment" (*CTSS2*, 226), take European vacations, and live in a handsome house. In the course of the story, the protagonist goes bankrupt, is accused of embezzlement due to the mismanagement of his brother-in-law, loses his house to a fire, and is accused of forgery. This final charge causes him to faint. When he comes to himself eighteen months later, he finds that his wife, rather than upbraiding him for the troubles and the poverty of their present life, has carried on and cared for the family, and that the army officers have believed his story: "A West Point man might be a fool in business matters, but never a rascal and never a liar . . . even the best soldier could botch a trade which he was not fitted for" (*CTSS2*, 259)—so too, perhaps, might an author.

19. I rely on William Macnaughton's 1979 study for information on manuscripts in progress.

Knowing Twain's personal history, it is difficult not to see Livy in the saintly, uncomplaining Alison; it is also difficult not to see Susy in the author's portrait of Bessie. Although H. K. Bush, in his 2002 article, rejects Pamela Boker's assertion that Twain was "unable to accept and grieve in a healthy way any permanent loss"—quite rightly, I believe—and argues against applying Freud's either/or proposition of mourning and melancholia, our understanding of "Which Was the Dream?" can benefit from another of Freud's contemporaneous theories—*The Interpretation of Dreams*.[20] As a fictionalized account of wish fulfillment, the tale assuages grief and stress through an active, conscious act of imagination. It represents an acting-out of the theory of a dream self, a spiritualized self that transcends the positivistic, mechanized theory of self that was competing in Twain's mind at the time. The story "tries on" an alternative to his more pessimistic views in "What Is Man?" and allows Twain's dream self, at least, to interact with memories of Susy in what Freud would call mourning—the "normal" process of grief as opposed to what he called melancholia, mourning's abnormal counterpart.[21] The dreamlike quality of Tom's early life demonstrates the fleeting nature of the "real" life and the swiftness with which it can change. As a portrait of Twain's own life, the story is notable for the nobility of its characters in the face of adversity and their eventual triumph over it. The family's personal happiness does not rely on monetary wealth—an idea that would have appealed to Twain as he escaped from debt without any clear understanding of exactly how much financial security he might have, or what his income would look like in the future.

In Freudian terms, the fantasy balances the guilt Twain felt over Susy's death and what he saw as his responsibility in the family's financial hardships with his natural wish that the storybook family life of the Clemenses had remained untouched by financial and personal tragedy. In that sense, the fictionalized "dream" can be seen as beneficial to Twain's grieving process. Through an act of creative imagination, Twain temporarily escaped

---

20. Quoted from Bush, "Broken Idols: Mark Twain's Elegies for Susy and a Critique of Freudian Grief Theory," *Nineteenth-Century American Literature* 57:2 (September 2002): 237–68 (239).

21. John S. Tuckey elaborates on these two key competing ideas in Twain's late work in "Mark Twain's Later Dialogue: The 'Me' and the Machine," *American Literature* 41:4 (January 1970): 532, 542.

from the problems and losses of his personal reality into a fictional "dream." According to Freud, the "dream work" prepares the ego—one's "real" or rational self—to accept reality by reconciling the three theoretical parts of the personality—the id, ego, and superego. Instead of performing this work through his actual dreams, Twain's dream work was conscious, performed through the creative act of writing. On a different level, Twain's narrative structure also demonstrates Tuckey's proposition that Twain was vacillating between two competing philosophies: "or one might say more particularly, two competing psychologies—the somewhat older, positivistic one, already in vogue when he had been maturing, which viewed human beings as mechanisms, entirely the product of environment, and the newer one, emphasizing the force of the unconscious and dreams."[22] He was attempting to work out for himself in fiction the relative strength and efficacy of a "spiritual self." In Walter Blair's words, Twain was "fighting for faith."[23] The fight that Tuckey defines is clearly seen in many of Twain's unfinished projects, particularly in the *Mysterious Stranger* manuscripts, "The Great Dark," and "3000 Years among the Microbes." Thus, while in Twain's essays, interviews, and nonfiction, as noted earlier, we see a man reevaluating his political views and moving toward a more sophisticated and modern approach to multiculturalism, in the fiction we see a man debating nineteenth-century positivistic philosophies of man's inner life and the more modernistic and subjective approach to consciousness that Freud ushered in at the turn of the century. In this sense, Twain presaged the popularity Freudian psychology would achieve in the 1920s.

Twain's other published fictional piece during this period offers a portrait of mankind quite opposite in its nature. In "The Man That Corrupted Hadleyburg," the townspeople represent the corruptibility of mankind in the face of monetary temptation. The story is a reflection of his more pessimistic view of a mechanized self—one he had already aired in "What Is Man?" which was written during the Vienna years but remained unpublished until 1905, the year after Livy's death. Ozick sees Hadleyburg and its inhabitants in direct relationship to Vienna, particularly its theme of contagion, and the "smugness that arises out of self-righteousness": "the towns-

22. Ibid., 533.
23. Blair, *Mark Twain and Huck Finn* (Berkeley: University of California Press, 1960), 343.

people slide deeper and deeper into ethical perversion and contamination that was not far from a portrait of Europe undergoing the contagion of its great communal lie [anti-Semitism]."[24] Her assessment is supported by a reading of "Hadleyburg," although the tale's fascination for scholars lies in its ability to cover more ground than the particular instance of European anti-Semitism. It also addresses more subtle, philosophical questions that arise from the relationship between public opinion and the written word, displays elements of carnival, and in addition makes rhetorical use of mythology to comment on Western moral ideology.[25] It is a tale of the dark side of the brotherhood of man: his mechanistic corruptibility when forced to choose between personal gain and public morality, and the moral evil of hypocrisy generated by the opposition of these two choices.

Mary is living in a town noted for its honesty and incorruptibility; yet her first thought upon reading the stranger's note is to lock her door, obsessively worrying about burglars while awaiting her husband's return. When Edward returns tired and discouraged from his business, Mary's first response to their poverty is "we have our good name" (*CTSS2*, 393). On the heels of this self-righteous comment, Edward's reaction to the money's presence is to bury it, burn the papers, and keep the proceeds for themselves. In the course of the telling, Edward also reveals that he could have saved Reverend Burgess's reputation by revealing knowledge of his innocence; yet because his defense would contradict the town's public opinion of the minister, and he is dependent upon their good opinion for his livelihood, he does not. The townspeoples' continuing slide into corruption hinges upon a contrast between public and private morality; their inexperience with temptation leaves them subsequently susceptible when temptation is applied. Not surprisingly, the only Hadleyburgians exempt from temptation are Goodson, whose financial position allows him to ignore public opinion, and Burgess, whose status as a pariah allows public opinion to afford him no further harm.

24. Ozick, "Twain and the Jews," 56.

25. These alternative interpretations of the story are discussed, respectively, by Peter West, "To the Reader Sitting in Darkness: Mark Twain's 'The Man That Corrupted Hadleyburg,'" *South Atlantic Review* 65:1 (Winter 2000): 58–77; Peter Messent, "Carnival in Mark Twain's 'Stirring Times in Austria' and 'The Man That Corrupted Hadleyburg,'" *Studies in Short Fiction* 35:3 (Summer 1998): 217–32; and Thomas Werge, "The Sin of Hypocrisy in 'The Man That Corrupted Hadleyburg' and Inferno XXII," *Mark Twain Journal* 18:1 (1975–1976): 17–18.

Without commenting on the moral issues Twain asserts in "Hadleyburg," I would like to focus on what may seem a smaller issue: the possibility of freedom from the need to express "corn pone" opinions—by Twain's own definition, opinions that are based entirely on conventional wisdom and the opinions of one's peers without benefit of one's own native intellect and education. Twain had used the relative freedom of the outcast earlier to good effect in *Adventures of Huckleberry Finn*. Huck's status as an outsider allowed him to interrogate slavery's cultural establishment—in the church and in the legal system. It seems clear from both the novel and such later pieces as "My First Lie and How I Got Out of It" (1899), "Corn Pone Opinions" (1901), and "United States of Lyncherdom" (1901), among others, that Twain saw a complete financial and ethical freedom from social ties and mores as the only possibility for honesty in moral dealings. Dependence of either kind forced one to consider the opinions of others and their reactions to one's own, precluding one from making well-thought-out, reasoned choices that considered what might best serve mankind in general. That being the case, "The Man That Corrupted Hadleyburg" might also be read as Twain's manifesto on the value of public opinion and his desire to be independent of it. While he may not have completely worked out his own stances on some issues, he seems clearly to have formed them without regard for their popularity. As a direct result of his own travel experiences, his cosmopolitan lifestyle in Europe and elsewhere, and his observations of Viennese bigotry, he was ready to take a more independent view of political issues of his time.

Twain's experience in Vienna, coinciding as it did with the end of his self-imposed American exile, his newfound financial security, and the losses of his closest family that would follow, both signifies an end and ushers in a new beginning in his career as author and public figure. The earlier innocent, naive "Mark Twain" became the more experienced, less humorous, and more socially conscious Samuel Clemens, although it would be a mistake to believe that the change happened all at once. In 1885, Mark Twain imagined independence from conventional mores and public opinion for his most famous character, Huck Finn. Huck gained his independence due primarily to his freedom from social indoctrination. In 1897, Samuel Clemens gained his own freedom by becoming the sophisticated, cosmopolitan Mark Twain who stepped out of the train in Vienna in September. Much like the

Goodson character in "Hadleyburg," Mark Twain had status as an iconic figure that placed him above the reach of public opinion, at least in his own mind. In part, his belief was rooted in the confidence he gained from having weathered the storm of personal bankruptcy unscathed and more popular than ever. Thanks to the judicious investments Henry Huttleston Rogers made on his behalf and his successful negotiations for editions of Twain's work, fears for his and his family's security were at an end. In addition, he had reached the point in his life where he felt that he could express his opinions without regard for public reaction or its effect on his book sales; and Livy's death in 1904 removed the last impediment to the publication of his more radical opinions.

Twain felt comfortable enough in his newly established celebrity to spoof earlier worries about social blunders. In a February 3, 1898, letter to Twichell, he described the social protocol for meeting royalty: "we long ago found out that when you are noticed by supremacies the correct etiquette is to go, within a couple of days, and pay your respects in the quite simple form of writing your name in the Visitor's book," a protocol that he and Livy promptly performed (*Letters,* 657–58). The guards at the Archducal Palace seemed to breach this protocol by inviting the Clemeses in and insisting that they stay; he wished for Twichell's presence, as he "can't make all the rightful blunders himself" and teasingly suggested that Livy was the only one worried that they might be "imposters" (not the Americans expected by Her Highness). He ended the letter by remarking to Twichell: "we chatt[ed] along comfortably, and no one suspecting us for imposters." In point of fact, Twain was far too well known to remain unrecognized, but in any event, he appears to have considered himself enough above the social niceties of European royalty to joke about it.

With his celebrity and financial security as proof against social and political faux pas, Twain was free to indulge his responsibilities as a democratic citizen of America and an unofficial diplomat to the world. His lifelong belief in Jeffersonian ideals of democracy would not allow him to shirk his duty to speak his mind. What remained was for him to decide which causes deserved his attention and to formulate the ideas he would espouse. The freedom from monetary worries left him both the time and the inclination to delve into political, philosophical, and moral issues of importance. Unpublished work dating from the Vienna years illustrates the difficulties he encountered as he attempted to incorporate his sociopolitical stances into his fiction.

The triumphs (and blunders) that surfaced in his public interviews and private writing while he was in Vienna show his attempts to channel the more specific ideas of imperialism and Viennese anti-Semitism into the larger, more philosophical picture of morality and the moral sense that permeates his later fiction and his essays. To cite one example, in addition to the publication of "Stirring Times" and "Concerning the Jews," the incidents he witnessed in the Augsleich in October 1897, and the effect on the Jewish community in the aftermath, caused him to shift the setting of his *Mysterious Stranger* manuscript to Austria. His political commentary in *Following the Equator,* though it does remain inconsistent in its treatments, shows him gaining the political sophistication to challenge an all-or-nothing acceptance of imperialist ideology and groping toward an understanding of how these new ideas might fit into a conception of Western civilization's responsibilities to uphold the rights of undeveloped nations' minorities. His responses to the anti-Semitism he experienced in Austria, juxtaposed as it was with his experiences in Australasia, Africa, and India, show him coming to grips with the realization that the progress of imperial rule comes at a price to the indigenous populations of the nations into which it comes in contact.

His own inability to untangle the twentieth century's vagaries with a mind firmly rooted in the nineteenth century is perhaps most clearly seen in the fact that much of his more sustained work remained unfinished and unpublished within his lifetime as well as in the variety of his narrative choices in these pieces. In dream sequences like "The Great Dark," in which Twain's efforts were stymied at the point where the protagonists are endlessly floating in a microscopic waterdrop for all eternity, we see an author at the mercy of elements beyond his control. In "3000 Years among the Microbes," even Bkshp's radically expanded lifetime is still not long enough to answer the philosophical questions of human nature that Twain ponders. Even the eternal Satan cannot narrate the answers Twain seeks in the several *Mysterious Stranger* manuscripts and *Letters from the Earth.* Though Twain may never have worked out answers to these questions, the Vienna years seem to indicate that the turn of the century would see a shift from the "bounded" Twain of the early years. That such a shift did occur is indicated by his published anti-imperialist essays—"The Czar's Soliloquy," "King Leopold's Soliloquy," and others. Twain's letters, manuscripts, and published work all combine to illustrate an older, wiser author who antic- ipates the freedom from the intimidation of public opinion that his finan- cial situation and status as a celebrity promise, and welcomes that freedom as an opportunity to voice his objections to political and social inequities that he observes in the world around him. He looks unflinchingly at "the nasty underside of American and of human life in general: its brevity, self- ishness, and meaninglessness, its hypocritical religiosity, and its devotion to mammon."[26] To look long and hard at the underbelly of western European civilization would ultimately shift the nature and style of Twain's humor. Al- though from our perspective we can see the shift progressing through the Twain canon from even the early works, his last prolonged lecture tour and its finish in turn-of-the-century Vienna served as the dividing line for Twain both psychologically and politically. He began to slough off the cornpone opinions and inconsistencies of his youth for more considered and careful- ly thought out critiques of human nature. While Twain would never com- pletely lose his nineteenth-century positivistic approach to politics and morality, he could and did shift his own thinking toward the more mod- ernist concerns of transnational politics, religious skepticism, and pes- simism that would pervade the early-twentieth-century authors we now think of as modernists. He anticipated the psychological fascination with Freud of the early twentieth century, made broad strokes toward cultural pluralism, continued to defend the natives of underdeveloped countries during his lifetime, and used his rhetorical skill to debunk what he saw as religious fanaticism. Indeed, his presence at the century's turn as America's most celebrated author, lecturer, and pundit, along with his secure position as an unofficial diplomat without pay to the world, gave him the confidence to confront issues of the modern world, whether or not he could resolve them.

---

26. Fred Kaplan, *Singular Mark Twain* (Athens: University of Georgia Press, 2003), 553.

# A Room of His Own

## Samuel Clemens, Elmira, and Quarry Farm

MICHAEL J. KISKIS

> I have said that poetry is the spontaneous over-flow of powerful feelings:
> it takes its origin from emotion recollected in tranquility: the emotion is
> contemplated till by a species of re-action the tranquility gradually disap-
> pears, and an emotion, kindred to that which was before the subject of
> contemplation, is gradually produced, and does itself actually exist in
> the mind.
>
> —William Wordsworth, Preface to *Lyrical Ballads*

> After 30 days I go to Elmira, 1,000,000 miles from New York.
>
> —Samuel Langhorn Clemens to William Dean Howells

CRITICS have argued that Samuel Clemens's sense of outrage and his passion for acting as conscience to the "damned human race" were tied to some innate sensibility or to his contact with a variety of oppressed peoples (Asians during his time in San Francisco; African Americans during his Missouri childhood and eastern adulthood; Aboriginal peoples in New Zealand and Australia; and caste-bound Indians during his world tour of 1895–1896). His early writings were seasoned with a sense of outrage and a willingness to prick social convention; however, Clemens's intense concern for the world had at its heart both hope and dread based on intimate personal and domestic relationships. His moral voice gained timbre only after his careers as typesetter, pilot, miner, reporter, and writer of books were complicated and complemented by his becoming a husband and a parent, both of which roles were intimately tied to Elmira and the Langdons' summer home at Quarry Farm.

Olivia Louise Langdon Clemens called Elmira home. Her father, Jervis Langdon, made his fortune in the coal, timber, and transportation industries: he, his wife (Olivia Lewis), and their adopted daughter Susan[1] settled in Elmira, where Olivia Louise (Livy) was born on November 27, 1845. A son, Charles Jervis, was born four years later. Jervis Langdon was one of the leaders of the growing community, and he devoted his and the family's fortune to a variety of social causes, most notably abolition. In 1846, the Langdons were among the founders of the First Independent Congregational Church (later known as Park Church), and he is listed among the founders of Elmira College, which opened its doors as a women's college in 1855. The Langdons were progressive in both their religious practice and their politics, which left open the door for the more than slightly disheveled, self-educated, and somewhat ambivalently Christian westerner whose reputation as the "Wild Humorist of the Pacific Slope" and "The Moralist of the Main" was made poking at conventional beliefs. The Langdons, though careful of their youngest daughter, were progressive enough (perhaps intuitive enough) to see value in the young man who arrived on their doorstep already convinced of his affection for the young woman.

Samuel Clemens was drawn to the upstate New York town after Charlie Langdon introduced him to his sister, Olivia, first as an image in a miniature aboard the steamship *Quaker City* and later in person in New York City.[2] Sam accompanied the family to a public reading by Charles Dickens on New Year's Eve of 1867. Ron Powers comments, "The Langdons were as wealthy and cultured as any people the former printer's devil from Hannibal had yet encountered, *short of the Tsar's family*" (emphasis added).[3] That juxtaposition (from printer devil to tsar) suggests the wide experience that Sam Clem-

---

1. Born Susan Dean in 1836. Her family was disrupted by the early deaths of both parents: her mother died in 1837 when Susan was nineteen months old; her father died in 1840.

2. For Clemens's version of that first glimpse and his extended description of Livy as "both girl and woman" see *MTOA*, 23.

3. Powers, *Mark Twain: A Life* (New York: Free Press, 2005), 229.

ens had already accumulated by the time he showed up on the Langdons' doorstep in Elmira. By 1868, Clemens had learned the typesetting trade; traveled and supported himself during a journey that arced through New York, Philadelphia, and Washington, D.C.; earned his Mississippi riverboat pilot's license; mined for silver; been both correspondent and reporter for a variety of newspapers; lived in Nevada and San Francisco; visited the Sandwich Islands; crossed the isthmus of Panama; spent time in New York; and traveled throughout the Mediterranean. He was working on his first big travel book (*The Innocents Abroad*). His arrival in Elmira prompted Charlie Langdon to ask, "You've got some other clothes, haven't you?"[4] Inflated expectations, deflated hopes, worries, imagined affronts, pleas, and conscious and strenuous attempts at conversion (by Sam) erupted as Sam argued his case to Livy. A more-or-less rocky courtship followed, one marked by at least one refusal by Livy (though she did not close the door completely to a relationship and set the rules for Clemens to continue his campaign to win her) and an extended search for character references by Jervis and Olivia Lewis. As an example, on December 1, 1868, Livy's mother wrote to Mary Mason Fairbanks, one of the pilgrims on the *Quaker City* tour, who became a close friend to young Sam Clemens. An extended portion of the letter is valuable here:

> I cannot, & need not, detail to you the utter surprise & almost astonishment with which Mr. Langdon & myself listened to Mr. Clemens declaration to us, of his love for our precious child, and how at first our parental hearts said no.—to the bare thought of such a stranger, mining in our hearts for the possession of one of the few jewels we have. All this I must pass by, for today I have to deal with that, with which the judgment only has to do. . . .
>
> Now what I am about to write, must be plainly and frankly spoken. I do not ask as to his standing among men, nor do I need to be assured that he is a man of genius that he possesses a high order of intellectual endowments, nor do I scarcely crave your opinion of his affectional nature, but what I desire is your opinion of him *as a man;* what is the kind of man he *has been,* and what the man he now is, or is to become.

4. Ibid., 242.

I have heard from Charlie & I think the same idea has pervaded
your conversation, or writing or both,—that a great change had tak-
en place in Mr. Clemens, that he seemed to have entered upon a new
manner of life, with higher & better purposes actuating his conduct—
    The question, the answer to which, would settle a most weaning
anxiety, is,—from what standard of conduct,—from what habitual
life, did this change, or improvement, or reformation; commence?
    Does this change, so desirably commenced make of an immoral
man a moral one, as the *world* looks at men?—or—does his change
make of one, who has been entirely a man of the world, different in
this regard, that he resolutely aims to enter upon a new, because a
Christian life? (*L2*, 286–87)

Fairbanks helped soothe the mother; the father eventually took his daughter's suitor into his confidence. And, in a manner befitting the training of a
world-class writer and as a preview of a portion of their married life when
Sam was off lecturing or traveling for business, a good deal of Sam and Livy's
courtship was epistolary. All this sound and fury resulted in the marriage of
Sam and Olivia in the Langdon home in Elmira on February 2, 1870.[5]

    After their marriage much of Samuel and Olivia Clemens's family life cen-
tered on Elmira: they lived either all or a part of every summer there during their first twenty years together. They helped nurse Jervis Langdon during his bout with terminal stomach cancer and were at his bedside when he
died in August 1870. During this time, Livy was pregnant with the Clemenses' first child. After Jervis Langdon's death, Susan (married to Theodore
Crane) inherited the summer home at Quarry Farm. Elmira and the farm
became a hub for the Clemens family. Langdon Clemens (named after the
family patriarch) was born in Buffalo, New York, on November 7, 1870; he
was buried in Elmira's Woodlawn Cemetery in June 1872, just months after Olivia Susan (Susie) Clemens was born in Elmira and only days after she
was christened at Park Church (the Clemenses kept their membership in

---

5. Sam and Livy's courtship has been not only a part of longer biographies but has also the
specific focus of several books. See *LLMT;* Resa Willis, *Mark and Livy: The Love Story of Mark
Twain and the Woman Who Almost Tamed Him* (New York: Atheneum, 1992); and Susan K.
Harris, *The Courtship of Olivia Langdon and Mark Twain* (New York: Cambridge University
Press, 1996).

Park Church as Livy's family congregation). Clara Langdon Clemens was born on June 8, 1874, and Jean Lampton Clemens, the last of the children, followed on July 26, 1880. Each of the girls was born in Elmira and spent her earliest days at Quarry Farm, and in what must have seemed an omen of the farm's beneficence, especially after the troubling health and short life of Langdon, each baby was strong and healthy (Susie weighed in at four pounds; Clara, at seven and three-quarters pounds; and Jean, at seven pounds). Two days after Clara was born, on June 10, 1874, Clemens wrote to his brother Orion and his wife, Mollie, "The babe is a girl, & weighed nearly 8 pounds—which is colossal for Livy; Susie weighed only 4 pounds, & Langdon 3 ½. However the child is really but a small creature, but is very round & compact & solid. It could whip Susie at four weeks, with one hand tied behind it—& yet Susie is not a weakling" (L6, 155). As they grew, the Clemens daughters played in the surrounding fields and embraced the farm fully and joyously. Jean loved cows. They all loved cats. Clemens's first attempt at his (later patented) history game was tried out by pounding sticks with the chronology of the English monarchy attached into the expanse of the front lawn.

Clemens's development as a writer progressed alongside his embrace of family life, and Quarry Farm and its environs contributed both physically and atmospherically to much of Clemens's literary work during 1870–1890. The Langdon family's openness brought Clemens into contact with a strongly liberal form of Christianity that helped to cement his belief in the value of sympathetic ties and intellectual expansiveness. While some amount of his free thinking harkened back to his father, John Marshall Clemens, and a portion of his sympathy for those down and out was owed to his mother, Jane Lampton (Clemens described her as "this Friend of Satan"[6]), the open atmosphere of the Langdon household and of the members of their extended circle (which included both liberal Congregationalist preachers and progressive advocates for social change) fostered in Clemens both a care for social change and a reinforced and hearty social and personal conscience. Combined with Clemens's own interest in adopting

6. *Mark Twain's Hannibal, Huck and Tom*, ed. Walter Blair (Berkeley: University of California Press, 1969), 45.

and adapting to the muscular Christianity of the East as shaped and taught by Clemens's acquaintances and friends Henry Ward Beecher, Horace Bushnell, Thomas K. Beecher, and Joseph Twichell, the Langdon family's legacy of activism and Livy's ties to Alice Hooker Day, her mother Isabella Beecher Hooker, and Dr. Rachel Gleason brought Clemens to a new and deeper interest in the world and a certainty of the need for social engagement. While one reason for Clemens's attraction to Hartford was the location of his first publisher, the American Publishing Company, another and perhaps more important influence was Livy's (and Sam's to some extent) attraction to the intellectual and spiritual community. And while, once married, Livy focused on home and children (in keeping, perhaps, with both Sam's and her own acceptance of the dominant ideology of the Cult of Motherhood), she continually and profoundly influenced her husband's perspective of the world and shaped him not merely into a reactionary against social oppression but also into an advocate for social and (in its more fundamental and philosophically pure form) Christian justice. In short, the Langdon family and its circle became Samuel Clemens's Harvard. And it was a co-ed education.[7]

Conventional wisdom sees Clemens as completely formed by his western experience; however, Clemens was still young and unpolished when he came east in 1867. He was, after all, in his early thirties and had for all intents and purposes been rootless as he bumped along among various western communities. After his marriage, Clemens deepened his experience not only on the "local" path he and his family traveled between Hartford and New York and Elmira but also on the various regional paths of his lecture tours during both the 1870s and 1880s. He also returned to England and to Europe. Before his marriage Clemens managed to accumulate experience,

7. For an account of the coeducational aspect of Sam Clemens's education see Laura E. Skandera-Trombley, *Mark Twain in the Company of Women* (Philadelphia: University of Pennsylvania Press, 1994). For a broad understanding of the progressive influences on Clemens see Harold K. Bush, *Mark Twain and the Spiritual Crisis of His Age* (Tuscaloosa: University of Alabama Press, 2007). Biographers who have dealt with the progressive influences on Clemens include Powers, *Mark Twain: A Life,* and Fred Kaplan, *The Singular Mark Twain* (New York: Doubleday, 2003). On the relationship between Clemens and Harriet Beecher Stowe, see Leland Krauth, *Mark Twain and Company: Six Literary Relations* (Athens: University of Georgia Press, 2003), and Kenneth Andrews, *Nook Farm: Mark Twain's Hartford Circle* (Cambridge: Harvard University Press, 1950).

and he developed a sense of unbridled intellectual (and most likely spiritual) curiosity, but he had not yet formed a strong philosophical center. That
center took shape as he traveled more broadly and was able to bring more
rigorous analytical and synthetic powers to bear. More important, his interpretive prism revealed a broader spectrum as he grew into his adult and
family responsibilities.

During the 1870s and 1880s, Samuel Clemens expanded his talents and
developed his sensibilities toward and his creative responses to community, whether it was the tightly focused community of home and family or
the broadly constructed city, nation, or world. During his summers in
Elmira and when he looked out from the porch and into the horizon,
Clemens saw a world plagued by and in the clutches of the human moral
sense. The hearth and the porch, primary locations that affect domesticity, primed Clemens creativity and sparked his darkening conscience. In
1874, Clemens used the porch at the farm as the setting for "A True Story, Repeated Word for Word as I Heard It," his first piece to find an audience through the *Atlantic Monthly*. It is a tale told by Mary Ann Cord, the
cook at the farm.

"A True Story" is a profoundly sentimental piece that hangs on the
metaphor of the lost child (hence the symbolic change of Mary Ann Cord's
name to "Aunt Rachel") and that offers the central contrast between the
white and the black experience of family. The sketch starts with a fully conventional and foolish appraisal of the life of "Aunt Rachel" by the thick-
headed "Misto C—" when he assumes a familiarity with Rachel's experience
well beyond his ability: "why you *can't* have had any trouble. I've never
heard you sigh, and never seen your eye when there wasn't a laugh in it"
(*SNO*, 203). Here is the egocentricity of the white gentleman who somehow
believes that a servant—a black servant—is completely known to him. He
never considers that she has a life separate from him or his family; and he
takes for granted his own perspective on the world. This egocentricity is
Clemens's target.

Immediately Rachel's voice dominates the sketch as she points out the
human quality of her life and the similarity of her emotional ties to those so
freely assumed by the white family gathered around her:

"Has I had any trouble? Misto C—, I's gwyne to tell you, den I leave it to you. I was bawn down 'mongst de slaves; I knows all 'bout slavery, 'case I ben one of 'm my own se'f. Well, sah, my old man— dat's my husban'—he was lovin' an' kind to me, *jist as kind as you is to yo'wife.* An' we had chil'en—seven chil'en—*an we loved dem chil'en jist de same as you loves yo' chil'en. Dey was black, but de Lord can't make no chil'en so black but what dey mother loves 'em an' wouldn't give 'em up, no not for anything dat's in dis whole world.*" (*SNO,* 203; emphasis added)

Rachel here expresses the deep emotion of motherhood, an emotion that was firmly understood in the Clemens and Langdon household, as well as (Clemens would bet) in the households of his readers. This tie is reinforced by the experience of loss. As Aunt Rachel tells of the auctioning of her children, there is also an underlying emphasis on the loss of a child, a loss so clearly a part of nineteenth-century family life. By 1874, the Clemenses had lost one son and celebrated the birth of two daughters. Rachel's story is kin to Sam's. It is, perhaps more important, tied to Livy's.[8]

The story concentrates Clemens's writing with a growing sense of sympathy. The penultimate paragraph aligns "Misto C—" with Rachel's son Henry, perhaps an extension that allows the identification of Clemens not only with his lost brother Henry, who died in 1858 in the explosion of the steamboat *Pennsylvania,* but in a more profound way with the recently lost Langdon. The implied stage directions embedded in the paragraph reinforce the identification and, in the end, bring "Misto C—" and the reader to understand the true value of family:

"I was a-stoopin' down by de stove,—*jist so, same as if yo' foot was de stove,*—an' I'd opened de stove do' wid my right han',—so *pushin' it back, jist as I pushes yo' foot,*—an' I'd jist got de pan o' hot bisuits in my han' an was 'bout to raise up, when I see a black face come aroun'

8. Clemens's neighbor Harriet Beecher Stowe used the loss of her son Samuel Charles (Charley) to ignite her imagination and her sympathy. Stowe wrote to Eliza Cabot Follen on December 16, 1852: "I have been the mother of seven children, the most beautiful and the most loved of whom lies buried near my Cincinnati residence. It was at his dying bed and at his grave that I learned what a poor slave mother may feel when her child is torn away from her . . . I have often felt that much that is in [*Uncle Tom's Cabin*] had its root in the awful scenes and bitter sorrow of that summer" (*Uncle Tom's Cabin* [New York: W. W. Norton, 1994], 413).

under mine, an' de eyes a-lookin' up into mine, *jist as* I's a-lookin' up close under yo' face now; an' I jist stopped *right dah* [sic], an never budged! Jist gazed, an' gazed so; an' de pan begin to tremble, an' all of a sudden *I knowed!* [sic]. De pan drop' on de flo' *an' I grab his lef' han' an' shove back his sleeve—just so, as I's doin' to you,—an' den I goes for his forehead an' push de hair back, so, an 'Boy!' I says, 'if you ain't my Henry, what is you doin' wid dis welt on yo' wris' an' dat sk-yar on yo' forehead? De Lord God ob heaven be praise',* I got my own ag'in!'" (*SNO*, 207; emphasis added)

Throughout this ending, the reader is brought into the action and is both observer and participant in the drama of redemption. Clemens understands the value of that emotional trauma, and he uses the setting and the occasion of a family gathering at the farm to underscore the primacy of the domestic bond. The piece demonstrates that Clemens found his voice in the midst of home: exiling himself far from the demands of Hartford's and New York's social and business centers, he soaked in the calm and peace of Quarry Farm and in his own private study stoked his increasing outrage.

At the farm, Clemens's moral gaze gained focus through his wife, daughters, and, I believe, the ghost of his dead son, whose grave was merely a long walk from the farm and whose presence shaded home and hearth. A case can and needs to be made for the deep impact of Langdon Clemens's death on his father's major fiction. In a 1906 autobiographical dictation published in "Chapters from My Autobiography," Clemens offered his first extended account of how he saw his responsibility for Langdon's death, a death that had happened more than thirty years before:

> I was the cause of the child's illness. His mother trusted him to my care and I took him a long drive in an open barouche for an airing. It was a raw, cold morning, but he was well wrapped about with furs and, in the hands of a careful person, no harm would have come to him. But I soon dropped into a reverie and forgot all about my charge. The furs fell away and exposed his bare legs. By and by the coachman noticed this, and I arranged the wraps again, but it was too late. The child was almost frozen. I hurried home with him. I was aghast at what I had done, and I feared the consequences. I have always felt shame for that treacherous morning's work and have not allowed myself to think of it when I could help it. I doubt if I had the courage to make

confession at that time. I think it most likely that I have never con-
fessed until now. (*MTOA,* 63)

Biographers and critics have noted that Clemens spoke sparingly of Langdon's death, and they have used that silence to suggest that Clemens was
touched only minimally by the loss. It pays to keep in mind Huck Finn's silence on the trauma of Buck Grangerford's death: "I ain't agoing to tell *all*
that happened—it would make me sick again if I was to do that. I wished
I hadn't ever come ashore that night, to see such things. I ain't ever going
to get shut of them—lots of times I dream about them" (*HF,* 153). Clemens
knew the power of those dreams.

Setting also influenced Clemens's creativity. Hartford offered the physical and social opportunities to advance his professional life (which, in turn,
made possible his opportunities to revel in and relish his family ties). Elmira offered the quiet that Clemens increasingly needed to write. The contrast
was immediately clear to Clemens. During his summers of extended work
at Quarry Farm, Clemens used his writing about his experiences to create
and adapt to his mature literary voice; for the most part, he would save his
formal writing for his returns to Elmira and to Quarry Farm. On April 27,
1874, Clemens explained to John Brown: "This town is in the interior of the
State of New York—& was my wife's birth-place. We are here to spend the
whole summer. Mrs. Clemens will be confined in about a month [antici-
pating Clara's birth]. It gets fearfully hot here in the summer, so we spend
our summers on the top of a hill 6 or 700 feel high, about 2 or 3 miles from
here—it *never* gets hot up there" (*L6,* 121). Clemens added, "I am going to
work when we get on the hill. Till then I've got to lie fallow, albeit against
my will" (*L6,* 122). Serious work was relegated to the farm, most often because of its separation from city concerns and interruptions.

For Clemens, who was placed as an apprentice to the local print shop
soon after his father died in 1847 and whose adolescence and young adulthood were spent making his living and his way, the farm fairly sung with
peace and stability. In Elmira, Clemens, wanderer that he was, found love
and support and the discipline to write; like the children, he thrived at the
farm. As he wrote to David Gray on April 18, 1874: "We reached here yes-
terday evening, & Susie and her mother show but slight traces of what was
a very wearing & arduous journey. In the course of two weeks we shall be

housed at the farm on top of the hill—can't feel settled till then" (*L6*, 108). Feeling "settled" was the aim of the move to the farm. It was a place far away from social and business duties and responsibilities: Susan Crane had christened Quarry Farm "Do as you please hall," and Clemens embraced the opportunity. Quarry Farm gave Clemens the chance to tack away from day-to-day cares and to place himself above and beyond usual and mundane worries. To Charles E. Perkins he wrote on May 8, 1874:

> Your reference to the sidewalk matter reminds me that I am a citizen of Hartford—a fact which I was forgetting; for since we have perched, away up here on top of the hill near heaven I have the feeling of being a sort of scrub angel & am more moved to help shove the clouds around, & get the stars on deck promptly, & keep all things trim & ship-shape in the firm-ament than to bother myself with the humble insect-interests & occupations of the distant earth. But still, the pecuniary difference between a four-foot & a six-foot side-walk is a thing which even a new angel cannot afford to snub—& if you & Hall carry your point, there is one such spirit up here on high that will flap his wings & rejoice. (*L6*, 138)

All of this was made even more spectacular when, during the summer of 1874, Clemens happily took possession of the small octagonal study that his sister-in-law Susan Crane had built on a outcropping that overlooked the Chemung River valley. Clemens mentioned to Robert Watt in a letter dated July 15–16, 1874, that the house was filled with "babies and cats" (*L6*, 188). The study had only cats. No doubt Clemens's need for solitude was one reason for Susan Crane's compassion and investment in the small building; another reason may have been the need to get Clemens out of the corner of the front parlor where he had set up his writing desk. On June 11, 1874, Clemens described his new lair to Joe and Harmony Twichell:

> Susie Crane has built the loveliest study for me, you ever saw. It is octagonal, with a peaked roof, each octagon filled with a spacious window, & it sits in complete isolation on top of an elevation that commands leagues of valley & city & retreating ranges of distant blue hills. It is a cozy nest, with just room in it for a sofa & a table & three or four chairs—& when the storms sweep down the remote valley & the

A portrait of Samuel Clemens in his study at Quarry Farm taken in 1903 while the Clemenses were visiting Elmira hoping that the environment would improve Livy's health. The view in this photo, one of a series later published in the *Saturday Evening Post,* suggests the relationship between the domestic space inside the study and the natural and panoramic views just outside its windows. (Courtesy Mark Twain Boyhood Home and Museum, Hannibal, Missouri)

> lightening flashes above the hills beyond, & the rain beats upon the roof over my head, imagine the luxury of it! It stands 500 feet above the valley & 2 1/2 miles from it. (*L6,* 158)

Again to John Brown, Clemens wrote:

> We have spent the past four months up here on top of a breezy hill six hundred feet high, some few miles from Elmira, N.Y., & over-looking that town, (Elmira is my wife's birth-place, & that of Susie & the new baby). This little summer house on the hill-top (named Quar-ry Farm because there's a quarry on it,) belongs to my wife's sister, Mrs. Crane. A photographer came up the other day & wanted to make some views, & I shall send you the result per this mail. My study is a snug

little octagonal den, with a coal-grate, 6 big windows, one little one, & a wide doorway (the latter opening upon the distant town.) On hot days I spread the study wide open, anchor my papers down with brickbats & write in the midst of hurricanes, clothed in the same thick linen we make shirt bosoms of. The study is nearly on the peak of the hill; it is right in front of the little perpendicular wall of rock left where they used to quarry stone. On the peak of the hill is old arbor roofed with bark & covered with vine you call the "American creeper"—its green is already bloodied with red. The study is 30 yards below the old arbor and 100 yards above the dwelling-house—it is remote from *all noise*. (*L6*, 222)

This is the real legacy of Clemens's time at Quarry Farm. It offered the peace and solitude in the midst of family that fostered his creative work.

Silence and tranquillity are powerful allies to the creative process, and Clemens increasingly needed a haven. The study allowed Clemens to separate from the household so that he could work in unobstructed peace. It was designed in keeping with Susan Crane's allegiance to the ideal of the picturesque, which drove her to open the cottage to the outdoors with pocket windows and sliding doors so the family could extend the front room onto the covered porch and to erect several outlying buildings and shelters that welcomed the family into the hills alongside the cottage. The study's windows opened fully to invite nature in among the papers and cigar smoke (or to allow papers and smoke to escape into nature). Clemens was energized by the combination workroom and observatory: he could wrap himself in his imagination as well as look up to see the family cottage and, later, to watch his daughters play just below in a scale playhouse Sue had built for them. The blend of domestic care and imagination pushed him to write.

While Clemens's writing resulted in a full-faced American realism, his creative process was more clearly linked to the notions of the artist expressed in William Wordsworth's "Preface" to *Lyrical Ballads*. Wordsworth focused on the need for the writer to establish a distance between the experience and the creative act. To repeat from the epigraph to this essay: "poetry is the spontaneous over-flow of powerful feelings: it takes its origin from emotion recollected in tranquility: the emotion is contemplated till by a species of re-action the tranquility gradually disappears, and an emotion, kindred to that which was before the subject of contemplation, is gradually produced, and does itself actually exist in the mind."[9] Like Wordsworth, Clemens was able to find the shape and direction for his composition only when he was fully set apart from the experience. He was otherwise too much a part of it, too much a participant.

Because of the foundational beliefs that he formed during the 1870s, Clemens was better able to use the physical experience of travel to inform his literary work; for example, the trip to England in 1873–1874, the tour of the continent in 1878–1879, and the visit to the Mississippi in 1882 all helped inform the works that grew during that period: *A Tramp Abroad* (1880), *The Prince and the Pauper* (1881), *Life on the Mississippi* (1883), and *Adventures of Huckleberry Finn* (1885). The trips to England and to the American South would also carry over later to *A Connecticut Yankee in King Arthur's Court* (1889). One need only listen to his voice in *The Innocents Abroad* (1869) and its sequel *A Tramp Abroad* (1880) to hear the deepening timbre.

Of course, by 1870 Clemens had already been introduced to world geography (at least of the American West and Mediterranean); however, during his marriage he became a more polished and sophisticated world traveler. Gone were the days of his narrow dreams of travel as a way to show off on one of the Mississippi steamboats, as he described in *Life on the Mississippi*:

> When we presently got under way and went poking down the broad Ohio, I became a new being, and the subject of my own admiration. I was a traveler! A word never had tasted so good in my mouth before. I had an exulted sense of being bound for mysterious lands and distant climes which I never felt in so uplifting a degree since. I was in such a glorified condition that all ignoble feelings departed out of me, and I was able to look down and pity the untravelled with a compassion that had hardly a trace of contempt in it. . . . I kept my hat off all the time, and stayed where the wind and the sun could strike me, because I wanted to get the bronzed and weather-beaten look of an old traveler. Before the second day was half gone, I experienced a joy which filled me with the purest gratitude; for I saw that the skin had

---

9. Wordsworth, "Preface to the second edition of several of the foregoing poems, published, with an additional volume, under the title 'Lyrical Ballads,'" ed. W. J. B. Owen, *Anglihstica* 9 (1957): 128–29.

begun to blister and peel off my face and neck. I wished that the boys and girls at home could see me now. (*LOM*, 70–71)

That immature wish to be the object of the gaze, to be a spectacle and envied (a decidedly Tom Sawyerish dream), was dominant when Clemens made his way to upstate New York.

Travel, or more accurately life, was instructive, and Clemens filled his notebooks with jottings, ideas, and reactions; however, travel (or life) recalled in tranquillity allowed for a more effective and more affected understanding and for concentrated, creative work. His most effective writing was expressly shaped by his being separated from the world in a way that allowed him to concentrate fully and without distraction on the recomposition of experience through the prism of fiction. Tale telling, for Clemens, relied on the conjuring of character and conversation and setting, much of which he dredged out of his primary experiences. This is not to say that Clemens wrote exclusively autobiographical fiction. At times he did. Most often he did not. He did, however, allow the tranquillity of his Quarry Farm study to form a creative bubble within which he practiced an organic process to form his characters and their stories.

The atmosphere of the farm allowed Clemens to sit back, contemplate, and reinvent his experience. While it is tempting to consider Elmira and Quarry Farm as wholly separated from and, indeed, as a fundamental contrast to the blur of the social and political and economic responsibilities of Hartford or, more emphatically, as a counterpoint to the lessons of travel (especially the European travel that resulted in both *The Innocents Abroad* and *A Tramp Abroad*), the reality is that the condensed circle of family at Quarry Farm made it possible for Clemens to think creatively and to shape the lessons learned from travel. It is not travel itself that broadened Clemens (or any individual). It is the thinking and the writing about the experiences of traveling; it is the opportunity to discuss and consider experience with an appreciative and informed and sympathetic audience that ignites insight and fosters true cosmopolitanism. Quarry Farm was the crucible in which Clemens distilled his experience.

Clemens's early comments connected to his work on *Adventures of Huckleberry Finn* serve as an example. When Clemens began Huck's tale, he had just ended *The Adventures of Tom Sawyer* and realized that the strength of

that novel was in its introduction of the outcast Huck. From Elmira on August 9, 1876, Clemens wrote to William Dean Howells, "I . . . began another
boy's book—more to be at work than anything else. I have written 400
pages on it—therefore it is very nearly half done. It is Huck Finn's Autobiography. I like it only tolerably well, as far as I have got, & may possibly
pigeon-hole or burn the MS when it is done" (*SMTHL,* 75). This quick reference, however, needs to be placed in a broader physical and emotional
context. Immediately preceding the comment about Huck's tale, Clemens
presents a complicated and fully developed physical description of a sun-
set watched from his small study. The quiet and Clemens's sense of contentment are palpable. Here is the paragraph in full:

> The farm is perfectly delightful this season. It is as quiet & peace-
> ful as a South-sea island. Some of the sun-sets which we have wit-
> nessed from this commanding eminence were marvelous. One evening
> a rainbow spanned an entire range of hills with its mighty arch, & from
> a black hub resting upon the hill-top in the exact centre, *black* rays di-
> verged upward in perfect regularity to the rainbow's arch & created a
> very strongly defined & altogether the most majestic, magnificent, &
> startling half-sunk wagon wheel you can imagine. After that, a world
> of tumbling & prodigious clouds came drifting up out of the west &
> took to themselves a wonderfully rich & brilliant *green* color—the de-
> cided green of new spring foliage. Close by them we saw the intense
> blue of the skies, through rents in the cloud-rack, & away off in an-
> other quarter were drifting clouds of a delicate pink color. In one place
> hung a pall of dense black clouds, like compacted pitch-smoke. And
> the stupendous wagon wheel was still in the supremacy of its un-
> speakable grandeur. So you see, the colors present in the sky at one &
> the same time were blue, green, pink, black, & the vari-colored splen-
> dors of the rainbow. All strong & decided colors, too. I don't know
> whether this weird & astounding spectacle most suggested heaven,
> or hell. The wonder with its constant, stately, & always surprising
> changes, lasted upward of two hours, & we all stood on the top of the
> hill by my study till the final miracle was complete & the greatest day
> ended that we ever saw. (*SMTHL,* 75)

A Wordsworthian recollection of the day and the moment, the description
is lush in its use of color. Clemens was not reporting in real time or sitting

in the open window looking out at the setting sun. He was re-creating the experience, most likely sitting among the bric a brac holding down his papers and thinking back on the experience. And thinking back made the re-creation more intense. Of course, he then undercut the high drama and romance of the moment when he reported in the next paragraph, "Our farmer, who is a grave man, watched that spectacle to the end, & then observed that it was 'dam funny'" (SMTHL, 75).

This combination of romance and realism can also be seen in Clemens's descriptions of Huck's reaction to the river, a combination of wonder and practicality (HF, 154–57). Clemens, in the guise of Huck, channeled the recollection of scenes along the Mississippi while sitting atop the ridge in Elmira so that he could create a young boy's wonder and worry over life along the river. The scenes that appear in the book emanated both from Clemens's childhood and, more important to this discussion, from his just finished 1882 tour of the Mississippi. Here we see Clemens relying on a form of emotion recollected in tranquillity. We also hear Clemens's contrasting views of the natural world: on the one hand, fully involved in the aesthetic (and quite possibly god-given) quality of a scene; on the other, offering a direct and practical description of the reality of the strangeness and perhaps danger lurking behind the aesthetic experience (LOM, 112–21).

But recollection is not only meant to focus on the physical setting. It can also bring the writer to a more pronounced relation to lives or a particular life. Here the recollection is not strictly a memory; rather, it is a creative use of the past in consort with the present that offers a chance to bring to life concerns growing out of contemporary events and needs. Years later when Clemens dictated his autobiography, he called this "a form and method whereby the past and the present are constantly brought face to face, resulting in contrasts which newly fire up the interest all along, like the contact of flint with steel" (MTOA, 3). Clemens, for example, admitted that the character Huck Finn was derivative: Huck is, more or less, a composite of at least two individuals out of Clemens's past: in "Chapters from My Autobiography" Clemens's memory vacillates as he identifies first Frank Finn and then Tom Blankenship as the source for Huck (MTOA, 191, 212). Sitting in his Quarry Farm study, Clemens, however, settled in and created a life out of his prior experiences seasoned with concerns out of the present moment: his youthful experience with Hannibal's concern over the poor and the orphaned (or lack of it) and his adult experience with urban life and, perhaps most important, with the Social Gospel movement of David "Father" Hawley and the City Missionary Society of Hartford aimed at the poor and disenfranchised. All this was a potent mix that led Clemens to create Huck as both a historical representation and a contemporary model of a forsaken and abused orphan.

Elmira, and especially Quarry Farm, made it possible for Clemens to sharpen that focus and to tune his voice. It made it possible for him to engage a wholly sympathetic audience, to write fiction of high sentiment, and to use his own family to gauge the success or failure of the story and style. Clemens often shared his day's writing with his family on the small cottage's porch. In "Chapters from My Autobiography," he tells a tale of the family's editing:

> The passages that were so satisfactory to [the children] always had an element of strength in them which sorely needed modification or expurgation, and were always sure to get it at their mother's hand. For my own entertainment, and to enjoy the protests of the children, I often abused my editor's innocent confidence. I often interlarded remarks of a studied and felicitously atrocious character purposely to achieve the children's brief delight, and then see the remorseless pencil do its fatal work. I often joined my supplications to the children's for mercy, and strung the argument out and pretended to be in earnest. They were deceived, and so was their mother. It was three against one, and most unfair. Now and then we gained the victory and there was much rejoicing. Then I privately struck the passage out myself. It had served its purpose. It had furnished three of us with good entertainment, and in being removed from the book by me it was only suffering the fate originally intended for it. (*MTOA,* 49)

In another instance, Clemens revived Susie's description of his reading to the family. The passage is from her biography of her father, written in 1884–1885:

> Ever since papa and mama were married, papa has written his books and then taken them to mama in manuscript and she has expurgated them. Papa read "Huckleberry Finn" to us in manuscript just

before it came out, and then he would leave parts of it with mama to expurgate, while he went off up to the study to work, and sometimes Clara and I would 'be sitting with mama while she was looking the manuscript over, and I remember so well, with what pangs of regret we used to see her turn down the leaves of the pages, which meant that some delightfully dreadful part must be scratched out. And I remember one part pertickularly which was perfectly fascinating it was dreadful, that Clara and I used to delight in, and oh with what despair we saw mama turn down the leaf on which it was written, we thought the book would be almost ruined without it. But we gradually came to feel as mama did. (*MTOA,* 172)

Clemens's reaction to Susie's description follows:

I remember the special case mentioned by Suzy, and can see the group yet—two-thirds of it pleading for the life of the culprit sentence that was so fascinatingly dreadful and the other third of it patiently explaining why the court could not grant the prayer of the pleaders; but I do not remember what the condemned phrase was. It had much company, and they all went to the gallows; but it is possible that that specially dreadful one which gave those little people so much delight was cunningly devised and put into the book for just that function, and not with any hope or expectation that it would get by the "expurgator" alive. It is possible, for I had that custom. (*MTOA,* 172)

The custom, then, was also part of a family game, a game that took its cues from the writing that Clemens did while sequestered in his study.

The reality here is that Clemens was able to "try out" his fiction on a real and interested audience. And he prized their reactions and their judgments. His wife and children were his first critics, and he was able to use their response both to shape his fiction and to please himself as a father. Some years earlier, on March 11, 1880, he wrote to William Dean Howells to report Livy's reaction to *The Prince and the Pauper*: "Imagine *this* fact—I have even fascinated Mrs. Clemens with this yarn for youth. My stuff generally gets considerable damning with faint praise out of her, but this time it is all the other way. She is become the horse-leech's daughter & my mill doesn't grind fast enough to suit her. This is no mean triumph, by dear sir" (*SMTHL*, 145–46). Often, for Clemens, writing was a family activity.

This ready-made authorial audience made it possible for Clemens to work—so much so that he lamented those times it was necessary to forgo the summer's visit. From Hartford on April 23, 1875, he wrote to Mary Mason Fairbanks:

> We have determined to sweat it out, here in Hartford, this summer, & not go away at all. That is Livy's idea, not mine; for I can write ten chapters in Elmira where I can write one here. I work *at* work here, but I don't accomplish anything worth speaking of. Livy *wants* to go to Cleveland, but she can't. To carry the household would be like moving a menagerie; & to leave it behind would be like leaving a menagerie behind without a keeper. You mustn't suppose I am not *trying* to work. Bless you I peg away all the time. I allow myself few privileges; but when one is *in the workaday world,* there's a million interruptions & interferences. I can't succeed except by getting clear out of the world on top of the mountain in Elmira. (*L6*, 454)

Climbing to the top of the mountain was, indeed, Clemens's one way to assure that his work would flow. The surroundings, the calm, and the opportunity to re-collect his thoughts were a powerful conjure that brought Clemens more securely into his fictive world.

Perhaps one of the reasons for Clemens's increasing creative frustration during the late 1880s and 1890s was his loss of the farm. When the stresses of bad investments and bad business decisions loosed havoc on the family's finances, the Clemenses closed up the Hartford home in 1891 and sailed for Europe. Later, they would depart from Elmira when beginning the world tour of 1895–1896, leaving both Jean and Susie behind as they began their journey west. It would be the last time they would see Susie alive: she would die in the family house in Hartford from spinal meningitis in a fever that would strike her blind and delusional (*MTOA*, 23–24). And Jean would, in the late 1890s, become more and more hostage to her epilepsy until she was, in effect, exiled from home to various sanitariums and cures. In 1903 Sam and Livy would find their way back to Elmira and Quarry Farm for a last long visit, just prior to taking up residence in Florence, Italy, under doctors' orders for Livy's health. In 1904 Livy would die in Florence of congestive heart failure. Livy's funeral would be held in Elmira, where she was buried on July 14, 1904. With Livy's death, the family was irreparably broken. Clara married Ossip Gabrilowitsch in October 2009; Jean, only months into a reconciliation with her father that brought her back home (this time to Stormfield, in Redding, Connecticut), died on Christmas Eve morning in 1909. Clemens's final months were spent alone (except for the company of Albert Bigelow Paine, his biographer and eventual literary executor). He died on April 21, 1910, just days after being brought back from Bermuda by the ever-present Paine. He was laid to rest in Elmira on April 24, 1910.

The stone that marks Samuel Clemens's grave site in Woodlawn Cemetery, Elmira, New York, links him, and by extension Elmira, to the leadsman's call that he took as his own pen and professional name: Mark Twain. The obelisk is twelve feet high, or two fathoms. Around the marker is an array of family gravestones: the Langdons, Cranes, and Clemenses share the shade once more. Clara Clemens was the only immediate family member to survive her father, and she was responsible for her father's marker. Langdon, Susie, Livy, and Jean welcomed Clemens home to Elmira when he was laid next to them in the family burial ground. In 1962 Clara was buried alongside the rest of her family (her two husbands are buried near the Clemens family). Since 1966, Clemens's only granddaughter, Nina Gabrilowitsch, also lies there. Clemens never saw his granddaughter; she was born almost exactly four months after he died. Nina's death brought the family full circle and back to Livy's childhood home.

# About the Contributors

**James E. Caron** is Associate Professor of English at the University of Hawaii at Manoa. He is the author of *Mark Twain, Unsanctified Newspaper Reporter* and the coeditor of *Sut Lovingood's Nat'ral Born Yarnspinner: Essays on George Washington Harris*. He serves on the editorial board of *Studies in American Humor* and has published essays on the tall tale, antebellum comic writers, laughter and evolution, Mark Twain, George Washington Harris, Frank Norris, Hunter S. Thompson, Charlie Chaplin, and Bill Watterson, the creator of *Calvin and Hobbes*.

**Kerry Driscoll** is Professor of English at St. Joseph College in Hartford, Connecticut. In addition to her work on Twain, she is the author of *William Carlos Williams and the Maternal Muse*. Her current book project focuses on Twain's response to and representation of Native Americans.

**Michael J. Kiskis** is Leonard Tydings Grant Professor of American Literature at Elmira College, Elmira, N.Y. He is editor of *Mark Twain's Own Autobiography: The Chapters of the North American Review* and coeditor of *Constructing Mark Twain: New Directions in Scholarship*. He is past president of the Mark Twain Circle of America and of the Northeast Modern Language Association and past editor of *Studies in American Humor* and *Modern Language Studies*. He has been a contributor to *American Literary Scholarship* and will edit a special issue of *American Literary Realism* on Mark Twain for publication in Spring 2009. Along with his work on Mark Twain, he has published essays on Charlotte Perkins Gilman and on questions of pedagogy. He is currently working on a book project that examines the relationship between notions of domesticity and family and Samuel Clemens's fiction during his most prolific and successful years, 1870–1894.

**Joseph B. McCullough** is Distinguished Professor of English at the University of Nevada, Las Vegas. He is the coeditor of *The Bible According to Mark Twain* and *Mark Twain at the "Buffalo Express"* and editor of *Selected Letters of Hamlin Garland.*

**Janice McIntire-Strasburg** is Associate Professor of English at Saint Louis University. She has coedited *Mark Twain at the "Buffalo Express"* with Joseph B. McCullough and published a critical edition of *Modern Chivalry* at the University of Virginia's Electronic Text Center as well as several articles in *Kairos* and *Writing Instructor* concerning electronic publishing and technology.

**Peter Messent** teaches at the University of Nottingham in the United Kingdom. He is the author of *Mark Twain, The Short Works of Mark Twain,* and *The Cambridge Introduction to Mark Twain* and is coeditor of *A Companion to Mark Twain* and *The Civil War Letters of Joseph Hopkins Twichell.* He has also published on crime fiction, Ernest Hemingway, narrative theory, and a wide range of modern American writing. His forthcoming book is *Mark Twain and Male Friendship: The Twichell, Howells, and Rogers Friendships.*

**Bruce Michelson** is Professor of English and Director of the Campus Honors Program at the University of Illinois. His books include *Printer's Devil: Mark Twain and the American Publishing Revolution, Literary Wit,* and *Mark Twain on the Loose: A Comic Writer and the American Self.* He also writes the *Instructor's Guide* and the Web site for *The Norton Anthology of American Literature.*

**Ann M. Ryan** is Associate Professor of English at Le Moyne College in Syracuse, N.Y. She is coeditor of *A Due Voci: The Photography of Rita Hammond.* She is the past president of the Mark Twain Circle of America and the current editor of the *Mark Twain Annual.* In addition to her work on Mark Twain, she also writes on racial identity in nineteenth-century America, feminist history, and theories of humor.

# Index

WITHDRAWN